Peculiar Work

Also by Larry Anderson

Benton MacKaye: Conservationist, Planner,
and Creator of the Appalachian Trail

Peculiar Work

Writing about Benton MacKaye, Conservation, Community

Larry Anderson

Quicksand Chronicles
Little Compton, Rhode Island

Quicksand Chronicles
P. O. Box 205
Little Compton, Rhode Island 02837
www.quicksandchronicles.com

Copyright © 2012 Larry Anderson

Revised June 2013

ISBN 978-0-9855614-0-6

Library of Congress Control Number: 20122908439

For Nan

CONTENTS

‡

Peculiar Work

Ink, Paper

"Is there a theme or idea that connects the pieces"?

The question was put to me one day by the talented artist with whom I sometimes share morning coffee at the local café. She had already asked me about the progress of my current work, a subject of mild curiosity to a few bemused acquaintances. I told her I was gathering a selection of my articles and essays into a book.

"They're connected by the fact that I wrote them," I said, perhaps failing to conceal any pretense of humor. "I can hand the book to anyone who asks me what I've been working on."

My terse response may have indicated a certain thin-skinned frustration with the slow pace and intermittent public evidence of my literary output. In fact, though, there is a theme that connects this collection of articles, essays, op-ed commentaries, talks, and even a short story: they represent the essence of my own writing, interests, and activities over a long span of years. While the variety of subjects encompassed by these pieces may strike some readers as narrow, odd, even downright eccentric, they have a certain underlying unity, at least as far as I'm concerned. For one thing, they all address subjects I pursued by choice, not because they were assigned by an editor or boss. For another, they trace how one subject often led to another, as a tangential character or reference in one story planted a seed that sprouted years, even decades, later, in another burst of research and writing. I can also recognize where I became a subject in some articles—not just as the first-person narrator of a story about somebody else, but as an advocate or participant in the political and conservation activities to which I increasingly devoted time and energy (and for which I generated reams of writing, mostly unpublished, for purposes of advocacy, documentation, and dissent). From my perspective, then, these pieces possess a certain seamless continuity. Whether readers of this collection discern such connections is a question only they will be able to answer. In any case, as I told my inquisitive friend, I wrote them.

I borrowed the title of the book from one of its subjects, Edward G. Chamberlain, who spent more than half a century preparing panoramas and other hiking maps for fellow members of the Appalachian Mountain Club. "All this lifetime of peculiar work will be lost when I am gone," he once wrote of his unique variety of cartography, "for no one else understands just how to use it or would have patience to do it." Edward Chamberlain was considerably more disciplined and focused than I am, but his candid self-assessment of his solitary endeavors captures the stoic resignation with which many justify their own work. Unlike Chamberlain, I got paid—usually not much—for some of these pieces. In many instances, though, the work gathered here was its own reward.

The book's subtitle—"Writing about Benton MacKaye, Conservation, Community"—demands a different explanation. "Writing" (not "writings") of course encompasses two meanings: the actual writing represented by the pieces gathered in the book, and the act of writing that produced those pieces. The product and the process of writing are, obviously, intertwined and integral; but the combination of the two yields differing results and meanings for each individual writer. This book documents the process, the subjects, and the trajectory of my own work.

In the mid-1980s, when I was in my mid-thirties, I decided to write a biography of Benton MacKaye. I completed the job, which took considerably longer than I had originally planned. *Benton MacKaye: Conservationist, Planner, and Creator of the Appalachian Trail* appeared in 2002. Published by a good university press, the book sold modestly. The reviews, which appeared in an eclectic array of periodicals reflecting MacKaye's wide-ranging interests and activities over the course of a long life, were uniformly good. I was pleased with the result of my efforts. I had written the book I had envisioned at the outset of my long biographical trek, which I came to regard as the literary equivalent of an Appalachian Trail thru-hike.

Almost half of the articles collected here, then, are direct by-products of my work on Benton MacKaye. The rest, I came to see as I selected and gathered them together, in one way or other reflected two of the essential aspects of MacKaye's life and career: namely, conservation and community. An important reason I chose to write a biography of MacKaye was, of course, because I was personally interested in many of the ideas, activities, and goals to which he had devoted his own efforts. I did not consciously model my life on MacKaye's, and there were cautionary reasons why this would have been a bad idea: he had trouble holding a steady job; he was often broke; his personal life was sometimes solitary and unhappy. In fact, I was always wary of being sucked into the black hole of obsession, solipsism, and identification with one's subject that can doom a biographical project. The biographer, to have any chance of successfully re-creating another life on paper, engages in tense balancing act, constantly weighing warm-hearted empathy against cold-hearted critical analysis.

As I have written in the introduction of *Benton MacKaye*, other personal experiences motivated and contributed to my work on the book. I lived and worked for most of thirty years in the same landscape of north-central Massachusetts where MacKaye had lived for much of his life and which had inspired many of his ideas. Both of my parents had family roots in the same region. Furthermore, they had been in the printing and publishing business. In our house, there was no mystery about how ideas and words originally arising in imagination eventually find their way to publication in material form. Hence, the idea of writing and publishing a book was not an altogether daunting one, except for the actual work involved.

My driven, multi-tasking father, among his many other enterprises, for a time wrote and published a newsletter for the business-forms trade. Once a month, often surrounded by noisy children while watching a Red Sox game on our grainy black-and-white television, he meticulously laid out and wrote the newsletter. On a tiny Masonite drawing board, he produced a careful mock-up of the newsletter, rendered in his clear and distinctive handwriting. He then turned this dummy over to a typist and a graphic artist for preparation as camera-ready copy, with strict instructions that not a word or an element of his design be changed. A week or two later, the newsletter would come back from the printer, and some of us kids would be enlisted to fold and stuff the publication for mailing to subscribers. Eventually, this newsletter evolved into a substantial monthly magazine, which my opportunistic father was soon able to sell to a competitor in the same field, whom he had beaten to market. Ink on paper. I knew the smells, the sounds, the textures at every stage of the publication process. And I knew I would likely be involved in that business and tradition in one way or another.

In the mid-1970s, after completing an unfocused college career and listlessly pursuing a few other activities, I returned to the town of Harvard, Massachusetts, where my parents were then living. I went to work for a lively weekly newspaper, *The Harvard Post,* which had recently been launched by two talented and rigorous young writers and editors, Ed Miller and Kathleen Cushman, who published the newspaper from their often chaotic house. Under their tutelage, I had the opportunity to write about local history, environmental controversies, politics, art, books, and just about anything else that would fill space. Writing about people and events in the close quarters of a small town also offered some life lessons in judgment, tact, and choosing one's battles.

Soon, Ed, Kathleen, and I started our own small book-publishing company, The Harvard Common Press. We turned to friends and acquaintances for book ideas (my brother Bob earned a small equity share in the company by writing a concise history of the town of

Harvard). And the three of us co-wrote and published *How to Produce a Small Newspaper: A Guide for Independent Journalists* (1978), a combination handbook and manifesto that sold quite a few copies.

One of the book ideas we tried unsuccessfully to get off the ground was a photo-essay about the salvation of the Nashua River. The grossly polluted waterway that defined and demarcated our region had been cleaned up by a combination of citizen activism and government intervention, including the requirements of the Clean Water Act and large infusions of federal money. Kathleen's brother Jack Cushman, then writing for the *Harvard Post,* began work on the project, along with an excellent photographer, Mike Carroll. When Jack moved along on the next step of a career that eventually led to the Washington bureau of the *New York Times,* Mike and I for a time continued to pursue the Nashua River project. We couldn't find the sponsorship we needed to make it work financially, but during this effort I came to learn more about Benton MacKaye, who had only recently died. MacKaye had lived only a few miles from where I grew up and subsequently lived. As an elder statesman of the national conservation movement, he had bestowed his blessing upon the Nashua River clean-up crusade.

Nan and I were married during this time. She had recently earned a nursing degree. I was enjoying the opportunity to write regularly and to create a small business producing books. But a sober assessment of the practical economic prospects of these enterprises, under the supportive but constant gaze of my nearby parents and in partnership with a couple who were always frenetically juggling their own personal and business activities, impelled me to make a break.

In 1980, Nan and I moved to Rhode Island, closer to her family. We lived in Providence at the time, only a few blocks from Brown University. While searching for a potential purchaser of my majority share of the miniscule book-publishing business (which still survives as an independent company), I enrolled as a part-time graduate student at Brown, partly to patch some of the gaping holes in my undergraduate education. I had the good luck to take a seminar on American regionalism taught by the enthusiastic and demanding historian John L. Thomas, who shared and encouraged my interest in MacKaye. When I received a master's degree in American Civilization, I determined to plunge directly into researching and writing a biography of MacKaye, a project for which I had no institutional or financial support, other than my own resources and ambition (and, of course, Nan's patient encouragement). I estimated the job might take two or three years.

At about this time, partly as a result of a health scare, we abruptly decided to move from urban Providence to rural/exurban Little Compton, the coastal Rhode Island town where Nan owned some property that had long belonged to her family—and where she also had an opportunity to work as a home-health-care nurse. From that point in the mid-1980s, I scrambled, not always efficiently or effectively, to find some balance among the various obligations and commitments we had assumed. We moved into a new, not-quite-completed house, surrounded by acres of land that generated a perpetual round of chores; raised our son Sam; and gradually knit ourselves into the fabric of another small New England town. Nan dedicated herself to her nursing vocation. I traveled, sometimes for extended periods, to pursue my research into MacKaye's life and to interview the fast-dwindling cohort of his surviving acquaintances. I tried to interest agents and publishers in my prospective book, but the combination of an unknown writer and a little-known subject made this a tough sell. From time to time I would fend off inquiries from other potential MacKaye biographers, usually by intimating that I was close to completing my work. I wasn't alone in believing that MacKaye deserved a good biography, but I clung to the not necessarily rational notion that I was uniquely qualified to write it. Over the years several would-be MacKaye biographers had fallen by the wayside; indeed, there seemed to be something of a curse on the endeavor. The odds that I would complete and publish the book were not particularly good. *(Advice to aspiring biographers: Choose a subject who dies young—not somebody who lives almost a century, writes something almost daily from childhood until the moment of death, and belongs to a vast network of similarly literary friends and family members, almost all of whom save every scrap of scribbled-upon paper.)*

It helped, though, that Benton MacKaye was an incorrigible optimist. I always felt encouraged and refreshed after spending a long day in the

archives, reading his insistently hopeful correspondence and manu-
scripts. He was also a genuine idealist. Is it possible to maintain and
pursue one's ideals, while remaining rooted in reality? MacKaye tried.
"Work and art and recreation and living will all be one," he had san-
guinely envisioned, invoking the example of Thoreau. There could be
worse ways to envisage and pursue life, even if one fell far short of the
high-minded prospects depicted by such American originals as Mac-
Kaye or Thoreau.

My work on the MacKaye biography proceeded in fits and starts, as
time, finances, and other obligations and distractions permitted. I was
pulled into various local causes and controversies. Over time, it became
difficult for me to distinguish between vocation and avocation. I
uncomfortably and silently acknowledged that this pattern mirrored, in
some measure, the circumstances of MacKaye's life.

In my community, I gradually earned a reputation as a gadfly and
troublemaker. Although I had no local journalistic position or connection, I used my reporting experience to assume the role of self-
appointed explainer and commentator, churning out letters to the editor
and an occasional op-ed commentary. This kind of effort—criticizing,
complaining, and generally trying to stop bad things (at least as I saw
them) from happening—can take its toll on one's morale, mental and
physical energies, and social relationships. As a more positive outlet for
such local activism, I became increasingly involved with a non-profit
land trust. As its president for a few years, I tried with some success to
reinvigorate the venerable local conservation organization, which could
operate, for the most part, outside the control and influence of the well-
entrenched community political structure.

Eventually, partly because of persistence but primarily due to the
simple passage of years, I had become something of a town elder, if not
always a popular one, within the snug precincts of our small town. I was
even elected (and re-elected) town moderator, responsible for presiding
over the time-honored institution of town meeting. This was not
necessarily a major feat (I ran unopposed), but it was perhaps a sign that
I had earned a degree of trust and respect for my civic efforts.

In any event, while I pushed along with one big long-term writing project, MacKaye's biography, I also worked on other, shorter projects that offered the prospect of actual publication and, in some cases, payment. This book, then, is a representative compendium of some of these experiences, endeavors, and projects. It is loosely organized along the amorphous contours and blurred boundaries of the three subjects encompassed by its subtitle: Benton MacKaye, conservation, community.

The ten articles and essays that immediately succeed this introduction flow directly out of my work on MacKaye. These were, in part, efforts to try out and circulate some of the new material I was uncovering, to school myself in the practical expository techniques required for full-scale biography, and to build a record of publication that would, I hoped, improve my chances of finding a publisher for the book. In the end, I more or less achieved all these modest objectives.

The next five pieces address conservation issues, subjects, and personalities that are not directly related to MacKaye. Nonetheless, some are sidelong outgrowths of my work on his biography; others reflect several of MacKaye's preoccupations and priorities: the meaning and management of wilderness; the purposes and pleasures of hiking and outdoor recreation; the sustainability of life on the planet.

Finally, the last eleven pieces wander most widely across time and subject matter. They are all linked, somehow, to the notion of community, if on diverse scales ranging from the sometimes constricted sphere of small-town life to the sprawling arena of national politics.

A few comments are in order concerning the editorial principles (such as they are) involved in the organization of this book. First of all, readers will notice a certain degree of overlap and repetition in the series of articles describing MacKaye's early adventures in the mountains of northern New England. Early in my research on MacKaye, I had been excited and overwhelmed by the abundance of diaries, letters, photographs, maps, and other materials he had generated during these expeditions and tramps in the late 1890s and early 1900s. These resources had, as yet, been little exploited by other writers and scholars.

They revealed, among other things, what an ambitious, intrepid, and tough hiker and outdoorsman the young Benton MacKaye had been. This depiction of MacKaye as a genuine, on-the-ground trailblazer was somewhat at odds with the prevailing portrait that had evolved, both during his life and in the years immediately after his death. By these accounts, MacKaye was a pipesmoking "dreamer" rather than a "doer," an impractical intellectual who was happy to sit beside the campfire philosophizing about the virtues of outdoor life while others were doing the hard labor of cutting and maintaining trails. His remarkable 1897 excursion by bicycle and on foot from his Massachusetts home to and through the heart of the White Mountains, his 1900 tramp virtually the length of Vermont, and his 1904 White Mountain hike as the co-leader of a small band of young campers demonstrated just how much rugged, first-hand experience MacKaye had gained as a young adventurer.

The records of these tramps, canoe trips, and bicycle rides also revealed how early in life MacKaye had begun developing his ideas about the purposes and benefits of hiking, trailmaking, wilderness preservation, and conservation. Hence, as I began work on my planned biography of MacKaye, I wrote and published accounts of several of his youthful expeditions. These were partly exercises in narrative writing, not scholarly or theoretical articles. I hoped that by recounting closely his youthful adventures, I could illustrate in concrete terms the settings and circumstances in which his ideas began to take shape. I have chosen not to edit or revise these articles. Rather, I have included them as originally published.

In each of these trail chronicles, I found myself returning to an article he had written—the first of his writing ever published, as best I could determine—which thoroughly documented the hike he led through the White Mountains in the summer of 1904 with the boys of Camp Moosilauke. As its title suggests, this article, "Our White Mountain Trip: Its Organization and Methods," provides a nuts-and-bolts trail guide, at least for conditions as they existed in 1904. By the standards of our own era, some of MacKaye's advice may seem shockingly wrongheaded. But his article concludes with a peroration, titled "Camp Ethics," which outlined clearly and eloquently the precepts that shaped the rest of MacKaye's long life and career as a conservationist. With the permission of the Rauner Special Collections Library at Dartmouth College, I have included here a facsimile reproduction of MacKaye's article. His pen-and-ink sketches alone provide a sense of life along the trail many decades before the era of leave-no-trace camping practices and ultralight hiking gear.

In most cases, I have included articles here exactly as they were first published, altering only obvious grammatical or typographical errors. At the end of each piece, I have provided the year it was originally published or written. In a number of cases, I have also included postscripts that update events and developments since the articles first appeared. Readers will also notice that the pieces employ various forms of notation and citation. These inconsistent methods of documentation reflect the variety of publications and contexts in which the pieces originally appeared, including weekly and daily newspapers, magazines, literary journals, organizational newsletters, semi-scholarly journals, and talks at various conferences and events. The level and detail of documentation provided is, I hope, sufficient for the purposes of each article.

The concluding article about Las Vegas, previously unpublished, reflects another biographical project for which I have long been gathering and writing material. My late great-uncle Sam Gay, who died well before my time, was Las Vegas's leading lawman for almost twenty-five years at the beginning of the twentieth century. One of these days, there may be a book about his life and times. It's peculiar work, I know, but somebody has to do it.

(2012)

Benton MacKaye: Brief Life of a "Geotect"

"Speak softly and carry a big map," Harvard alumnus Benton MacKaye '00, A.M. '05, exhorted a 1930 gathering of outdoor enthusiasts who were building the 2,100-mile Appalachian Trail he had proposed nine years earlier. Adapting the more militant aphorism coined by fellow alumnus Theodore Roosevelt, an early champion of the American conservation cause, MacKaye (the name rhymes with *high*) evoked the technique and perspective he brought to his own idiosyncratic calling.

A self-styled "visualiser," MacKaye received the first graduate degree in forestry awarded by Harvard. His studies under such eminent Harvard earth scientists as Nathaniel Southgate Shaler and William Morris Davis inspired his long, fruitful career as a forester, writer, regional planner, activist, and "geotect." Indeed, MacKaye's work spanned and shaped the evolving American conservation and environmental movements during the first three quarters of the twentieth century.

From 1906 to 1910 MacKaye divided his time between cruising New England timberlands for the fledgling U.S. Forest Service and teaching forestry at Harvard. He lost his university position in a clash with the program's director, Richard T. Fisher, but soon won a full-time Forest Service job at the climax of the Progressive era. In Washington he helped organize an informal circle of journalists, radicals, suffragists, and reform-minded bureaucrats who dubbed themselves Hell Raisers.

Benton MacKaye on Hunting Hill, near Shirley, Massachusetts, July, 1937.
(Courtesy of Dartmouth College Library and Robert McCullough.)

In 1916 he went to work at another new agency, the Department of Labor. The provocative report that resulted from his official travels throughout the country, *Employment and Natural Resources* (1919), "ranks among the most mature and memorable fruits of the American conservation movement," in the words of historian Roy Lubove.

By the early 1920s the death of his wife, suffragist and peace activist Jessie Hardy Stubbs, and his disillusionment with the conservative turn of federal policies impelled MacKaye to assume the role for which he remains best known: father of the Appalachian Trail. His turn-of-the-century explorations of the New England northcountry stimulated his conception of the Maine-to-Georgia hiking path, which he publicly broached in the *Journal of the American Institute of Architects* in October 1921. By 1937 the Appalachian Trail Conference, a federation of hiking clubs he helped organize in 1925, had collaborated with state and federal agencies to complete a continuous trail along the ridgeline of the Appalachian Mountains.

In 1923 MacKaye joined writer Lewis Mumford, architect Clarence Stein, economist Stuart Chase, and other reformers to create the Regional Planning Association of America. Over the next decade this close-knit, farseeing group promoted a pathbreaking array of ideas about architecture, land-use, housing, and transportation.

Prodded by Mumford, MacKaye published *The New Exploration: A Philosophy of Regional Planning* in 1928. The book vividly portrayed his grim vision of the "metropolitan innovation" flowing out from the nation's cities but also outlined techniques for maintaining a harmonious balance between urban, rural, and "primeval" environments. Mumford described *The New Exploration* as worthy of "a place on the same shelf that holds Henry Thoreau's *Walden* and George Perkins Marsh's *Man and Nature.*"

MacKaye joined the newly created Tennessee Valley Authority in 1934 as a regional planner and was among the idealists who hope to make the TVA a model of multiple-purpose watershed planning. But he left the job after two stormy years, a victim of the political and ideological struggle for control of the controversial agency. After stints with the Forest Service and the Rural Electrification Administration, he would retire from government service in 1945.

Meanwhile, he had united with such conservationist luminaries as Aldo Leopold, Robert Marshall, and Robert Sterling Yard to establish The Wilderness Society in 1935. From 1945 to 1950, as its president, he encouraged the organization's small but influential staff, led by Howard Zahniser and Olaus Murie, to begin the long political battle that led to passage of the 1964 Wilderness Act.

In his later years MacKaye completed a long but unpublished autobiographical treatise, "Geotechnics of North America," detailing his distinctive vision of the "applied science of making the earth more habitable." His interest and writings during the 1940s and 1950s encompassed nuclear disarmament, world government, and population growth. Well into the 1970s this elder statesman of the cause continued to influence people and organizations at the forefront of ecological thought and environmental activism.

Throughout his life MacKaye's colorful, even eccentric personality attracted a legion of friends and followers. "He lives a very quiet abstemious life: plain living and high thinking," wrote Mumford in 1932, "and wastes less of his time on the *means* of living than anyone I know." A self-described "amphibian as between city and country," MacKaye punctuated his forestry and planning assignments with long stretches of solitary reflection and writing in Shirley Center, Massachusetts, his beloved rural home since boyhood. When he died there at 96, he had never held high government office; his literary reputation did not match that of his illustrious friends and colleagues. Yet on landscapes both physical and intellectual he left a considerable—and persistent—legacy. The Appalachian Trail and 95-million-acre National Wilderness Preservation System embody the prophetic, wide-ranging ideas that continue to inspire many environmental activists, adventurers, architects, and planners.

(1994)

POSTSCRIPT: By 2012, the National Wilderness Preservation System comprised 757 Wilderness Areas, totaling almost 110-million acres.

Benton MacKaye and the Art of Roving: An 1897 Excursion in the White Mountains

In "Walking," Thoreau's essay containing the unforgettable proclamation "that in Wildness is the preservation of the World," the Concord philosopher also mused about what the future might hold for saunterers such as himself. During the 1850s, when he was preparing the essay, Thoreau could still rove the Massachusetts country unimpeded, without fear of upsetting the privacy and equanimity of the commonwealth's more sedentary citizens:

> At present, in this vicinity, the best part of the land is not private property; the landscape is not owned, and the walker enjoys comparative freedom. But possibly the day will come when it will be partitioned off into so-called pleasure grounds, in which a few will take a narrow and exclusive pleasure only—when fences shall be multiplied, and man-traps and other engines invented to confine men to the *public* road, and walking over the surface of God's earth shall be construed to mean trespassing on some gentleman's grounds. To enjoy anything exclusively is commonly to exclude yourself from the true enjoyment of it. Let us improve our opportunities, then, before the evil days come.

Those evil days did come, of course. Highways, population growth, and all the paraphernalia of the industrial age have tremendously circumscribed the possibilities of practicing "this noble art" of walking—the unhurried, unstructured observation and experience of the natural environment. Thoreau advised his readers to walk "like a camel, which is said to be the only beast which ruminates when walking." To walk like a camel in the vicinity of Concord these days, needless to say, would be to take a good chance of being run over by an automobile.

Thoreau's attitudes about walking and wilderness were shared by a resident of another Massachusetts town a vigorous day's tramp west of Concord. Benton MacKaye (1879–1975), the forester, regional planner, and "geotect" best known for his conception of the Appalachian Trail, began prowling the countryside around the town of Shirley soon after he first came to the community in 1887 as a boy of eight. The landscape and rural way of life of Shirley just before the turn of the century were not so far removed in time or custom from Thoreau's Concord.

MacKaye spent the winter of 1890 and 1891 with his family in Washington, D.C. There he heard lectures by such legendary explorers as Major John Wesley Powell and Robert E. Peary. And he spent many days investigating the exhibition halls of the Smithsonian Institution. Indeed, so familiar a figure did the inquisitive and purposeful lad become at the museum that he was soon invited into the laboratories and libraries closed to the rest of the public.

His firsthand experience with these eminent explorers and men of science inspired MacKaye, upon his return to Massachusetts, to undertake some explorations of his own. He filled notebooks with sketches, maps, and comments describing Shirley's topography, wildlife, and vegetation. These studies were rudimentary versions of the wide-ranging geographic surveys he later compiled throughout his professional life. His older brother James jocularly referred to Benton's habit as "expedition nining" after the younger MacKaye returned from one of his investigative forays, which he systematically numbered in his notebooks. (For the rest of his life MacKaye employed the term as a metaphor for his own explorations, both physical and intellectual. Indeed, his last book, a slender volume published in 1969 on the occasion of his 90th birthday, was titled *Expedition Nine*; it included excerpts from his boyhood notebooks.) Mulpus Brook, the Squannacook River, Hunting Hill, Catacoonamug Brook, the profiles of mountains like Wachusett, Watatic, and Monadnock to the west and northwest—such were the features of the landscape imprinted in MacKaye's imagination. For MacKaye, this hometown geography became the focal point and the template for one aspect of an ideal "indigenous" environment, which held urban, rural, and "primeval" values in balance.

A bachelor for most of his life, MacKaye lived frugally in his family's small cottage near the common at Shirley Center. (His six-year marriage to suffragist and peace activist Jesse Hardy Stubbs—or "Betty," as she was familiarly known—ended tragically in 1921, when she took her own life.) He was known to a legion of friends for his colorful speech, faithful correspondence at birthdays and anniversaries, and single-minded devotion to the self-created discipline of "geotechnics," which he described as the "applied science of making the earth more habitable." A visionary with practical skills, MacKaye was a sort of transcendental engineer. During the course of his work with such agencies as the U.S. Forest Service, the Department of Labor, the Tennessee Valley Authority, and the Rural Electrification Administration, he attempted to identify and channel those forces which Thoreau had only vaguely foreseen as potential threats to both the landscape and the human spirit.

Just before the turn of the century, MacKaye was introduced to another New England environment also familiar to Thoreau—the White Mountains of New Hampshire. His experiences in the mountains during those years, as he would often recall later in life, sowed the seeds in MacKaye's fertile imagination for ideas about long-distance trails and wilderness preservation.

On the afternoon of August 14, 1897, MacKaye waded across the Swift River just north of James Shackford's Passaconaway House, a modest hostelry and a landmark for hikers in the settlement of Albany Intervale, not far from the present site of the U.S. Forest Service's Passaconaway Campground on the Kancamagus Highway. With two youthful companions, he began an adventure he later recalled as the time "I first saw the true wilderness." Eighteen years old, soon to start his sophomore year at Harvard, MacKaye was setting out on the first, and perhaps most memorable, of many hikes he would make over the next few summers in the mountains of northern New England. "It was a journey of Ulysses," he remembered thirty-five years later. "I graduated from dung to spruce—from the tang of the barnyard to the aroma of the virgin smoke amid the far night roar of Bolles Brook tumbling from Passaconaway."

MacKaye and fellow Harvard students Draper Maury and Sturgis Pray had set out by bicycle from Shirley ten days earlier. They made good time on their "wheels" over rugged New England back roads in that twilight of the pre-automobile era ("getting off every 10 rods to walk through 5 rods of mud from 10 to 15 inches deep"), working their way north through the picturesque hill towns of north-central Massachusetts and southern New Hampshire. In Dublin, New Hampshire, a resort for artists and writers, they stayed with family acquaintances and climbed Mount Monadnock. Another seventy miles or so brought them to Lakeport, on the shores of Lake Winnipesaukee. They were towed, bicycles and all, on a raft across lake, doing their laundry along the way. At Tamworth, MacKaye, Maury, and Pray stopped to visit friends and to admire Mount Chocorua. A fifteen-mile night-time bicycle ride from Conway brought them to Shackford's, where they prepared for the real aim of the trip—their tramp through the mountains. "We arrived here at 10 p.m. The moonlight on the wild and weird landscape of the Swift River Valley was something which I had never seen before and was as beautiful as anything I ever expect to see."

The White Mountains were a revelation to the wiry, observant, energetic MacKaye, who characteristically kept a vivid and meticulous record of his trip—in a journal, letters to his family and friends, and even a six-chapter semi-fictionalized account that he later wrote for his Harvard composition class. "The country we are about to traverse is one, I am told, undisturbed by civilization in any form," MacKaye recorded on the first morning of the hike. "Besides us, only the bear,

Sturgis Pray, Benton MacKaye, and Draper Maury at Shackford's, Albany Intervale, New Hampshire, August 14, 1897. (Courtesy of Dartmouth College Library.)

deer, catamount, porcupine and coon disturb the solitude of the primevial forest. *[Note: MacKaye's handwritten and usually legible journal is transcribed with spelling and punctuation unchanged.]* No longer will women folk look shocked or embarrassed as they did when they met me clothed in a sleaveless undershirt or stripped to the waist. We have said 'goodbye' to the bicycles and civilization and will now pursue our way on foot through the White Mountains."

Full of himself—as any eighteen-year-old discovering life—MacKaye took several liberties with circumstance. For one, logging companies had been active in the Albany Intervale area since at least the 1870s; the Bartlett Land and Lumber Company operated a railroad through Bear Notch to the settlement until just a few years before MacKaye's hike. And although the White Mountain National Forest would not begin to take shape until after the passage of the Weeks Act in 1911, hikers had been heading into the hills for recreation in growing numbers; the Appalachian Mountain Club's founding in 1876 was but one indication of the increasing popularity of the rigorous sport MacKaye was enjoying for the first time.

Even so, the profiles of Mount Tremont and its companion, Owl Cliff, presented a rugged prospect to MacKaye and his fellow refugees from civilization. Rising to the north of the Swift River across the broad, flat Albany Intervale, the palisade of Owl Cliff is surmounted by the 3,384-foot hump of Tremont, whose south approach is itself steep and craggy. The mountains, observed from the valley, were—and are—distant enough, wild enough, and solitary enough to quicken the imagination of a young man bent on discovery.

Starting as they did late in the afternoon, the trio covered a modest two-and-one-half miles the first day, making camp near a log hut along the way. The next day, a Sunday, their adventures began:

> We struck what is called a 'blow down'[,] the most horrible thing on earth. A hurricane comes, blows down half the trees which lay like jack straws interwoven with bushes and briers. Over these we must crawl over and under, balancing ourselves on a 4 inch fallen tree which at the same time we must ascend and which suddenly gives way under its 200 lbs.

pressure and leaves us five to ten feet below on our backs. Then after crawling like snakes under the debris we come out 20 minutes later about 10 feet beyond finding that we have gone about 5 feet in the wrong direction. By this time we have to wait and rest in order to gain our breath and then proceed to pull ourselves up with our teeth, fingernails and spikes over a precipitous, slipery, moss-covered crag, at the top of which we fall back to our starting place and roll another 6 feet in the wrong direction. Such is a 'blow down', and in going through one of these we spent last Sunday, making all day, about three miles.

MacKaye's sense of humor and irony remained intact throughout the trip, if his journals and letters are any indication. He and his companions were not sure what to expect along the trail, except perhaps for a taste of danger. After traversing the blow-down, the group "found a trappers hut in which Sturgis thought he saw a dead man which proved to be a lot of old clothes." Their nerves calmed, they camped nearby, using bark from the hut for their own shelter, constructed to protect them from the rain which fell that night. The account of their experiences the next day, August 16, deserves quotation at length, for it depicts a crucial moment in the making of the young Benton MacKaye:

It is cloudy, and we didn't get started till just past noon. After going over several preliminary hills each of which we thought was Tremont Mt., we finally struck the base of the latter. We then went up an angle of 45°, sometimes 50° for over 1500 feet. We found ourselves in a cloud with the rain coming down like "pitchforks". Suddenly everything would clear and the mountains would appear behind the vapor. The scene was beyond description. All this time the thunder kept up an incessant roar. After we had grubbed we started on, and were about to come on what we thought was the summit when the lightening struck within a few rods of us, almost giving us a shock.

We now beheld the summit about half a mile ahead and so after going through bushes and clouds once more we came upon what we supposed surely to be the summit. Sturgis here deposited a bottle containing our names etc.

We then went down into the woods a little ways and after some discussion as to location we started to erect a shelter with darkness upon us, a cloud around us, and a heavy thunder storm coming. The rain poured, the lightening was the only thing which enabled us to see to do anything. We were soaked, all our things were soaked, the shelter inside and out was soaked and still the rain poured. After about an hour and a half of this God or something took pity on us, and the shower chased itself not to return. Then it was that we denuded ourselves and stood by the fire writhing with the pain from the fire in order to dry our clothes from which the steam arose. Finally, about 12:30 we had dried the boughs of the shelter and turned in.

Tues. Aug. 17: . . . In two seconds I was asleep, but at 3:40 I was awake cold and wet. I started a little fire, got my shoes on and was up on our summit just as the sun was rising. The first thing I discovered was that the true summit was about 1/4 miles beyond ours. It was about 4:30, the clouds were in the valleys below and a brisk breeze was blowing from the southwest. The grandest sight I ever saw was now before me, nothing but a sea of mountains and clouds. I sketched Mt. Washington, and then, as I heard the fellows call, I returned to inform them that we had some distance yet before us to the summit.

We got together our wet packs, and with no breakfast, save a few crums of hardtack and dried apples and a swig of whiskey, the like of which had kept us alive through the night, we started out. We ascended our summit, took the bottle and in a few minutes were on the true summit from which the view is something immense.

We had been here about three minutes when I looked up and saw a Black Bear about 10 rods down on the rocks. I shouted to the fellows, and Sturgis jumped for his revolver. Bruin, however, didn't stay long but put himself out of sight over the edge of the mountain. About 5 minutes after we saw 2 eagles soar through the air and over the valleys.

The last 24, or as it is now 9 A.M., 21 hours have been great experiences for us. . . .

It was this moment, alone on the top of Mount Tremont as the sun rose and the weather cleared, that MacKaye would always remember as one of revelation, perhaps the closest thing to a religious experience that he ever mentioned or recorded. "A second world—and promise!" he wrote his close friend and fellow Wilderness Society founder Harvey Broome in 1932, recalling the occasion. The vista from Tremont that misty, mystical August dawn in 1897 made "the cold chills go up your back," MacKaye reported to a Shirley friend:

> I saw the sun rise over the mountains making one side of them day and the other, night. Several hundred feet below the valleys there were white clouds and occasionally parts of them would rise and chase themselves by me.
>
> On one side Mt. Washington would emerge now and then from a cloud, on another, to the northwest, the Franconia range was seen through Carrigain Notch; to the northeast I could see over into Maine, and on the south away in the distance I could make out the hills of old Massachusetts. I felt then how much I resembled in size one of the hairs on the eye tooth of a flea, to use a vulgar expression.

The wilderness movement "is philosophically a disclaimer of the biotic arrogance of *Homo americanus*," Aldo Leopold wrote in 1935, when he joined with his friend and one-time Forest Service colleague MacKaye to form The Wilderness Society. "It is one of the focal points of a new attitude—an intelligent humility toward man's place in nature." Adrift in "a sea of mountains and clouds" on the summit of Tremont, feeling no more substantial than a hair on a flea's tooth, Benton MacKaye was irrevocably educated in the meaning of just such an intelligent humility.

The hikers' adventures on the summit were only the beginning of their trek, however. For the next two weeks MacKaye, Maury, and Pray, joined at Crawford Notch by another friend, Rob Mitchell, traveled a circuit through the White Mountains, covering much of the territory that would later be incorporated into the White Mountain National Forest. From Tremont, the original trio worked its way northwest to the lumber settlement Livermore Mills and across another blow-down on the way up Mount Lowell.

Their route next took them over Mount Anderson, then along the rocky streambed of Nancy Brook, "jumping from rock to rock, and expecting to break our necks every other minute." They struck the road (present-day Route 302) and flagged a train headed north to Crawford Notch. Enjoying the comfortable atmosphere of the Crawford House for several days, the three regained some of the weight they had worked off ("I gained six pounds in one meal, 8 1/2 pounds in one day") and were joined by Mitchell and Sturgis Pray's father. The group made for Mount Washington over the Bridle Path (Crawford Path), receiving a rousing send-off from the other hotel guests ("a lot of lazy dudes who turned out in the morning in light suits and straw hats, and in the evening in dress suits").

Benton MacKaye, Sturgis Pray, Benjamin Pray, Draper Maury, and Robert Mitchell, Crawford House, Crawford Notch, New Hampshire, on or about August 22, 1897. (Courtesy of Dartmouth College Library.)

But MacKaye and his companions were forced to spend the next two days at a hut near Mount Clinton because of the "fiendish" weather. They beat a retreat to the Crawford House, "resembling frozen drowned rats" upon their arrival. The party now decided to assault Mount Washington from another direction. They traveled by train to Gorham, where Pray's father left the group. The remaining four took a day to climb nearby Mount Hayes, *without our packs. We had a grand view of the Androscoggin valley and made our farthest north 44° 25'*."

After walking several miles south on the Glen Road (Route 16), they begin their climb of the eastern approach to Mount Washington on a day that "was one in 1000 for clearness." MacKaye and Maury headed up the Carriage Road, while Pray and Mitchell ascended by way of Tuckerman Ravine. The group spent the night in comfort, each with a room in the Summit House, their presence documented in the daily newspaper, *Among the Clouds*, then published on the mountain.

The rest of the excursion must have seemed anticlimactic. From Mount Washington, the quartet scrambled over the Presidential Range to Crawford's Notch and caught another train, this time for Franconia Notch. They spent a night at the Profile House, "once more an object of interest to the occupants of white dresses and dress suits. The latter were even worn by boys in short pants here."

The hikers headed south from Franconia Notch, Sturgis Pray climbing Mount Lafayette and down the Franconia Range, while the three others planned to follow the road toward the Flume. After making their rendezvous at North Woodstock, the group convinced the "authorities" at the Henry mills, which maintained logging operations along the East Branch of the Pemigewasset and the Hancock Branch, to transport them by train to the company's Camp 7. The next day they climbed Mount Osceola, finding a camp near the summit.

On September 1, their last full day in the mountains, they walked to Waterville, then headed up Mount Tripyramid by way of Slide Brook, Avalanche Brook, and the north slide. They left the summit at 4:45 P.M., thinking it might be possible to complete their mountain excursion and reach "our Mecca, 'Shack's'" that night. But at 10:30 P.M., after negotiating the "worst 'blow-down' yet" in pitch-dark conditions, the exhausted trippers stopped in their tracks, and without making a meal or building a shelter they tried to get what sleep they could.

The dawn brought rain, "and the grog came in handy." MacKaye's feet, he noted in his journal, "were now fiendish and every step was a world of agony in itself. My shoes which by this time had almost disappeared were bound by Drape with his bandage tape and thus my underpinnings had a very unique aspect." Hiking the last few miles by way of Sabbaday Brook and Sabbaday Falls, the "happy but fagged" young men "arrived finally about 11 o'clock at the long sought 'Shack's.'" Their circuit of the mountains was complete.

Almost twenty years after his initial mountain expedition, in a 1916 article in the *Journal of the New York State Forestry Association*, MacKaye spelled out for the first time his original and ambitious ideas about outdoor recreation. He worried about decreasing opportunities for what he called "roving"—the footloose exploration of the landscape. He credited the term to his friend Allen Chamberlain, a writer and former president of the Appalachian Mountain Club, who had an influential hand in promoting the creation of the White Mountain National Forest. MacKaye made his 1897 trip by means of bicycle, boat, railroad, horse and wagon, and shoe leather. He and his friend slept in barns and farmhouses, in rustic hostelries and resort hotels, beside streams, and on mountain peaks. The opportunities for this serendipitous variety of travel, MacKaye wrote in 1916, "are being yearly restricted through the more rigid enforcement of the trespass laws"—just as Thoreau had feared. And he predicted that "the desire for such roving is likely to increase as the chances for indulging it narrow."

MacKaye's article, "Recreational Possibilities of Public Forests," outlined an even more bold scheme than the one he would describe five years later in his well-known article proposing the Appalachian Trail. Citing the growing number and size of the National Forests and National Parks, as well as the efforts of amateur organizations like the AMC and Vermont's Green Mountain Club, MacKaye suggested the "linking up" of publicly owned forests and parks, existing trail networks, and scenic rivers. "Here would be the basis of a land-and-water transportation system which would connect and unify a possible national recreation ground which would reach from ocean to ocean."

MacKaye's grand scheme for a national network of recreational facilities—intended for "not only those few of the people who can 'afford it,' but especially those who can not afford it"—would, he hoped, preserve the chance for all to practice "the art of living in the open and of using their camping ground." Such opportunities had been momentous ones for him, as they had been for other defenders of the wilderness—like Thoreau, in some of the same New England terrain familiar to MacKaye, and John Muir, in the Sierra Nevada Mountains of California. Many of MacKaye's own friends and colleagues in the wilderness preservation movement had shared similar experiences. Robert Marshall, in the Adirondacks and the Brooks Range of Alaska, Aldo Leopold, in the desert country of the southwest and the sand counties of Wisconsin, Ernest Oberholtzer and Sigurd Olson, in the canoe country of northern Minnesota, Olaus and Margaret Murie, in Alaska and the Rockies—each of these individuals, and many other people less articulate and less influential, had been able to "rove," physically, intellectually, and emotionally, across their own particular and beloved landscapes, finding inspiration and understanding along the way.

"If the people are to have something deeper than a perfunctory love of country, they must have the chance to see their country," MacKaye concluded. Written the year before the United States entered World War I, his comments about the nation's forests and mountains as the source of a genuine "love of country" take on a special resonance.

In the decade after his 1897 hike, MacKaye returned often to the mountains and forests of northern New England. In 1902 and 1903 he rendezvoused in the White Mountains with Sturgis Pray, "my super teacher of wilderness lore," then starting a career as an eminent landscape architect. MacKaye helped Pray, who at the time served as the AMC's Councillor of Improvements, lay out a new trail along the Swift River from Sabbaday Brook to Kancamagus Pass—roughly the route of the Kancamagus Highway—linking for the first time the trails of the Sandwich Range with those of the East Branch of the Pemigewasset and the Franconia Range. With another Harvard schoolmate and lifelong friend, Horace Hildreth, MacKaye in 1900 roved the Vermont countryside from Brattleboro to Morrisville, by railroad, farm wagon, and on foot, climbing Vermont's highest peaks ten years before the Long Trail was initiated.

In the summers of 1902 and 1904 MacKaye, as "master" at a New Hampshire summer camp, led groups of boys through White Mountain territory he had first visited on his 1897 hike. Once he was caught with his campers in a storm on Mount Washington, "crawling yard by yard, from one cairn to the next. I have never forgotten the sight of the cog railway, looming suddenly out of the fog, that would lead us safely to the Summit House."

Years later MacKaye recalled how these experiences nourished his idea for the Appalachian Trail. "It may have been this summer with Horace; or perhaps back in '97 on that trip with Sturgis when we used to talk about Mt. Mitchell [North Carolina] and the Ranges which lay between," he wrote Harvey Broome in 1932. He remembered telling the headmaster of his camp in 1902, a man with the evocative name of Virgil Prettyman, "that there should be a trail from Mt. Washington to Mt. Mitchell. He was sanguine for all my projects but this was a trifle beyond the imagination of that day. 'A damn fool scheme, Mac', was his blunt reply." Immediately after the publication of his seminal Appalachian Trail article in the *Journal of the American Institute of Architects* in the fall of 1921, MacKaye met with his former trail companions Pray and Hildreth to map out potential routes for the trail.

MacKaye left his imprint on the White Mountain landscape in more ways than one. The Appalachian Trail, of course, traverses these mountains, including some of the paths MacKaye hiked during that summer of 1897. And he had a minor, but significant, role in the creation of the White Mountain National Forest itself. The passage of the Weeks Act in 1911 permitted the federal government to purchase private lands for the creation of national forests in the east; the national forests in existence before that date had all been established on land already owned by the federal government in the western states. Uncertainties about the constitutionality of the measure, however, convinced the implementers of the bill that legal justification for such purposes might be found in the government's right to maintain navigable rivers and their tributaries. Thus MacKaye was sent to the White Mountains under the auspices of the U.S. Geological Survey in the autumn of 1912 to map the region's forest cover. His report on the relationship of forests to the flow of northern New England's rivers helped to buttress the technical argument for acquisition of the lands that compose the White Mountain National Forest.

Finally, the designation of more than 100,000 acres within the national forest as federal Wilderness Areas was in no small measure a result of the efforts of The Wilderness Society in drafting and promoting the 1964 Wilderness Act; MacKaye, besides being a co-founder of the Society in 1935, served as an officer or councillor of the organization until the time of his death. MacKaye's contributions to all these efforts are destined to be long-lasting. And they can all be traced, at least in modest degree, back to that August morning in 1897, when he ascended the summit of Mount Tremont alone to observe a sunrise that would remain vivid in his memory throughout a long and productive lifetime.

MacKaye's very first published piece of writing was based on his adventures in the mountains of New England during the years around the turn of the century. His article, "Our White Mountain Trip: Its Organization and Methods," appeared in 1904 in the *Log of Camp Moosilauke*, published by the camp where he worked. In the article MacKaye recounts in careful detail the outfitting and camping practices of the ten-member, ten-day hike he led across the White Mountains that summer. He considers such practical matters as food, equipment, and campsite selection ("The rule must be: 'The possible best rather than the impossible ideal.'"); "tramping" ("try to spend the same amount of energy for every given unit of time"); shelter (the hikers built lean-tos of poles and boughs); campfire palaver; and "breaking camp" ("a process very simple though surprisingly long").

MacKaye's informative portrait of life along the trail in an era long before Gore-Tex, rip-stop nylon, and freeze-dried eggs suggests how little the essentials of such an experience have changed, even if some of the trappings have. In fact, as in much of his writing, MacKaye articulated the fundamental and timeless attributes of outdoor recreation. The concluding passage of his article follows the heading "Camp Ethics"; it is a concise and pointed summation of his own sense of responsibility for the environment that he had come to know and enjoy so well over the course of eight years. "The simplest rule of conduct for a camper is to leave a place as he would like to find it," he recommended, adding that "such conduct is becoming more and more the tradition, and hence camping as an institution is giving greater enjoyment every year." But he was less approving of the behavior of the "picnicker," who leaves his litter everywhere and "improves the rocky summit of every mountain with his initials." MacKaye was especially distressed about the condition of the Appalachian Mountain Club's hut on Mount Madison, where the grounds and the woodbox were repository of "hundreds of tin cans and broken glass jars" despite the presence at the hut of a clearly identified dumping spot. "The pernicious principle illustrated here is one of disdain for those who are to come after." MacKaye in the summer of 1904 had just finished his first year in the graduate program in forestry at Harvard; his freshly attained background in the discipline led him to draw a telling parallel between the behavior of thoughtless picnickers and the rapacious lumbering he observed that summer long the East Branch of the Pemigewasset River. "The contempt shown by the unconscientious guest at Madison Hut for those who are to come afterward and that shown by the lumberman in the East Branch are both identical in principle."

Benton MacKaye's conception of "camp ethics" provides a down-to-earth, immediately practicable example of Aldo Leopold's land ethic. "Camping," a pastime at once careful and carefree, is nothing more than good citizenship, common sense, and self-respect:

> There is no other sport or mode of living which so clearly exemplifies the need of each to do his share and the dependence of all upon the resources of nature. If we are to have these resources, whether lumber or other; if things are to be used and not dissipated; if we are to have a camping ground and not a desert, we must work and fight for these ends. The

duty of the camper, as one with greater opportunities in this respect than the average citizen, is to preserve the resources which nature has bestowed and to cherish the land as he would his home.

Benton MacKaye—camper, rover, trailmaker, optimist, visionary—felt at home in the White Mountain wilderness, and cherished it, on the trail and in imagination. The lesson he learned there so well, and spent a lifetime trying to teach others, is that wilderness is the "known quantity from which we came"—the common home of humanity. Thoreau, considering the declining prospects for roving in the vicinity of Concord, had warned against the temptation to hoard the landscape for "a narrow and exclusive pleasure only." It was an admonition Benton MacKaye took to heart, in his own lifelong effort to practice what he called "the reverse art of leading civilization to the wilderness."

A Note on Sources
Benton MacKaye's 1897 trip through New Hampshire and the White Mountains has been reconstructed here from a number of documents among his papers at Dartmouth College; they are quoted by permission of the literary executors of Benton MacKaye and the Dartmouth College Library.

The main source is MacKaye's handwritten journal of the trip. According to a note accompanying the journal, it had been returned to MacKaye in 1933 by Sturgis Pray's widow, who found it among her husband's effects; Pray died in 1929, after serving for twenty years as chairman of the graduate landscape architecture program at Harvard University.

MacKaye also wrote numerous letters to friends and family recounting and embellishing his trip. Those relied upon in this article include: letter to Mary Medbery MacKaye, his mother, 7 August 1897; letter to Maud Hosford, 21 August 1897; letter to Emily von Hesse ("Aunt Emmie"), 25 August 1897; letter to Sarah Stetson Pevear ("Aunt Sadie"), 28 August 1897. MacKaye's 5 September 1932 letter to Harvey Broome, besides containing recollections about the origins of his idea for the Appalachian Trail, also includes many autobiographical details concerning, among other things, MacKaye's Shirley boyhood and his experiences in the U.S. Forest Service. MacKaye's article in *Log of Camp Moosilauke, 1904* is also among his papers at Dartmouth.

Expedition Nine: A Return to a Region (Washington, D. C.: Wilderness Society, 1969) is only fifty pages long, but it is a deft summary of MacKaye's ideas about wilderness preservation and nature study, based on the lore and landscape of the region surrounding his Shirley home. *The New Exploration: A Philosophy of Regional Planning* (1928; reprint, Urbana: University of Illinois Press/Appalachian Trail Conference, 1991) is MacKaye's keystone work. Prophetic in many ways, *The New Exploration* is the book in which MacKaye most thoroughly outlines his vision of an ideal balance among urban, rural, and "primeval" environments. This minor classic still makes rewarding reading as a pioneering and sophisticated study in the meaning of environmentalism. *From Geography to Geotechnics* (Urbana: University of Illinois Press, 1968), edited by Paul T. Bryant, is a representative collection of MacKaye's articles on "outdoor culture," regional planning, and "geotechnics."

"Recreational Possibilities of Public Forests" appeared in the *Journal of the New York State Forestry Association*, October 1916, pp. 4-10, 29-31; MacKaye relied extensively upon his friend Allen Chamberlain's article, "Recreational Use of Public Forests in New England," in *Proceedings of the Society of American Foresters*, July 1916, pp. 271-280. "An Appalachian Trail, A Project in Regional Planning" was published in the *Journal of the American Institute of Architects*, October 1921, pp. 325-330. The source for some of the information about MacKaye's early hiking trips, his friendship with Chamberlain, and "the reverse art of leading civilization to the wilderness" is his article, "Some Early A. T. History," in the *Potomac Appalachian Trail Club Bulletin*, October-December 1957, pp. 91-96. The results of MacKaye's 1912 White Mountain survey are incorporated in a report of the U.S. Geological Survey, *The Relation of Forests to Stream Flow* (1913).

Aldo Leopold's thoughts on nature and humanity are from "Why the Wilderness Society?" which ran in the first issue of the society's magazine, *Living Wilderness*, September 1935, p. 6. Sturgis Pray's ideas about trail-making in the White Mountains can be found in his article "The

New Swift River Trail and Its Bearing on the Club's Policy," in *Appalachia*, May 1903, pp. 173-179. For a flavor of the setting and history of Albany Intervale I have relied upon *Passaconaway in the White Mountains*, by Charles E. Beals, Jr. (1916; Conway, N.H.: Minuteman Press, 1983), and upon my own hikes in the area.

(1987)

A "Classic of the Green Mountains": The 1900 Vermont Hike of Benton MacKaye and Horace Hildreth

It was the summer of 1900. The two recent Harvard graduates, free for a few leisure months before facing the sobering responsibilities of autumn and adulthood, set out for a north country adventure. Little did they then know that their Vermont excursion would cement a lifetime friendship and help to inspire the 2,100-mile Appalachian Trail from Springer Mountain in Georgia to Katahdin in Maine.

The two young men were Horace Hildreth, a long-time resident of Harvard, Massachusetts, and his friend Benton MacKaye from the neighboring town of Shirley. The two had been close during the three years they shared at Harvard College; Hildreth had graduated in 1899, MacKaye in 1900. MacKaye, in fact, defrayed a share of his college expenses by reading for and tutoring Hildreth. But the two had first become acquainted in 1895, according to MacKaye's recollection, probably through mutual family friends.

Those years were truly the "Gay 90s" for cosmopolitan and educated families like the MacKayes and the Hildreths, who added an element of zest and culture to these rural hill towns. The Hildreths had deeper roots in the area; the MacKayes were relative newcomers and only part-time residents in the years when Benton and Horace came to know each other. Benton, son of the colorful playwright and actor Steele MacKaye, arrived in Shirley in 1887 at the age of eight. The family's financial situation often bordered on the disastrous, and the MacKayes found that they could live economically and comfortably, at least during the summer months, in their cottage at Shirley Center. There they could enjoy the country atmosphere without actually having to endure the responsibilities and tedious routines of farming. They could also share the company of other families who were, in the latter years of the nineteenth century, purchasing pastoral retreats in towns like Shirley and Harvard. Organizing concerts, dances, plays, hayrides, skating parties, and other diversions, the young men and ladies of such families reveled in the rural surroundings. "The summer people were generally welcomed and they added to the quality of life in the community," one friend of MacKaye's, a ninth-generation Shirley native, has observed. "Sometimes, however, the natives felt that they were regarded with a missionary or explorer attitude, like Rousseau's 'noble savage,' rustics to be observed and studied like Margaret Mead's Samoans."

MacKaye and Hildreth shared many of the same enthusiasms, including cross-country tramping, railroads, geology, and the works of Gilbert and Sullivan. The two-week trip they planned for the summer of 1900 permitted them to indulge some of these interests. They had studied geology and geography at Harvard under two of the most eminent earth scientists of the era, Nathaniel Southgate Shaler and William Morris Davis. These distinguished men of science had inspired their students to observe the regional landscape in a systematic and purposeful fashion. Indeed, Davis borrowed the name of Mount Monadnock, visible from Shirley and Harvard, as the generic term for a solitary mountain surviving in an eroded peneplain. And MacKaye, in his extensive later writings about regional planning, outdoor recreation, and wilderness reservation, often used examples from the "Montachusett" region to illustrate his ideas. (MacKaye was on hand at a 1929 conference when a close friend, a *Fitchburg Sentinel* editor, coined this term to describe the landscape bounded by the mountains Monadnock, Watatic, and Wachusett.)

MacKaye and Hildreth had already taken a number of more modest excursions before 1900. In April 1899, during a break from their Harvard studies, they explored a stretch of the Nashua River by canoe. And probably in the summer of that same year, which MacKaye spent on the farm of family friends in Brattleboro, the two made their first trip along Vermont's West River Valley, described by Hildreth years later as "the most beautiful place in the world." They rode the narrow gauge Brattleboro and Whitehall Railroad, "part way atop a bumping freight car," to what was then its northernmost point in South London-derry. "It was one of my expeditionary highlights," Hildreth wrote almost four decades later. "The sky was very blue and the clouds very white. The deciduous foliage was very green and the wild exalia [sic] very pink; what might be termed vivid indigenosity!" ("Indigenosity" was a play on one of MacKaye's favorite words, "indigenous," which he used in his own writing to describe communities and landscapes uncor-rupted by what he called the "metropolitan invasion.")

MacKaye, in the previous summers of his college years, had already become familiar with New Hampshire's White Mountains. His first and most rugged mountain expedition was a month-long 1897 trip with several other Harvard friends. That journey had taken them by bicycle from Shirley to the Swift River Valley west of Conway, New Hamp-shire. From Albany Intervale, then a remote valley settlement long before the Kancamagus Highway traversed those southern ranges of the White Mountains, MacKaye set out with his friends on a hike that led them across the Presidential Range and back eventually to their Albany Intervale starting point. This excursion, which included being caught in fierce lightning storms on mountain summits, a close call with a bear, exhausting bushwhacks where trails did not exist, and other rigors and rhapsodies, started MacKaye on his long and productive career as one of the leading figures of the American conservation movement in the twentieth century.

On the morning of July 14, 1900, MacKaye and his older brother Percy (himself a Harvard graduate who would go on to achieve a measure of fame as a playwright and poet) met Hildreth at Shirley Village, where they caught a westbound train. Headed for Vermont, their goal was to climb many of the state's highest mountains, beginning in the south and working their way north. At the turn of the century there were trails to the summits of many of these mountains. Today's Vermont hiker on a similar mission would stick to the Long Trail, the 265-mile footpath that follows the Green Mountains from the Massachusetts border to Canada. In 1900, though, no such trail yet existed to connect Vermont's summits. The idea for the Long Trail was not broached until 1910 by James Taylor, and the Green Mountain Club did not complete the footpath until 1930. So the route of the MacKaye-Hildreth expedition, by "back road, cart path, and sheer bushwhacking," as MacKaye later wrote, would be devised by the trampers themselves along the way. Forty-one years later, Hildreth remembered their journey as "our *Classic of the Green Mountains.*"

The details of the southern leg of their trip are sketchy, consisting of little more than scattered recollections in the correspondence between MacKaye and Hildreth. From Shirley they may have ridden the train west as far as the Hoosac Tunnel. There the main railroad line left the valley of the Deerfield River to enter the 25,000-foot tunnel. A branch line, the Hoosac Tunnel and Wilmington Railroad, followed the river north to the village of Monroe Bridge and across the Vermont border to the towns of Readsboro and Wilmington. Possibly they rode a stretch of this line on a flatbed car in front of the engine, from indications in Hildreth's later recollections. For years to come, as he rode the important east-west line of the Boston & Maine on his many business trips, Hildreth would often write to MacKaye en route, still inspired by the sight of the Deerfield River Valley—both the memories it brought back and the possibilities for future exploration it promised. "The Deerfield River Canyon is marvellous as ever," he wrote MacKaye in 1936 during one of his trips, remembering their 1900 expedition.

Over the course of the next week the trio made their way, perhaps following roads along the East Branch of the Deerfield River, to the summits of Haystack (3,420 feet) in Wilmington, Stratton (3,936 feet), and Bromley (3,260 feet) in Peru. (All of these mountains have since become the sites of downhill ski areas.) This was a region of the Green

Grout's Job, a logging settlement, south of Stratton Mountain, Vermont, 1900.
(Courtesy of Dartmouth College Library.)

Mountains that could still be described in the 1930s, according to one popular guidebook, as "densely forested and unpenetrated wilds that constitute the largest tract of wilderness in Vermont." In an era when concern was increasing about the rate at which northern New England's forests were being harvested, MacKaye and Hildreth visited "Grout's Job," a short-lived logging settlement near Stratton Mountain. The area around Stratton was one they would return to again and again over the years, measuring the changes in the forest and the landscape against their first experiences and observations in 1900.

On July 21, in Dorset, the hikers boarded the Rutland Railroad northbound. Percy took his departure at Rutland, leaving Benton and Horace to continue the journey. Percy presented his younger brother with a small notebook, inscribed with the exhortation: "Benton—record your details—and 'Keep a-peggin' away.'" The notebook survives among MacKaye's papers at the Dartmouth College Library, and his account of the trip from Rutland to Morrisville not only provides a sense of MacKaye's animated personality but gives a lively and personal portrait of the turn-of-the-century physical and social landscape of central Vermont.

MacKaye and Hildreth made their way on foot east on the "Notch Road" towards the next mountain on their itinerary, 4,235-foot Killington Peak in the town of Sherburne. "Stop to get drink; thug came along in wagon," MacKaye tersely recorded in his journal. "I left the axe which he took. Met another old buck Irish going other way, said thief was called 'Henkley.' Probably lied." They found lodging that night at the rustic home of a French-Canadian woman who made her living taking in lodgers. The "old man" resident at Mrs. Mercy's sold butter and other farm goods "to the 'dark complexion folk in the city who now speak English or French' the Roumanians," as MacKaye transcribed the man's conversation. After a night's sleep next to a flea-infested dog and a "greasey" breakfast in the company of chickens that roamed freely through the house, MacKaye and Hildreth made for Killington. Near the summit, they were offered a drink by some raucous hikers who had hauled a keg of spirits up the mountain the previous night. They enjoyed a panoramic view of the White Mountains to the east, the Adirondacks to the west, the southern Vermont mountains from which they had just come, and the mountains to the north they had yet to explore.

MacKaye was alert both to the ethnic distinctions evident in these Vermont hills and valleys and to the lay of the land—a reflection, perhaps, of the influence of his professors Shaler and Davis, who promoted the theory that geography shaped the behavior and character traits of different human races. Back on the road again toward North Sherburne, they "Guffed with [an] Irishman who said three things he would not change, 'his name, his religion, and his politics.' He would vote for Bryan, tho' he 'might get beat again.'"

After a night in another bug-infested house, MacKaye and Hildreth were glad to be on their way the next morning. "The people in this Otter Creek Valley are mostly French and Irish. A man's shanty in the woods where he used to camp was burned because he locked it up. Specimen of the people's conduct. We are anxious to get into the Conn. R. valley again," MacKaye wrote. A height of land not 200 yards from

Benton MacKaye on the road in Vermont, summer, 1900.
(Courtesy of Dartmouth College Library.)

their lodgings, he observed, marked the divide between Otter Creek and the Tweed River, a tributary of the White (and thereby of the Connecticut), which they followed by way of Pittsfield ("had a moxie") to Gaysville. They caught a freight train to Bethel, and another to Roxbury. "The country is less bold than toward Rutland," MacKaye noted, "tho' the hills are still very high. Rail and board fences, more than stonewalls."

Hiking west along the steep road leading over the Northfield range, the trampers secured lodging at a hill farm. "An old buck, his wife apparently, an *aged* man and a young man, made up the family. They had no horse on the place; used oxen; raise cattle; had just begun haying. Said wolves have been seen further north within 2 yrs. Not much

lumbering now, because first growth had all been cut off. . . . Best
night's rest on trip. Had sheets."

The next day, the 24th, Hildreth and MacKaye ambled along hot and
unshaded roads (present-day Route 100) through East Warren and
Warren, and north along the Mad River to Irasville. The next summit on
their route was 4,083-foot Camel's Hump. They headed west along a
back road toward North Fayston to begin their approach to the mountain. J. B. Thompson, proprietor of the farm where they spent the night,
was a paragon of Yankee virtues, in MacKaye's eyes; he had "taught
school, been to the legislature, etc. now on school board." The hikers
spent much of the next day, a rainy one, helping out around Thompson's farm, pitching hay and cleaning harnesses.

Thompson directed them to a Mr. Johnson up the road, "a fat genial
old cuss. . . . He puts up barns. Says a close barn gives cattle tuberculo-
sis." Johnson told MacKaye about the 10,000-acre forest preserve in
Fayston and Ripton donated by Middlebury's Joseph Battell and the
extensive farm being developed by the wealthy Webb family in Shel-
burne. Concerning local forestry practices, however, the barnbuilder
was less approving. "Lumbering is done by cutting clean," noted
MacKaye, who was three years away from making the decision to
become a forester. "He thinks poor thing."

Johnson, after putting up the two young men for the night ("Cost for
lodging & breakfast—*zero.*"), gave them directions across the rugged
terrain to Camel's Hump. There was a good trail from a sawmill at the
base of the mountain, but to reach it they had to cross "a blow down,
swamp & general damnation on top" of an intervening mountain. Not
far from Camel's Hump's rocky, cold, and windy summit they built a
"lead-to" [sic] for the night. It took two hours to start a fire for their
oatmeal supper, but they spent a comfortable night on the mountain
top. "The only sound which startled us was a weird cooing."

The next morning, MacKaye and Hildreth descended the north slope
of the mountain, and walked along the Winooski River to North
Duxbury and Waterbury, meeting on the way a young fellow who
worked in an electric plant on the river. "He asked us if we were 'jack
tars,' seeing the U.S.N. on our knapsacks. Offered us a drink of whis-

key. Quite upset that we refused & in general dismayed at our conduct and walking apparently with no end in view."

Walking for its own sake, of course, was the whole point of the excursion. But after stocking up on provisions in Waterbury ("quite a place, swell, with side walks, shade trees & croket [sic] grounds"), they were glad to take advantage of the electric trolley that ran to Stowe, a town whose prosperous appearance and atmosphere seemed to unsettle MacKaye slightly. "[A] strange air prevaded [sic] everything." He sketched the "unique form" of the church's steeple, noted the prevalence of brick architecture, and was amused by the town's various signs announcing such matters as "'ice cream & cake at Unity Church at eight o'clock' etc."

On the road toward Mount Mansfield, they negotiated with a sullen couple for a place to bed down. "[A]fter going from the woman in the home to the man milking cows in the barn across the road, and back again, we finally got in for the night. The woman would 'leave it to the man,' the latter would say, 'it is just as the woman say.'" The ramshackle farmstead "was in a sorry condition: loose boards, stray chickens, naked kids, slouchy mother, stinks, etc. etc. In this we had breakfast. The slush to go on the potatoes was the worst yet." Rural life on the hill farms of Vermont seemed somehow less civilized than what MacKaye was used to back home in Shirley.

MacKaye and Hildreth had one more mountain to climb in their peak-bagging expedition, 4,393-foot Mount Mansfield, Vermont's highest point. Following the carriage road, the trampers reached the "Nose" of the mountain, the southern peak of its long ridgeline. MacKaye had nearly exhausted the supply of superlatives available to describe stunning mountaintop views, so he reached for a classical analogy. Observing Lake Champlain to the west as the sun descended, he noted that "the islands showed up distinctly & reminded me of the Isles of Greece"—islands he had never seen except in his mind's eye. From the "Chin" of the mountain, its true peak, he observed that it "was here that the effect [of the sun] on the lake was so glorious. The Isles of Greece from Olympus, if such could have been." He essayed a rough sketch of this vista in his journal, but it falls short of capturing the sublime spirit that so inspired him.

They roamed around the mountaintop until sunset, then scrambled down the carriage road. "We heard one beast prowling in the woods, otherwise the walk was uneventful." At the home of Mrs. Luce, a "funny, fat, old few teethed thing" who took them in for the night, they were provided a late supper of crackers and milk. The next day, a Sunday, MacKaye and Hildreth help the friendly Mrs. Luce with her chores, listened to her reminisce, then walked back into the village of Stowe, passing by "the house of the man with the kids & loose boards." In Stowe, the two stopped for services at the Methodist church. "The text was 'Where art thou' of Adam, Eve, the Serpent, etc. We howled fairly loud." The sermon lasted almost an hour, and MacKaye escaped being recruited for Sunday school, "a feat which an urgent stomach ache of the time did not allow."

The last leg of their hike was along the road to Morrisville, which they followed at a leisurely pace, stopping so that MacKaye could recover from his stomach troubles; nonetheless, he was able to enjoy the lunch of maple sugar and bread that Mrs. Luce had packed for them. He photographed the riverside pastures and noted the changes in the landscape, which appeared as "something like that to the north of White Mts. in N.H." They spent an unsettled night in Morrisville, sleeping in a box car. "A freight train came along about 11 o'clock. We were afraid of discovery & lighted out. Got back again; heard 'noises' all night till 1.00 a.m."

The next morning, July 30, they rose early, had breakfast at the railroad station, and boarded a 6:15 train homeward bound. MacKaye calculated their expenses for food, lodging, and train fare since leaving Rutland ten days earlier at $12.01, which the two explorers split—one of them apparently picking up the extra penny. Hildreth, shortly after his arrival back in the town of Harvard, reported to MacKaye that "I spent all my time eating."

That fall Hildreth returned to his studies, this time at M.I.T., where he took an engineering degree in 1901. His varied career included an early stint working for railroads in New York and Pennsylvania; then he pursued a number of other business ventures, such as banking, mining, and family manufacturing business in Harvard. He was also active in many community organizations in Harvard, including the library, the Historical Society, the Bromfield Trust, and local Republican politics.

MacKaye took his first full-time job in the fall of 1900, tutoring schoolboys from well-heeled families in New York City. He returned to Harvard University in 1903 for a degree in the new profession of forestry (his tuition and other expenses covered in large measure by a substantial loan on generous terms from Edwin A. Hildreth, Horace's father). His career as a bureaucrat, writer, regional planner, and philosopher of "outdoor culture" brought him into contact with scores of important figures in American politics and reform movements from the time he joined the United States Forest Service in 1905 until his death at age 96 in 1975. While his reputation is modest, his impact on several generations of planners, environmentalists, politicians, and writers has been substantial. As the author Lewis Mumford, MacKaye's long-time friend and colleague, has written: "Nobody else in our time has pointed out more clearly the terms upon which modern man, and in particular the American people, may occupy the Earth and use judiciously all our resources, natural, technical, and urban, without making the land itself uninhabitable and our own life unendurable."

MacKaye's most influential piece of writing was his 1921 article in the *Journal of the American Institute of Architects,* "An Appalachian Trail: A Project in Regional Planning," which outlined his ambitious scheme for a footpath the length of the Appalachian Mountains. Soon after the piece appeared, MacKaye, who had lived in Washington and traveled the country extensively on official duties during much of the previous decade, returned to his Shirley home, where he began plotting a route for the trail as well as a campaign to implement its creation. One of the first people he called on for advice was his old hiking companion Horace Hildreth. And in July 1922 the two returned to some of the southern Vermont terrain they had traversed more than two decades earlier. (Hildreth's son Edwin recalls that MacKaye coined the term "shrining" to describe this nostalgic and almost ritualistic return to the

Horace Hildreth at Camp Webster, on the Long Trail, south of Stratton Mountain, Vermont, July, 1922. (Courtesy of Dartmouth College Library.)

sites of past explorations.) MacKaye wanted to use the area in the vicinity of Stratton Mountain as a sample chapter for a handbook he was writing (and never saw published) about the geography through which the Appalachian Trail would pass. Their three-day hike took them along the Long Trail from near Bennington some twenty-odd miles over Stratton Mountain. They observed other dramatic changes in the landscape since 1900 besides the presence of the Long Trail. Grout's Job, the busy logging camp they had visited in 1900, was now abandoned. The headwaters of the Deerfield River had been dammed for the production of hydroelectric power, creating such new bodies of water as the Somerset and Harriman Reservoirs. Hildreth returned to the Stratton area once again in 1934 on one of his country excursions. He climbed Stratton Mountain and visited the site of Grout's Job. Writing to MacKaye, then on the planning staff of the new Tennessee Valley Authority, Hildreth reported that "now a complete forest cycle has elapsed and Grout's Job is again active."

Hildreth died in 1945. That same year MacKaye retired from a career of government service that had spanned forty years. He then began a five-year stint as president of the Wilderness Society, which he had co-founded ten years earlier with other luminaries of the conservation movement, including Aldo Leopold and Robert Marshall. Though virtually blind in his very last years, he remained active and articulate in the promotion of his favorite causes right up until his death in Shirley. And MacKaye often remembered his 1900 expedition through Vermont with his close friend Horace Hildreth, "a pioneer in the reverse art of leading civilization to the wilderness," as one of the experiences that most influenced his vision of the Appalachian Trail.

"We walked up through the trailless woods to the top of Stratton Mountain and climbed trees in order to see the view," MacKaye wrote in a message to the 1964 Appalachian Trail Conference, vividly recollecting the experiences of that summer of 1900. "It was a clear day with a brisk breeze blowing. North and south sharp peaks etched the horizon. I felt as if atop the world, with a sort of 'planetary feeling.' I seemed to perceive peaks far southward, hidden by old Earth's curvature. Would a footpath someday reach them from where I was then perched?"

MacKaye and Hildreth did indeed live to see the result of their tree-climbing exploits on Stratton Mountain. By 1937, volunteers had cleared a footpath along the mountains from Maine to Georgia. Benton Mac-Kaye's Vermont hike with Horace Hildreth, their "Classic of the Green Mountains," has by now become part of the folklore of the Appalachian Trail.

(1986)

Where Paths Cross, a Path Begins

The trail was nearly level where it crossed the open glade of hardwoods, spruce, and fir. There, perhaps fifty yards ahead and to the left, the animal entered my field of view. Alert and wary, possibly more surprised than I, it stopped in the middle of the trail. I stopped too. Leaning back on its tensed haunches, the creature offered me a brief but clear look at its profile: dark, almost black; a long, bushy tail; small ears. It wasn't a dog, a coyote, a bear cub, or a bobcat. Plenty of people claim they've seen evidence of mountain lions in New England in recent years. But this animal was too small, its form was too stout to be really feline—and anyway, black panthers were entirely out of the question.

Two curious species, one at home, the other passing through, we froze in place for only a few seconds, our eyes meeting momentarily. Then the animals sprang out of sight, vanishing into the woods. Unsettled, adrenaline flowing, I resumed my pace, only gradually regaining my breath and rhythm.

Poring over guidebooks later, I determined that what I had seen must have been *Martes pennanti*—a fisher. This larger cousin of the marten and weasel "was common throughout New England during early settlement," observes Alfred Godin in his definitive *Wild Mammals of New England*, "but soon disappeared in most of New England due to overtrapping, logging, and clearing of the forest for agriculture." The fisher has made a comeback in the region, however, "[I]ts speed of dispersal seems to be related to hilly country," Godin writes, "regardless of the kind of forest cover present in New England."

I had been walking along the Sleeper Trail, a short, gentle path that connects Mt. Whiteface with Mt. Tripyramid in the Sandwich Range, the southernmost hills in New Hampshire's White Mountain National Forest, between the lake country to the south and the higher peaks, including the Presidential Range, to the north. The trail takes its name from the Sleepers, a pair of barely discernible knobs in the forested gap between Whiteface and Tripyramid. As it traverses the Sleepers, the trail demarcates the watershed of the Mad and Swift rivers.

Godin's account exactly fit the setting and the situation. Fishers, he continues, "travel greatly in search of food." To describe their cross-country scavenging, Godin cited another naturalist, who "stated that fishers prefer to travel along ridges, usually crossing small streams to get to the next ridge, and added that such a 'crossing may be used by generations of fisher.'"

I had started early that morning, making good time on the trail that ascends steadily from the Kancamagus Highway to the ridge, following Downes Brook. I wanted to get ahead of the crowds on this late fall weekend, which always bring hordes to the White Mountains. I hadn't yet seen another hiker. Somewhere along the way, though, as I knew from the map at the trailhead, I had crossed a surveyor's line marking the boundary of a designated federal Wilderness Area. Established in 1984 and covering roughly 25,000 acres, the Sandwich Range Wilderness is one of five separate Wilderness Areas which together comprise about 15 percent of the 772,000-acre White Mountain National Forest.

My hike was an historical pilgrimage, an act of homage to a man who had walked the same woods in the late 1890s and early 1900s. I was following the footsteps of Benton MacKaye, the long-lived (he died in 1975 at the age of 96) forester, regional planner, conservationist, author, and visionary best known for his conception of the Appalachian Trail. I was retracing the first and last legs of a two-week hiking circuit of the White Mountains he completed with several fellow Harvard students in the summer of 1897.

MacKaye's hike through the mountains that summer, he later observed, marked the time "I first saw the true wilderness." The experience changed his life—and changed as well, in subtle but significant ways, the prospects and the uses of America's remaining wild lands. MacKaye's adventures and observations right here, on the slopes and summits of Passaconaway, Whiteface, Tripyramid, and the surrounding hills, contributed directly to the area's protection as Wilderness— indeed, to the protection of Wilderness Areas around the country. MacKaye was one of that hardy tribe—including the likes of Muir, Marshall, Leopold, the Muries, Zahniser, and Brower—who nurtured the organizations, the spirit, the philosophy, and the laws that preserved the possibility for such modest but meaningful encounters as I had experienced on Sleeper Trail. They saved a space where a fisher and I might cross paths.

In a windowless, climate-controlled archive, I had read MacKaye's original handwritten journal of his 1897 mountain excursion. Though, by his own account, he and his companions endured more than one fierce storm when rain came down like "pitchforks," he had managed to protect his pocket notebook from the elements. Now, years later, the quills he had gathered from a dead porcupine still pierced the journal's pages. His crude sketches yet evoked the stunning mountain vistas that so inspired him.

The hikers completed a loop covering much of the mountain terrain that would later be incorporated into the White Mountain National Forest. From the remote Swift River Valley settlement of Albany Intervale, or Passaconaway, near where I had begun my own day hikes, MacKaye and his companions headed north over such mountains as Tremont, Lowell, Anderson, Washington, and other summits of the southern Presidentials. Following roads south along the Franconia Range, they completed their hike by climbing over Osceola and Tripyramid—the latter mountain my destination as I followed the Sleeper Trail—to return to their starting place.

It had been on the very first day of MacKaye's hike, though, that a mountain experience struck him with the force of revelation. During their rigorous approach to the modest 3,384-foot summit of Mt.

Tremont, the hikers crossed a blowdown, and ascended the steepest part of the mountain in a torrential downpour; then, in the middle of a fearsome lightning storm, they set up camp during the night on what they thought was the mountain's summit. Awaking cold and wet before sunrise the next morning, MacKaye determined that they were in fact a quarter-mile from the "true summit." Alone, he ascended Tremont. "The grandest sight I ever saw was now before me," he noted in his journal, "nothing but a sea of mountains and clouds." The sunrise view from the mountain was panoramic, taking in much of the White Mountain range as well as "the hills of old Massachusetts" to the south. "I felt then," he wrote a friend, "how much I resembled in size one of the hairs on the eye tooth of a flea, to use a vulgar expression."

A century ago, in many respects and by whatever definition, this New Hampshire terrain was less of a "wilderness" than it is today. These mountains and forests had a different aspect in the 1890s. MacKaye's trip came at the climax of the region's timber boom, when logging railroads wound up every valley. He walked among the ruins of the logging epoch, camping in abandoned lumber camps and hitching rides on the railroads. The tide was turning, as the century turned, and MacKaye was riding the flow. The timber barons of New England were frantically shaving spruce and fir off the mountain slopes. The ravages of the lumberman sparked a response, however, from a growing legion of hikers, resort owners, and reformers. In 1876, some of them had created the Appalachian Mountain Club. By the turn of the century, a movement to create an Appalachian national reserve was growing in such southern states as Tennessee, North Carolina, and Virginia. North and south along the Appalachian range, activists joined forces. After passage of the 1911 Weeks Law, which authorized creation of the first National Forests in the East (including the White Mountain National Forest), some of the East's highest, wildest terrain began to be retrieved for common use and enjoyment.

One of MacKaye's trail companions was Sturgis Pray, then on the threshold of a career as an eminent landscape architect. Trained in the Brookline, Massachusetts offices of Frederick Law Olmsted, Sr., Pray

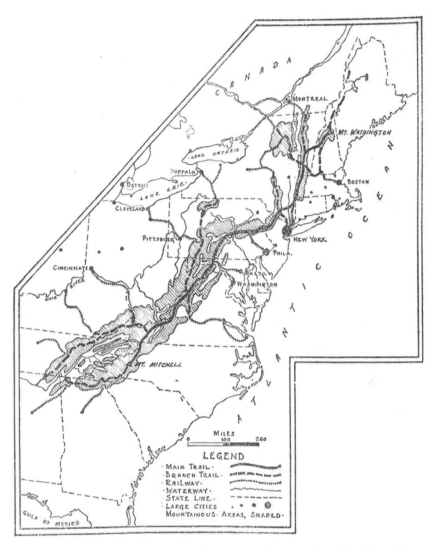

Benton MacKaye's original map of the proposed Appalachian Trail, from his article, "An Appalachian Trail: A Project in Regional Planning," published in the *Journal of the American Institute of Architects*, October, 1921.

would go on to head Harvard's pioneering landscape architecture program. Until failing health and professional obligations overtook him at a relatively young age, he also maintained an intense interest in the mountains. For the Appalachian Mountain Club, he oversaw the maintenance and expansion of the network of hiking trails spreading across the White Mountains.

Pray, MacKaye later observed, held to a simple axiom for the design of a hiking trail: it should be wide enough for "one fat man to barge through." MacKaye often credited his hiking partner's notion of a "path through a pathless wood" as a key inspiration for his own vision of the Appalachian Trail. In October 1921, MacKaye's article, "An Appalachian Trail: A Project in Regional Planning," appeared in the *Journal of the American Institute of Architects.* By 1937, Eastern trail enthusiasts had completed the continuous footpath, which today stretches for more than 2,100 miles between Georgia and Maine. The Appalachian Trail became a model for trails and greenways throughout the country. Its success inspired passage of the 1968 National Scenic Trails Act. In combination with that year's Wild and Scenic Rivers Act, the legal framework was in place for what MacKaye, as early as 1916, had envisioned as a "linked-up . . . national recreation ground which would reach from ocean to ocean."

But the Appalachian Trail was just one of MacKaye's important contributions to the reclamation of the American environment. And recreation was not the only—or even the principal—element of his evolving vision of the American landscape. From the utilitarian conservationism of Gifford Pinchot's Forest Service, which he entered as a fledgling forester in 1905, to the land ethic of his friend Aldo Leopold, whose *Sand County Almanac* he championed, MacKaye's life, work, and thought encompassed the American conservation and environmental movements in this century. In 1935, along with other conservationist luminaries such as Robert Marshall, Robert Sterling Yard, and Leopold, MacKaye co-founded the Wilderness Society.

Indeed, outliving many such friends and colleagues, he witnessed the realization of numerous ideas to which he devoted his life—ideas at first declared utopian or ignored outright. The 1964 Wilderness Act, for example, established by law the principle (if not always the practice) that untrammeled wilderness is the highest and best use of certain American lands and resources. MacKaye had drafted a federal wilderness law in 1936. A decade later, during his tenure as president of The Wilderness

Society, he had another version on Howard Zahniser's desk when the principal author and proponent of the 1964 law took over as the organization's executive secretary. Today, some 100-million acres of federal land are designated under the Wilderness Act.

This legal variety of wilderness, like the Sandwich Range acreage tucked among the ski areas, tourist resorts, and factory-outlet stores in New Hampshire's White Mountains, is still something novel on the American landscape. We're not quite sure what to make of it. Bureaucrats and academics gather for conferences, coolly analyzing the management, philosophy, ethics, and politics of wilderness. Activists of varied persuasions and extremes challenge the premises of the Wilderness Act—either complaining that designated Wilderness represents a paltry gesture at real wilderness protection, or railing against wilderness as an assault on freedom and their own uncompromising notion of the "wise use" of natural resources. Photographers bring back stunning images. Scientists study acid rain, ecosystems, endangered species. Hikers and climbers seek solitude, challenge, beauty, a measure of danger. Some, like myself, stalk other prey—exploring back through history, trying to see a wild place through other eyes, imagining what it might have been like to walk here in another time.

My momentary encounter with the Sleeper Ridge fisher remains with me. I remind myself that there was nothing mystical about our meeting—that I had not experienced another "epiphany around every corner," as author Terry Tempest Williams sardonically describes one commonplace literary response to the natural world in the late twentieth century. A fisher, these days, is not that rare an animal.

Nonetheless, this ridge route, the naturalists suggest, could have been favored by "generations of fisher." MacKaye's journal didn't mention any ancestors of my erstwhile trail acquaintance. But he and Sturgis Pray did startle a bear on the summit of Mt. Tremont; then they watched in awe moments later as two eagles soared above the mountain's cliffs.

Now, almost a century later, a fisher and I cross paths. It is in its element. But where am I? I do not—by law, I cannot—remain. I am a transient here. In America today, the paradoxical landscape I traverse is called "wilderness." For Benton MacKaye, the same terrain inspired the vision of an environment reclaimed, renewed, always evolving. Acting on his vision, he left a legacy that is incalculably significant—whether measured in miles of trail blazed, acres of Wilderness designated by law, species of wildlife protected, or numbers of activists inspired. Mac-Kaye's example endows us with hope and optimism in a gloomy time.

Today, almost a hundred years later, a fisher's domain still offers the prospect of new visions, new hopes, and new explorations. A century hence, will this modest spot on a quiet trail in the New Hampshire forest provide similar possibilities and prospects?

(1996)

POSTSCRIPT: Passage of the 2006 New England Wilderness Act added 10,800 acres to the Sandwich Range Wilderness Area. The law also created a new Wild River Wilderness Area, now comprising 24,030 acres, located in the White Mountain National Forest just west of the Maine border. Today, designated Wilderness constitutes 153,052 acres of the national forest.

As it happens, MacKaye, while working for the U.S. Department of Labor in 1918, collaborated with a Forest Service colleague, Austin F. Hawes, to develop plans for a government-sponsored forestry community at the site of an abandoned logging camp in the Wild River valley. Their proposal, under the auspices of a short-lived U.S. Wood Fuel Corporation, was projected to support 200 people. The residents were to include the families of loggers who would harvest lumber from the national forest on a sustainable basis, producing firewood, pulpwood, and "turnery" wood for a local bobbin factory. The plan was one of many wartime federal schemes and proposals to meet a projected national fuel emergency and to avert an anticipated postwar unemployment crisis. But the project was suspended immediately after the armistice of November 1918. Now, not quite a century later, that Wild River terrain is considered "wilderness."

"Our White Mountain Trip:
Its Organization and Methods"

BY BENTON MACKAYE

Log of Camp Moosilauke, 1904, yearbook of the boys' camp on Upper Baker Pond in Orford, New Hampshire, where Benton MacKaye worked as a councilor that summer, is reproduced here in its entirety by courtesy of the Dartmouth College Library. At the time, MacKaye had just completed his first year as a graduate student in Harvard's then new forestry program. His article in the *Log,* "Our White Mountain Trip: Its Organization and Methods," was the first article published by MacKaye in a long writing career; it is reprinted here on pages 61 through 68. In addition to other news and information about Camp Moosilauke, the *Log* also includes a narrative by Knowlton "Cub" Durham, "The Tramp of the Tattered Ten," which also describes the White Mountain hike he and his fellow camp councilor MacKaye led that summer.

My article about this excursion, "Benton MacKaye's 1904 White Mountain Hike: Exploring a Landscape of Logging, 'Camp Ethics,' and Patriotism," appears in *Nature and Culture in the Northern Forest: Region, Heritage and Environment in the Rural Northeast*, ed. Pavel Cenkl (Iowa City: University of Iowa Press, 2010), pp. 153-170.

Log

OF

Camp Moosilauke

1904

INTRODUCTION.

The Log of Camp Moosilauke, published annually, aims to give a resume of the life in Camp.

It is hoped that the articles contained in this number will be pleasant reminders of the life in the woods.

Our thanks are due to those who have reviewed for us the good times of our vacation of 1904.

Camp Moosilauke presents its greetings to members and friends.

CAMP COUNCIL.

Benton MacKaye, Harvard

Knowlton Durham, Columbia.

Gerald Curtis, Columbia.

George B. Leggett, Yale.

C. W. Prettyman Ph. D., University of Pennsylvania, Assistant Director.

Parley Monroe M. D., Columbia, Camp Physician.

Virgil Prettyman, Director.

CAMP ROSTER.

BOX I.

Archie Burchell
Lawrence Curtis
Adrian de Luna
William Herbert
Edward Johnstone
Thomas Meehan
Lloyd Richards
Dayton Smith

BOX II.

Jasper Campbell
Theodore Kenyon
Arthur Lawson
Tracy Lewis
Henry Naylor
Guy Steeves
Cyrus Turner

BOX III.

Ralph Baldwin
George Carrington
Richard Imhoff
Alfred Klüpfel
Salvador Rionda
William Sondheimer
John Steeves

BOX IV.

Wyman Herbert
Roland Klüpfel
Arthur Labaree
Irving Larom
Rufus Sommerville
Townsend Van Glahn
William Wollerton

BOX V.

Langdon Adams
Erskine Sanford
Leonard Thomas
Philip von Saltza

Our White Mountain Trip.

ITS ORGANIZATION AND METHODS.

BENTON MACKAYE.

Our party consisted of ten members, two masters and eight boys. The latter had been chosen from the candidates for the White Mountain trip, all of whom had been tested by several short preliminary trips. We left Camp Moosilauke on August 9th and were gone ten days. The purpose of this article is to outline the organization of the trip and the methods of camping employed.

OUTFIT.

The outfit included those articles alone which were absolutely necessary for comfort. For convenience, these articles were classified into five lists: Individual Outfit, Cooking Outfit, Medical Kit, Equipment, and Provisions. The "Individual Outfit" consisted of those articles which each member obtained for himself, and which he alone would use.

INDIVIDUAL OUTFIT.

Clothing—Woolen undershirt, or sleeveless jersey, woolen drawers or trunks, two pairs of woolen socks, trousers made of khaki or of other stout material, belt, flannel outing shirt, grey or blue jersey with sleeves, sweater, boots, "sneakers," hat with brim.

Blankets—One rubber blanket, (not a poncho); one heavy woolen blanket.

Other Articles—Tin cup, soap, comb, toothbrush, handkerchiefs, extra shoe lacings, safety pins, sewing kit, twine, knife, postal cards, pencil.

It is very important to wear the right kind of clothing. Woolen underwear is necessary to resist exposure to cold and dampness. The jersey with sleeves and the sweater, taken as extra clothing, were both required on account of the possibility of sudden mountain storms and of unusually cold nights. A pair of heavy easy boots is usually worn, but it is often a great relief to change them to "sneakers."

The blankets form the chief bulk of the load, so that a single blanket is usually preferable to a double one. The blankets during our trip were folded and pinned with large safety pins so as to form a sleeping bag with two thicknesses above the sleeper and one below him. This seems to be the only method of preventing the feet and legs from becoming uncovered.

The rubber blankets were supplied with eyelets along the sides, and a short string was tied into each eyelet. The rubber blanket when in use was placed upon the ground, rubber side down, and upon it was placed the sleeping bag. In this way one was able, after getting into the sleeping bag, to tie the rubber blankets around his legs. The Individual Outfit was contained in very small space. All the clothes were worn except the sweater, jersey, sneakers, one pair of socks, and sometimes the underwear. All of these except the sneakers were rolled with the blankets and carried on top of the knapsack. The tin cup was carried on the belt; the knife, handkerchiefs and safety pins were carried upon the clothing, so that only the sneakers and a few small articles were left to take up space in the knapsack.

CAMP MOOSILAUKE

COOKING OUTFIT.

2 frying pans, 2 sauce pans, 1 tin pail, 10 teaspoons, 2 table spoons, 2 long handled spoons, 1 kitchen knife.
The frying pans were of the small size used in the army, with folding handles. A tin plate for each person is sometimes convenient, but during our trip the tin cups were found to serve every purpose of the plates.

MEDICAL KIT.

Whiskey, half pint; absorbent cotton, gauze, adhesive plaster, bandages, bi-chloride of mercury tablets for sterilizing water used for bathing cuts, Cascara tablets, quinine, soda mints.
All these articles, except the whiskey, were contained in a small canvas bag labelled "Medicine." The importance of such an outfit cannot be too much emphasized. Bandages in case of a severe axe cut, or whiskey in case of exposure, may be the only means of saving life, while the other small articles aid much in daily comfort.

EQUIPMENT.

10 knapsacks, 7 canteens, 3 axes, 3 hatchets, 17 canvas food bags, 1 folding lantern, 6 candles, 1 extra rubber blanket, matches (in tin box), wire nails ("spikes"), twine, wire, extra straps, sapolio, boot grease (in tin box), compass, maps, time tables, note book, pencils, money bag, kodak.
The knapsacks were of canvas—those used by the U. S. Marine Corps—one for each member of the party. The folding lantern was of great service, though not necessary where a good camp fire was burning. Card sulphur matches were used because they occupied the least space and were not likely to blow out. A few boxes of "Blazers" were taken to be used in case of a high wind. Wire spikes are often a necessity in building the shack, as will be explained later. Such small articles as the folding lantern, candles, "spikes," matches, boot grease, compass, maps, kodak, also the medical kit and whiskey, were carried in the knapsack of the writer. The canteens were carried by straps over our shoulders, the axes and sauce pans in our hands. The other nine knapsacks were thus left free for the remaining cooking utensils and the provisions.

PROVISIONS

(taken at the start)—Salt, 1 bag, 3½ pounds; potted ham, 17 cans, 13½ pounds; boned chicken, 4 cans, 13½ pounds; pea soup, 19 tablets, 2½ pounds; macaroni, 3 packages, 3½ pounds; rice, 1 bag, 9 pounds; cocoa, 2 boxes, 1½ pounds; coffee, 1 bag, 3 pounds; pepper shaker, ½ pound; German chocolate, 100 cakes, 25 pounds; oatmeal, 2 bags (6 quarts), 5½ pounds; bacon, 3 bags (147 slices), 13½ pounds; pilot crackers, 6 bags (168), 12½ pounds; sugar, 2 bags, 12 pounds; total, 105½ pounds.
These provisions were distributed equally by weight among nine of the knapsacks, except that the 100 cakes of chocolate were distributed among all ten knapsacks, 10 cakes in each. The bags were all labelled in ink, according to the contents, as "Oatmeal," "Sugar," etc. These labels remained visible for the ten days we were camping.

CAMP MOOSILAUKE

Of the provisions given above, only those from oatmeal down had to be renewed during the trip. Seeded raisins were bought to give flavor to the rice, and cheese for the macaroni. The effect of carrying so many provisions from the home-supply was to make the knapsacks much heavier during the first part of the the trip. The average weight at the start was about 25 pounds, 11½ pounds being food, so that at the end of the trip the weight was reduced to about 14 pounds,

TRAMPING.

There are few suggestions regarding camping which are not axiomatic. The axes, canteens and saucepans should each be assigned to particular persons, who should take the responsibility for them during the trip. While on the trail we always walked single file; each member had his own place in the line, one master leading, and the other walking last. During the ten days we walked 80 miles with the packs, and 40 miles without. The least distance tramped during any one day was 6 miles; the greatest 18½. Our method was to walk every other day with packs, stopping for two consecutive nights at the same camping place, and spending the intervening day in a side trip without packs. Such side trips were taken to the Flume and to the summits of Mount Carrigan and Mount Willey. This method greatly eased the strain of carrying the knapsacks. While walking one should try to spend the same amount of energy for every given unit of time, thus quickening the pace on easy stretches, and slackening it on every steep climb.

CAMPING.

The most critical moment of making camp is that of selecting the spot. On this depends both the final comfort to be derived from the conditions and the degree of exertion necessary to obtain it. The selection must be made quickly and then held to. The essentials of a good camping place are few, but the right combination of them is very difficult to find. On the banks of rivers or on islands this combination is generally found; on the mountain slopes it is often rare. The rule must be: "The possible best rather than the impossible ideal." The essentials are, first, a supply of wholesome water; secondly, an appropriate place for the shack, which should preferably be built on a spot dry and level, where two trees may serve as corner posts. The fire, placed near the front of the shack, should be on the least thickness of vegetable mould, in order, if possible, to avoid a ground fire. These necessities will become more apparent as the development of the camp-making is outlined.

MAKING CAMP.

In making camp the organization of a party is peculiarly tested. Such a party represents an independent community, equipped with certain provisions and outfit by the civilized world, and now dependent only upon Mill's two requisites of production, "Labor and appropriate natural objects." As in all communities, division of labor is essential; and, in order that each member of this community may know his place, his work must be specifically defined at the outset.

The work to be done is, briefly, to change any given place in the woods into a temporary habitation. By habitation here is meant not only the shack, but the other requisites of comfort, the most important of which is the fire. There can be comfortable camps in good weather without a shack, but without fire there is neither food, warmth nor cheer. On our trip the labor was divided as follows: One master took charge of the fire and cooking. He had two assistants, one to start and keep up the fire, the other to aid in the cooking proper. A third boy collected kindling. Two others were detailed to get medium sized wood and back logs for the "camp fire," which replaced the "cooking fire," after the latter had served its use. The remaining three boys helped the other master to build the shack, one having the duty of cutting long, slim trees for roof rafters, the other two acting as levellers on the shack floor. They also made the general bed of boughs and spread the blankets ready for use. It usually takes between two and three hours to make camp and get supper, so that the site should be selected as soon before sunset as the day's walk will allow. In August any time before five o'clock will do very well. When our camping place had been selected our first duty was to deposit our knapsacks in order, numbered from one to ten, in the spots selected by the masters. The master in charge of the cooking, having his list of the provisions and equipment in each knapsack, was now able to find any desired article. After this each member went immediately to his own work.

THE FIRE.

The most convenient kind of fire-place is one made of stones. This can be easily built when camping near a brook bed. When once made it serves as a rough stove, the stones arranged to form a circular wall, enclosing the fire, and having the stones near enough together to support the edges of the saucepans and frying pans.

STONE FIREPLACE.

Small iron bars placed upon the stones to support the pans were used once on the trip with great convenience. These were found on the camping ground, but would not generally be of enough use to warrant their carriage in the packs. Steward Edward White, however, in "The Mountains," recommends carrying such bars, and where the service of horses is to be had, this is probably advisable.

A more usual fire-place for the woods consists of two parallel logs, four or five inches thick, to support the saucepans over the fire, which is built between the logs. The old method of having two upright crotches with a cross bar and suspended pail over the fire is very useful in cooking coffee or any food that requires no stirring.

COOKING FIRE.

The "cooking fire" itself should be of small sized wood or large chips, and the cooking postponed till the blazing is over and a good bed of hot coals is secured In starting the fire the sticks should be laid in the form of a cone in order to make a draught. Often when the ground and wood is wet, birch bark will be found very convenient to start the fire. When supper is ready the small "cooking fire" may be transformed into the "camp fire" of any desired size, by piling up the back logs — from six to twelve inches thick each—on one side, and building up the bed of the fire with sticks of smaller sizes, from two to four inches thick.

CAMP MOOSILAUKE

CAMP FIRE.

The fire should, if possible, be placed opposite the open front of the shack, toward which the heat should be thrown from the back logs piled carefully for this purpose.

In the woods the fire must almost always rest upon vegetable mould, but this should be made as thin as possible. The chief danger from the camp fire is, of course the ground fire already mentioned. This danger is greater because not immediate, for if not put 'out before leaving, it is very likely to continue to smoulder and creep, hidden for weeks. until it covers a large surface. It is then ready to start an open fire and commit the ravages which make the forest fire the greatest natural problem of forestry, as constituting a perennial menace to the lumber supply. Thus it is very important that this ground fire be absolutely extinguished before leaving, and if the same camp be used for more than one night, that it be kept within certain narrow limits until finally put out.

THE SHACK.

The "Shack" or "Lean to," is the simplest form of house. Two standing trees, or posts, connected by a cross-bar, form the front. The cross-bar is usually supported in the middle by an upright post. Long slender poles, the rafters, form the frame work of the roof, which is slanting. One end of each rafter, the higher end, rests on the cross-bar and the other end on the ground. The sides are formed by upright poles, placed parallel to the corner trees, and becoming shorter as the roof slants to the ground. (No. 4). The body of the roof and sides may be

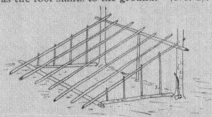

FRAMEWORK OF SHACK.

made in several ways. The usual method is to weave spruce and balsam boughs between the rafters and side poles as thickly as possible. Thus a shack can be made which which gives protection from the wind and to some extent from the rain, though it will never be tight. In fact no roof of boughs capable of keeping out a heavy rain can be built in the short time allowed to make a temporary camp. With permanent camps, good roofs may be built of bark or even of boards. The method adopted during our trip was to tie the rubber blankets upon the rafters and to the side poles. Each rubber blanket had strings already tied into the eyelets, so that a roof was thus made very quickly that could keep out enough rain to make the shack comfortable. Other rubber blankets were laid over the balsam boughs which formed the general bed, the eleven blankets in the party being sufficient for both roof and floor.

The only tools necessary for such a construction are the axes, or hatchets, and wire nails ("spikes") about five inches long. When there are no branches on the corner trees to support the cross-bar, the latter must be nailed upon the trees by the spikes. This greatly simplified the problem of selecting the site for the shack, as one is then independent of the occurrence of branches on the corner trees. The bark should be cut away on both cross-bar and trees so that the two will fit as closely as possible before nailing.

Four persons were engaged in making the shack. It was especially necessary to have the ground upon which we were to sleep as level and as free from snags as possible. Two of the boys thus prepared the ground and then laid a bed of balsam and spruce boughs, upon which the rubber blankets were spread. One other boy helped the writer to cut the rafters, trim them and build the framework of the shack. The rafters had to be made from small straight trees (spruces), not more than three inches in greatest diameter and not shorter than ten feet. After the roof had been made as outlined above, boughs were sometimes piled on top and around the sides in order to make the whole structure more snug.

THE GRUB.

The foregoing tasks have served to convert the average woods into a comfortable camp. Concentrated attention is now given to that *desideratum omnium* technically known as "grub." This in the daily regime of three meals, consisted of the following:

Breakfast—Oatmeal, 3 cups (dry); coffee, 6 table spoons; potted ham, 1 can, pilot crackers, 20.

Lunch (cold)—Sweet chocolate, 10 cakes; potted ham, 1 can; pilot crackers, 20.

Supper—Bacon, 30 slices; potted ham (or boned chicken), 1 can; pilot crackers, 20; cocoa, ½ box; rice (¼ cup, dry) and raisins; or, macaroni (1 pkg.) and cheese.

Combined with the above we had, as opportunity afforded, apple sauce, blackberry, raspberry and mountain-cranberry jam, and blueberries. We always had cold lunches, because too much time would have been required to make a fire and do any cooking. The duty of washing the dishes after supper and breakfast was given to two of the members other than the cooks.

AFTER SUPPER.

Supper might be supposed to celebrate the end of the day's work, and it usually did. But general rules are bound to be modified in a life as rough and irregular as that of camping. Provided, however, that the shack be as tight as need be, and that the supply of fire wood be sufficient, nothing remains to be done after supper except to pile up the small cooking fire into the large camp fire as described above. It is now that the camp as known to the general reader is realized; and there can be no more cheering host than the roaring fire lighting the tree trunks to the crowns and radiating its supply of warmth and good feeling. Itself a creature of the wilds, it seems animated with their hidden spirit, which flashing into life, welcomes all comers as guests. Bed time begins any time after supper and ended when the two of the party, usually the masters, decided to prepare for the night. The boys turned in one by one as sleep dictated, and after each had had the necessary verbal "scrap" with his nearest neighbor regarding his resting accommodations, quiet reigned, and snores alone interrupted the crackling of the fire.

Such is the making and enjoying of camp when the weather approves. In case of hard rain these are modified. The chief struggle then is for fire. Birch bark, blowing and determination will get the start, and finally back logs will triumph. The rubber blankets should be used to cover the knapsacks while the shack framework is being built. A comfortable camp can be made in spite of the elements, though it will require a harder and longer struggle.

DANGERS.

Next to the danger from fire is that of a cut by an axe or hatchet. An axe can and should be used so that it cannot possibly reach the user. Chop at arm's length away from the body, and keep the feet as far as possible from the axe, and danger is practically removed. Don't be induced to use the methods of old lumbermen, whose long experience may allow them with safety to handle an axe in a way most dangerous to the average good camper. The only other danger from chopping is in cutting one's neighbor. This may be absolutely removed by working at safe distances apart.

The chief dangers from walking are in turning the ankle and in running some twig into the eye. "Eyes and ankles" should be the warning when on trail in the woods. Warnings of all snags should be given by the ones ahead.

BREAKING CAMP.

Breaking camp is a process very simple though surprisingly long. Cooking breakfast takes most of the time and for this reason it is well to boil the oatmeal the night before. The first thing to do is to start, or revive, the fire and get some water boiling. It is best to have the cooks attend to this before the others get up. As soon as each camper rises, he should roll up his blanket and collect his own things. After breakfast the dishes must be washed, the fire put out and the last things picked up. All rubbish should be burned before the fire is put out. The two masters, on our trip were usually up at four o'clock and the party was ready to start at seven.

CAMP ETHICS.

The simplest rule of conduct for a camper is to leave a place as he would like to find it. The man who carries out this rule will do his fellow camper a greater benefit than by any other one thing. Fortunately such conduct is becoming more and more the tradition, and hence camping as an institution is giving greater enjoyment every year. But the signs of the "picnicker" are as yet all too plentiful. Stately pine groves, picturesque brooks and shores of lakes are the particular prey of this desecrator. Old pasteboard boxes, tin cans, broken glass jars, egg shells and chicken bones are among the prizes which he donates. He improves the rocky summit of every mountain with his initials. The "camper" should take him as a warning. A very remarkable example of this sort of treatment we saw at Madison Spring Hut where we spent one night. This hut made of stone is situated on the

CAMP   MOOSILAUKE

side of Mt. Madison, one of the Northern peaks of the Presidential Range, in a little valley or "coll" separating Mt. Madison from the next peak. A small stream runs close by and the upper scrubby growth of balsam furnishes plenty of fuel. The hut is owned by the Appalachian Mountain Club and is kept open by the club for all who wish to use it. In return for this courtesy the people using the hut have strewn the ground all about it with hundreds of tin cans and broken glass jars. The wood-box inside has been used for this same purpose. This is done in spite of specific printed instructions as to the place to throw rubbish and a request from the club to use no other spot. There seems no help for such action except to create a stronger public opinion against it, and thus to raise the standard of camping as a sport to an elevation which other forms of athletics have already reached.

The pernicious principle illustrated here is one of disdain of those who are to come afterward. Another example of this same principle on a scale far vaster than that just cited, was called to our attention while tramping from Franconia to Crawford Notch. A large commercial lumber plant near North Woodstock, N.H., has been engaged for several years in cutting off the timber on the mountains in the basin of the East Branch of the Pemigewasset River. A view of this region may be had from Mt. Willey near Crawford Notch. The method of lumbering is the primitive one of "shaving" the slopes and leaving them in the ruined condition, as regards the lumber supply and water conservation, which such methods always cause. The beauty of this region, the wildest of the White Mountains, was in great part destroyed, the slashes of the lumbermen branding the mountains like unsightly scars on a beautiful face. But worse than this was the evidence of ruin everywhere present in the tangled mass of wasted lumber strewn for miles over the shaven land ; a wasted resource which may in some places be regained by hard labor and decades of time, in other places, never. The present owner occupies the land, partakes of the resource to make a fortune and leaves a barren land for posterity. The contempt shown by the unconscientious guest at Madison Hut for those who are to come afterward and that shown by the lumberman in the East Branch are both identical in principle.

Camping thus serves to teach a lesson in patriotism which few other opportunities afford. There is no other sport or mode of living which so clearly exemplifies the need of each to do his share and the dependence of all upon the resources of nature. If we are to have these resources, whether lumber or other; if things are to be used and not dissipated; if we are to have a camping ground and not a desert, we must work and fight for these ends. The duty of the camper, as one with greater opportunities in this respect than the average citizen, is to preserve the resources which nature has bestowed and to cherish the land as he would his home.

THE TRAMP OF THE TATTERED TEN

KNOWLTON DURHAM

A ten days' walk in the White Mountains had been talked of all through July in Camp Moosilauke. Repeated trying-out trips for a single night in the woods (rain preferred) reduced the number of candidates to eight; and these eight, together with Farmer and Cub, as guide and financeer, composed the band of the Tattered Ten. As we left the camp, one hot afternoon in early August, our line wound along the path through the woods in this order: "Farmer" MacKaye, "Beer" Klüpfel, "Babe" Sommerville, "Pretzel" (Beer's brother), "Von," short for Von Saltza, "Shanks" Larom, "Feet" Herbert, "Jack" Steeves, "Jill" Rionda, and "Cub" Durham, each bearing a thirty-pound pack—containing provisions, extra clothing and blanket roll—and either canteen or axe.

The glory of the day was, I fear, somewhat lost sight of by most of the ten, for the day was hot, the burdens, because of unfamiliarity with them, heavy, and the pace rapid. Welcome indeed was the first sight of the old deserted barn, which was to be our first camp. Rest and food soon brightened spirits, where natural beauty had failed. A jolly evening around the camp fire, singing to mouth organ accompaniment and story telling made all feel contented, and a good night's sleep in the barn, or in the tall grass without, prepared each for the hard mountain climb on Wednesday.

The ascent of Mt. Moosilauke was completed by ten o'clock the next morning, two hours and forty minutes from the foot. The day was dark, but nevertheless there was a splendid view to be had from the summit, for those who preferred it to time-worn magazines in the Tip-Top House. At twelve we were off again, bound for the little cluster of houses in the valley far below. The descent was not only steep but very slippery—two facts which, combined with rapidity of motion and an entire absence of protective padding in the seat of khaki trousers, resulted in rather amusing complications—amusing to all, except perhaps Jack and Jill, who played the title rôles. The foot of this trail left our party in the Lost River valley, whence a lumber road led into the village of North Woodstock. The last three miles, in a dismal rain, brought us to Johnson's lumber camp and an old disused barn (made famous by a previous visit of the Hungry Hoboes), in which we were just comfortably settled, beginning preparations for supper, when the "boss" of the camp appeared and ordered us out, because of a fear of fire in the neighborhood. But what promised to be a doleful calamity proved an unmixed blessing—instead of a barn, old and dirty, we were given an old ground-floor room in one of the camp's buildings, were we found a stove for our cooking purposes and mattresses for our beds. As a result we passed a comfortable night, not even disturbed by the swarm of rats that infested the place and made a camp of the lumbermen's dining table.

Thursday, the eleventh, was voted a day of rest. Shanks particularly was out of gear and needed repose, which was equally welcome to all, and the occasion was eagerly seized for a swim in the Pemigewassett and a visit to the Flume.

CAMP MOOSILAUKE

On Friday we were on the road again by half-past five. At Lincoln a hurried visit was made to the Henry's pulp mill. A four-mile ride on a lumber train up the East Branch was a welcome change from walking; but the Ten were soon on foot again and counting the ties of an old disused and dismantled railroad track up the Hancock Branch. All morning we plodded up a valley wasted by the Henrys, and at noon were climbing the trail over the divide to the Swift River valley. A long and difficult day's walk was compensated for by some glorious views. An abundance of giant huckleberries, and a cool swim in Swift River, where we were entertained by the sight of Beer, dressed as a water nymph, shooting Niagara. That evening camp was made in a sheltered hemlock grove on the bank of Sawyer's River, where, after a hearty supper of rice, bacon and crackers, we spent as comfortable a night on a bed of boughs as ever we had known in the soft luxury of mattress and sheets.

Again a day of rest was declared for the benefit of the wounded. Shanks and Jack kept camp on Saturday, while the other eight left for a climb up Mt. Carrigain (4500 feet). From Livermore Mills, at the foot of the trail, the ascent was accomplished in two and three-quarter hours. Our labor was without reward, the top of the mountain was enveloped in cloud, and one of the finest views in the White Mountains was lost to us. But there was real joy in returning to a delicious supper of boiled macaroni and cheese, bacon, potted chicken and crackers, and to a sound night's sleep undisturbed by rain.

Sunday's walk brought us without special incident into the valley of the Saco and the famous Crawford Notch, where we were housed for two nights in the Willey barn. The following day opened clear, so all but Feet and Shanks, the invalids, made an early start for the top of Mt. Willey (4200 feet). The path leads straight up the side of the mountain without a turn or a rest.* But the wonderful view from the summit well repays one for the difficult climb. It seemed as if we were in the very heart of an undiscovered, enchanted land; on all sides mountain peaks, shading from dark green to light blue, and flooded in sunshine; and away to the northeast lay the most splendid of all—the Presidential peaks, one rising above another, and all but foothills to their chief, Mt. Washington. As we looked the clouds slowly lifted from its top and disclosed the whole range, wonderfully grand and beautiful beyond expression.

On Tuesday we were up before the sun, and, after an early start, passed through the Notch to Crawford's, up Mt. Clinton by the bridle path and along the range to Washington. It was here that the song of the Tattered Ten first took form in the mind of the head cook—the other minds, Farmer's excepted perhaps(?) were too busily engaged in contemplation of the expected "feed" at the Summit House for other thoughts. I shall not attempt to describe the Summit House. Those who have been there know its charms; those who have not can but imperfectly imagine them. Suffice it to say that it was all that could have been expected; that the supper came and went, like all good suppers, and that even Farmer admitted the exquisite pleasure to be had from the combination of ravenous appetite, plenty of good food and a pretty waitress. That Von outdid us all, even

CAMP MOOSILAUKE

Jack the Guzzler, with twenty-nine helpings; that Babe made excellent use of a most bewitching childlike expression in securing extras; and that all ate and slept and felt like kings are matters of history which the Ten will not soon forget, but which will appeal so forcibly only to those who have been in a like situation.

Wednesday morning brought us more cloud and only fleet glimpses of distant valleys. By mid-afternoon we had covered the rest of the Range and arrived at the Madison Hut, where our last night was passed. Space will not permit me to detail the events of our stay there, but our party, reinforced by four other trampers, two of whom were recent Holyoke College Alumnæ, was very jolly, and the evening passed quickly amid great hilarity, with singing and story-telling. The charm of this company, the adventure with the porcupine, the climb up Madison, the walk to the railroad and the journey back to camp, are all matters which I must leave to the memories of those who shared them. The welcome of the returned wanderers back to camp, the swim at the boat-house, the supper and the songs are camp traditions which only those who have experienced such a trip can fully appreciate; and which, once experienced, remain delightful reminiscences always.

BASE BALL TEAM

Woolerton, Catcher.
Larom, Pitcher
A. Klüpfel, 1st Base.
R. Klüpfel, 2nd Base.
Sanford, 3rd Base.

Thomas, Short Stop.
Baldwin, Right Field.
Imhoff, Center Field.
J. Steeves, Left Field.
Mr. Leggett, Manager.

SCORES OF BASE BALL GAMES

Wednesday, August 24.

Moosilauke	0	2	0	1	0	0	0	2	1	6
Masters	1	0	1	0	1	0	3	1	x	7

Friday, August 26.

Moosilauke	0	0	0	0	1	0	0	0	3	4
Wentworth	1	0	2	0	1	0	7	1	0	12

Saturday, August 27.

Moosilauke	2	2	0	1	3	1	1	0	3	13
Masters	3	0	0	1	0	3	7	3	1	18

Tuesday, August 30.

Moosilauke	1	2	0	1	1	0	1	2	2	10
Masters	0	1	2	1	0	3	2	2	x	11

TO MOOSILAUKE

Tune "Cornell's Alma Mater."

W. L. THOMAS.

I.

Where the breezes of the forest,
Stir the mountain Pine
Where the moon-beams on the water
Through the ripples shine.

(CHORUS:)

Raise your voices—loud and hearty
Make the echoes talk—
Give a cheer and make it sound
Long life to Moosilauke.

II.

There among the lofty hemlocks
On a sun-kissed hill
In the shadows stands old Moos'lauke
Camp we love so well.

III.

In the evening by the camp-fire
On the moon lit shore
Sing of all the joys before us
Sing of days of yore.

IV.

Taps is sounding ov'r the mountain
Ringing o'er the hill
All the voices of the evening
Sink—and then grow still.

V.

Then we'll sing one song together
For we part 'ere long
Just a tribute to old Moos'lauke
Just a farewell song.

TO OUR ABSENT FRIENDS

Tune "Old Black Joe."

W. L. THOMAS.

Come, sing one song for the stars that shine so bright,
Come, sing one song for those away to-night,
Gone are the friends that we all have learned to love,
We know they're gazing at that same old moon above.

Come, pledge them
Come, pledge them
Upon this happy day—
Just give one thought to all our friends so far away.

TRAMPING SONG

Tune "Marching Thro' Georgia."

W. L. THOMAS.

I.

Give a cheer together boys we'll give it good and strong,
Give it with a spirit that will make it roll along,
Give it as we used to in the days that now are gone,
    While we go tramping the mountains.

(CHORUS:)

Moos'lauke! Moos'lauke! May luck be ever thine
Moos'lauke! Moos'lauke! Yell all along the line
Oh! Whoop 'er up again now boys and make it loud and fine
    While we go tramping the mountains.

II.

How the old White Mountains learned to know our footstep's beat
How the moon beams glittered as they shot from peak to peak.
How the pines put us to sleep with incense soft and sweet.
    While we were tramping the mountains.

CAMP MOOSILAUKE

DIARY.

Sept. 1902.—Camp site discovered.
June—Sept. 1903.—Mess hall, ice house and boat house built.
May 1904.—Sleeping boxes built.
June 16—Mr. Durham, Larom (and his gun) Van Glahn, J. Steeves, A. Klüpfel,
  Wyman Herbert, Sommerville, Matthew and Lucy arrive.
  " 18—Larom and Van Glahn catch and cook a trout. First stone in fire place
  " 24—Mr. Leggett arrives.   [laid.
  " 30—Camp party arrives at Mess Hall at 9 P. M.
July 2—Gerry shows Campbell how to upset a canoe.
  " 3—First ascent by camp party of Mt. Cuba.
  " 4—Noise.
  " 6—Matthew makes apple pies.
  " 7—Box No. 2 spend evening on North Shore.
  " 8—Ruf rests in hammock. Box 2 camp out, and are visited by cattle, etc.
  " 13—Box 4 visits North Shore. Shades of former owner investigated by Larom
  " 14—Trail to Mt. Moosilauke blazed.   [and Herbert.
  " 20—Box 3 celebrates Dr. Monroe's birthday.
  " 21—Mr. Meehan visits Camp. Ascent of Cuba by Box 4. Cub fusses.
  " 22—Mr. and Mrs. Campbell visit camp. Box 2 camps on Cuba.
  " 25—Mr. Adams visits Camp.
  " 26—Party camps on Pierremont.
  " 27—Larom used an ax. Adams arrives.
  " 29—Box 1 camps on Cuba.
  " 31—Fire brigade does efficient work in woods.
Aug. 1—Tramp to Indian Pond. "Pewee" celebrates his birthday.
  " 4—Timmy and Ruf guide Box 2 on Mt. Moosilauke trail. Mt. Carr ascended.
  " 8—"Fat" climbs mountain at 1. A. M.
  " 9—Mr. Mac Kaye, Mr. Durhan, R. Külpfel, A. Klüpfel, Wyman Herbert,
  Larom, Sommerville, Rionda, J. Steeves, von Saltza start on White
  Mountain trip.
  " 13—"Buck" arrives.
  " 16—Dr. Prettyman demonstrates his sailing ability.
  " 18—White Mountain party returns.
  " 19—Mr. Baker, Mr. Leggett, Adams, Lawson, Kenyon and Carrington start
  on Franconia trip.
  " 20—Tommy (big) and Mr. Durham arrive.
  " 23—Franconia party returns.
  " 24—Masters defeat Camp base-ball team.
  " 25—Pajama parade after taps.
  " 26—Base-ball game with Wentworth. "Babe" visits Camp.
  " 27—Camp team again defeated by masters. Mr. Curtis visits Camp.
  " 30—Camp team plays masters.
  Annual show.
  " 31—Packing. Questions. Last Camp fire on the beach.
Sept. 1—Farewells.

Bake Oven Knob, 1931:
On the Appalachian Trail with Myron Avery and Benton MacKaye

Adapted from a talk sponsored by the Appalachian Trail Museum Society, Harpers Ferry, West Virginia, June 2, 2007, upon the dedication of an exhibit at the Appalachian Trail Conservancy about Benton MacKaye and Myron Avery.

A photograph from the archives of the Appalachian Trail Conservancy is the only one I've seen that depicts Benton MacKaye and Myron Avery together. The conventional history of the Appalachian Trail (AT) portrays MacKaye and Avery as adversaries and rivals, who, during the mid-1930s, engaged in an increasingly intense, bitter, and personal debate—which evolved into a genuine feud—over control of the Appalachian Trail Conference, the future of the Appalachian Trail, and indeed the very idea of the Appalachian Trail. Yet this photograph, which was taken, as best I can tell, on October 11, 1931, on the Appalachian Trail at Bake Oven Knob, in Pennsylvania, captures two apparently relaxed and cheerful men, side by side.

When Appalachian Trail Museum Society President Larry Luxenburg invited me to participate in today's activities commemorating the indispensable contributions of these two giants in the conception and creation of the AT, I immediately thought of this photograph and of the moment and the spirit it captures. Today, on this 15th National Trails Day, I don't want to paper over or ignore the differences of personality, policy, tactics, and philosophy that led to the final break between MacKaye and Avery in early 1936: those differences were genuine and important. They sacrificed their personal relationship, such as it was, in their dispute over the principles and practices they each believed should guide the destiny of the Appalachian Trail. As time passes, though—and I think the new exhibit captures this spirit—it becomes possible to see and understand that Benton MacKaye and Myron Avery, on most essential points, in fact shared a substantially common vision of the Appalachian Trail.

They agreed, for instance, that it should be created and maintained primarily by amateurs; but they also understood that the trail would likely require legal protections that only government involvement could provide and secure. Although they sometimes differed over trail standards, they agreed that the trail should be wild and rugged in character, and that it should be open to all who are willing to tackle it on those terms.

It's important to recognize that Benton MacKaye and Myron Avery were men of different generations. In 1931, MacKaye was 52 years old, twenty years older than Avery. When Avery was born in 1899, MacKaye was entering his senior year at Harvard College. But the two shared certain personal attributes: a New England upbringing, which may explain their flinty stubbornness as well as their love for the region's mountains and forests; native intelligence, which they expanded and honed with professional educations, including stints in Harvard graduate programs, MacKaye as the first to receive a masters degree in forestry, Avery at the Law School; literary skill, which they could deploy with facility and effect, even if that effect was sometimes intensely personal and even hurtful; careers with the federal government, which they pursued with professional dedication and competence; and—not least important—passion, which they both devoted to the Appalachian Trail and other related conservation causes. It is also a testament to the

Benton MacKaye and Myron Avery on the Appalachian Trail at Bake Oven Knob, Pennsylvania, October 11, 1931. (Courtesy of the Appalachian Trail Conservancy.)

professional integrity of both men that they didn't air their intense personal differences publicly. In their public statements and articles, they refrained from direct personal assaults on each other—although the personal context of their sometimes veiled language is possible to decode. In any event, at least in their public comments, they put the welfare of the Appalachian Trail project above their personal differences.

I'm not going to re-tell today the full story of the intense debates of the 1930s over how the trail community should respond to the threat posed to the Appalachian Trail and the east's mountain terrain by the Skyline Drive, the Blue Ridge Parkway, and other proposed eastern scenic mountain parkways. I've already told one version of it in my book, from MacKaye's perspective. And other writers and scholars have addressed these issues from other points of view.

But let me relate what MacKaye himself understood to be the principal philosophical difference between him and Myron Avery over the purpose of the Appalachian Trail. This passage is from a November, 1935 letter, part of the remarkable exchange of correspondence between the two men as their dispute reached its climax.

"The purpose of the A.T. Conference, we all agree, is to preserve the primeval or wilderness environment," MacKaye wrote:

> One means to this end, and only one, is a "connected trail." To preserve the wilderness the trail must of course be a *wilderness* trail (as to sounds, sights, and tread). There are hundreds of *non* wilderness ways well connected from Maine to Georgia; to make one more is pointless. Here then is the first issue between us. You are for a *connected* trail—whether or not wilderness; I am for a *wilderness* trail—whether or not connected.
>
> . . . Your ideas on the skyline road seem not to be consistent. Your ideas on the trail itself seem wholly consistent and I do not agree with them: you put *connected* trail first while I put *wilderness* trail first. You have put great zest and energy into a connected trail from Maine to Georgia, and I have praised you for it, privately to you as well as publicly. But this very *zest* for a *means* (a connected way) has dimmed apparently your vision of the *end* (a wilderness way). . . . *Wilderness, not continuity, is the vital point.*"

Within months of writing this, MacKaye and Avery had permanently parted ways over this philosophical difference. They were talking past each other. Their continuing separate efforts had the eventual effect, however, of strengthening the two essential aspects of the trail that have always been the foundation of its enduring popularity and success—that is, its uninterrupted continuity over more than 2,100 miles and its wild character.

Let's return to Bake Oven Knob on that day in October of 1931. I believe the moment captured in the photograph of MacKaye and Avery represents an important turning point in the history of the Appalachian Trail, in several important respects.

We have a relatively detailed contemporary account of the Bake Oven Knob gathering from Raymond Torrey, another important figure in the early history of the Appalachian Trail. Torrey described the event in his popular weekly column, "The Long Brown Path," which appeared in the *New York Evening Post*. Torrey was, among other things, also a founder of the New York-New Jersey Trail Conference, a prime organizer of efforts to build the first new links of the Appalachian Trail west of the Hudson River in the early 1920s, and the author of the original *New York Walk Book*. He was the "supreme ombudsman in the boiling consortium of New York hiking clubs," in the words of trail historians Laura and Guy Waterman. Like MacKaye, Torrey would eventually clash with Avery over a variety of AT-related issues.

What brought MacKaye and Avery to Bake Oven Knob? At the time, there were at least two explicitly and publicly stated reasons for the gathering. And, at least in retrospect, there was also a more complicated context for the event.

"Inspired Appalachian Trail Meeting," read the headline on Torrey's story about the gathering at Bake Oven Knob. The event was organized by the Blue Eagle Mountain Climbing Club, a unique hiking group established by a group of Reading, Pennsylvania men in 1916 (that is, five years before the initiation of the Appalachian Trail project). One purpose of the meeting was to celebrate the tenth anniversary of Benton MacKaye's original article proposing the Appalachian Trail, titled "An Appalachian Trail: A Project in Regional Planning," which appeared in the October, 1921 issue of the *Journal of the American Institute of Architects*.

The second purpose of the event, Torrey reported, was to mark "the practical completion of the Appalachian Trail across Pennsylvania," except, he claimed, for the marking of a few miles between Lehigh and Wind gaps. The work was the culmination of a five-year effort that had begun when the club's members had met in 1926 with Eugene Bingham, a professor at Lafayette College in Easton and a member of the Blue Mountain Club (a different club than the BMECC). At a subsequent Pennsylvania AT conference in May, 1927 organized by Bingham, the Blue Mountain Eagle Climbing Club, under the leadership of Dr.

Harry Rentschler, took responsibility for locating more than 100 miles of trail between the Lehigh and Susquehanna rivers.

MacKaye did not attend the 1927 Pennsylvania trail conference, but he did send a message, couched in the sort of high-flown, often abstract language that some listeners found inspiring, even life-changing, but that left others scratching or shaking their heads. "The object of the Appalachian Trail," he exhorted, "is to develop the Indigenous America," as a bulwark against what he called the "metropolitan invasion" of commercialism, "chaotic growth," "suburban massings," and "an over-wrought mechanized civilization." For Benton MacKaye, the Appalachian Trail was never merely a footpath. Development of the Appalachian Trail, he said in his 1927 comments, was "the backbone of our strategy," as he put it, "to institute Public Parks and Forests along the mountain ridgeways in the populous portion of the country. This move is a vital one—to put the vantage ground in public ownership." The Appalachian Trail, that is, was the axis of what he envisioned as a vast expanse of protected public land, stretching along the mountains between Maine and Georgia.

Back to Bake Oven Knob. Club secretary Rentschler presided as master of ceremonies for the October 1931 event, which attracted more than 500 people, by Torrey's estimate, making it the "largest and most enthusiastic" Appalachian Trail gathering yet held in the ten years since the project's inception. Most had arrived by a nearby road and approach trail, but more than 100, including MacKaye, Avery, and Torrey, had walked six miles from a roadhead to the 1500-foot Bake Oven Knob.

"I talked on the 'second stage' for the second decade of the A.T. (this being the 10th anniv. of the A.T.)," MacKaye recorded in his diary that day. "Your deed has made a mark upon the map," he told the audience when his turn came to speak. "By little or much you have altered the geography of Pennsylvania, and of the Eastern United States," he said.

By Torrey's account, MacKaye made reference to a statement he had prepared for the fifth meeting of the Appalachian Trail Conference, which had been held in June of 1931 in Gatlinburg, Tennessee. At that meeting Myron Avery had been elected to the first of his many terms as chairman of the Appalachian Trail Conference, replacing his mentor, Arthur Perkins, who had suffered a serious stroke the year before.

"A realm and not a trail marks the full aim of our effort," MacKaye had decreed to the trail enthusiasts gathered in Gatlinburg, looking ahead to the trail's "second stage." He warned that the trail should not be used as a "race course," an "amusement park," or the setting for what he called "make-believe."

Rather the trail should provide a setting for "a policy of 'expansion,'" as put it, both in terms of "territory" and "human understanding." "Miles measured on the trail should be expanded to square miles of public reservation," he commented. "Our realm must be broad as well as long."

I don't know what Myron Avery may have been thinking as he heard MacKaye's wilderness gospel read to the Gatlinburg gathering by Harvey Broome, the young president of the host Smoky Mountains Hiking Club. *"Primeval history is the story of the ages,"* MacKaye's message said. "The ridge is to the sky what the shore is to the sea," he continued, that is, the border "between earth and full-fledged atmosphere."

On Bake Oven Knob a few months after the Gatlinburg conference, MacKaye offered similar thoughts in person. He "was overcome by his feelings in observing the size and enthusiasm of the party and the realization as to how far his project had carried," Torrey observed. An important promoter of the project since meeting MacKaye in early 1922, Torrey offered his own emotional response to the event. "The gathering was an inspiring one to some of the older workers, who were early persuaded of the value of Mr. MacKaye's idea when he launched it in 1921, and who steadily sought to ally outdoor groups and individual groups to carry the trail forward," Torrey wrote. "They had seen the project grow from the thoughts of a few whom Mr. MacKaye inspired, and from a pencilled line on the United States Geological Survey maps, to the completion this year, of 1,200 out of 2,000 miles of the route."

Myron Avery also spoke that day on Bake Oven Knob. Torrey only summarized Avery's remarks, in which he described plans for "filling out the gaps [in the trail] yet unmarked," and described as the "next step" the construction of shelters similar to those in use in New England, the Adirondacks, and Europe.

MacKaye, in his comments for the 1931 Appalachian Trail Conference, had described its newly installed chairman, Avery, as "that indefatigable young Titan of the Trail," "a certain son of Old Katahdin who bobs up these days all along the trail from Maine to Georgia and sends in his reports straight from the bush." Already, after only four years of involvement with the trail project, Avery had won a reputation for his prodigious trail-building efforts and energy. For Avery, this year, 1931, and this major gathering of trail enthusiasts on Bake Oven Knob, provided him an opportunity to lay his claim to being the principal organizer of the yet-uncompleted task of building the Appalachian Trail. This is one sense in which the 1931 gathering at Bake Oven Knob represented a pivotal point in the Appalachian Trail's history. It was here that, as matters of both fact and symbolism, the baton of Appalachian Trail leadership effectively passed from MacKaye to Avery. Avery was bursting to place his own imprint on a project yet in progress, the success of which was in no way assured. While MacKaye continued to look beyond the horizon, imagining an ever-expanding wilderness realm, Avery kept his eyes focused a few feet ahead of his measuring wheel, intent on completing the continuous trail.

Indeed, Avery acknowledged but defended his focused goal. Shortly after the Bake Oven Knob gathering, he heard from Harvey Broome, who would become one of MacKaye's closest friends and one of the eight founding members of The Wilderness Society.

"Personally, Myron, I think you lay too much store by the thought of a *completed* Trail," Broome wrote. "As I once wrote, my belief is that much of its value is in the stimulus to get out-of-doors. Within limits, the rougher it is, the greater its challenge to a trifle-ridden people. I don't think we should welcome the mediocre when we may have the magnificent."

"You are probably right in saying that I overstress the value of the completed trail," Avery responded. "After all, this is my task. Its value to the public depends upon its existence and use. There will always be plenty of exploring and pioneering work to do when the through route is completed. It is a practical matter too. The only way we can keep people and organizations interested is by accomplishing something. In the last analysis, it is a humanitarian project and this work is a definite contribution. This is perhaps why I over emphasize activity rather than project. This is, of course, just our usual frank interchange of views." Within a few years, their exchanges of views would remain frank—but they would become considerably less civil.

Back again to Bake Oven Knob. Another important figure in the history of the Appalachian Trail was almost certainly on hand that day. Daniel K. Hoch, a local political figure, was one of the leaders of the Blue Mountain Eagle Climbing Club. He would eventually become its president. As we will see, Hoch played an important role almost 15 years later in promoting the notion of a national trail system, under the aegis of the federal government. That initiative would, at least at a political level, unintentionally re-connect the ruptured relationship between MacKaye and Avery. In a real sense, the existence of today's National Trails Day is linked directly to that moment on Bake Oven Knob, with Benton MacKaye and Myron Avery side-by-side, and Daniel Hoch somewhere nearby, possibly not far out of the photograph's frame.

As I noted earlier, there was another subtext to this October 1931 gathering, based on rapidly unfolding events to the south of Bake Oven Knob that would have a significant impact on the physical environment of the Appalachian Trail, the future of the ATC, and the relationship between MacKaye and Avery.

1931 was epochal in AT history because it was the year that work began on the 105-mile Skyline Drive. The scenic motorway would bisect lengthwise the narrow, only recently authorized, but not yet formally established Shenandoah National Park. On a Sunday morning in the autumn of 1930, President Herbert Hoover rode out on horseback from his weekend retreat near the headwaters of the Rapidan River, on the eastern slope of Virginia's Blue Ridge. Accompanied by a small party that included National Park Service Director Horace Albright, the president pulled his horse to a stop at the ridgeline, near an open expanse called Big Meadows. "You know, Albright," Hoover declared, "this mountain top is just made by God almighty for a highway. There's nothing like it in the country, really, where you can see such vistas. . . . I think everybody ought to have a chance to get the views from here."

Hoover thereupon instructed his Park Service chief to begin a survey for the Skyline Drive. In March 1931, the Department of the Interior and the Bureau of Public Roads announced plans to build a 34-mile section of road from Thornton Gap to Swift Run Gap, using recently appropriated drought-relief funds. By July, only a matter of months after Hoover's mountain-top revelation, parkway construction began. There had been no environmental impact statements, no congressional hearings, no specific congressional authorization for a scenic highway, barely a peep of public opposition. The few objections registered against the skyline road, Albright was informed by his Park Service assistants, came from "only two or three members of the Appalachian Trail Club."

In fact, though, on his horseback rides along the Blue Ridge, President Hoover may have crossed a narrow footpath, recently blazed with a small diamond-shaped marker comprising the letters "A" and "T". In these Virginia mountains, an enthusiastic amateur army of hikers had been at work building a link in the more than 2,000-mile Appalachian Trail. Indeed, the same year that Hoover ordered Albright to initiate the Skyline Drive, members of the Washington-based Potomac Appalachian Trail Club, which had been founded in 1927, had just finished building a 143-mile section of the trail through the region, including the full length of Shenandoah National Park. Now, based on Hoover's whim, all their trail-blazing was threatened with ruin. Avery, of course, as a founder and president of the PATC, had been a leader of the local trailbuilding effort.

The Hoover "road blitz," as a historian of Shenandoah National Park has called it, attained unstoppable momentum on the Blue Ridge by the time Benton MacKaye, Myron Avery, and other voices in the eastern trail community raised their voices in protest. In early 1931, as work began on the Skyline Drive, the Appalachian Trail's best known and most active leaders were unanimous, but virtually alone, in voicing concerns that the politically popular road might ruin the integrity and wild character of the trail and the park. Avery at first tried unsuccessfully to convince the Park Service's landscape architects to route the road to the east of the ridgeline, thereby preserving what he called "the best wilderness area in the park." MacKaye, for his part, met several times with Arno Cammerer, then assistant Park Service director, with whom he had been acquainted since the earliest days of the trail project. For MacKaye, the imminent construction of the Skyline Drive raised fundamental questions about the federal government's conception of its responsibilities for the eastern mountain terrain. "Does it mean the extension of the policy of motor skyline vs. foot-path skyline in the National Parks?" MacKaye asked Cammerer. Cammerer's tentative reply provided an early warning to MacKaye and other wilderness advocates that the Park Service, especially after Cammerer assumed its directorship in 1933, could not be relied upon as a guardian of the American wilderness.

Throughout 1931, then, MacKaye, Avery, and other trail activists had been in frequent contact about how the ATC and other trail clubs should respond to the Skyline Drive. They corresponded about the issue and met at several trail gatherings and for long conversations when MacKaye was in Washington, D.C. In July of 1931, just as ground was begin broken for the scenic highway, they rendezvoused at Skyland, along with other trail activists familiar with the terrain, such as Avery's fellow PATC founder Harold C. Anderson and Dr. H. S. Hedges of Charlottesville, the original Appalachian Trail scout along the Blue Ridge. All evidence suggests that communications between MacKaye and Avery during this period were frank and constructive.

But not long after the Bake Oven Knob gathering in October of that year, it appears that MacKaye and Avery began to part ways over the ATC's response to the federal government's role in promoting scenic mountain parkways, a movement that would gain momentum with Franklin D. Roosevelt's election in 1932 and the onset of the New Deal.

MacKaye was not alone in his growing concern that the ATC, under Avery's leadership, was not taking a sufficiently aggressive position in opposition to scenic mountain parkways. Among the most upset of trail activists was one of Avery's fellow colleagues in founding the Potomac

Appalachian Trail Club, Harold Anderson, a Washington accountant. In the fall of 1932, having just driven the first completed section of the Skyline Drive, he vented his frustrations to MacKaye in a lengthy letter.

"I cannot help feeling that Myron with all his indefatigable energy and enthusiasm has not yet fully grasped the idea of the Appalachian Trail," Anderson wrote. ". . . The whole question of road vs. trail is very fundamental. We outdoor folk who love the primitive are accused of selfishness in trying to have preserved inviolate a narrow strip of the little that we have left of the primitive area and preventing the enjoyment (?) [*sic*] by multitudes of the scenery of this area if roads were built therein. It seems to me that it narrows down to the question of whether it is worth while to preserve the primitive."

Anderson essentially failed in his efforts to serve as an intermediary between Avery and MacKaye on the question of "road versus trail." But his passion and persistence on the point would instigate the organization of The Wilderness Society in 1934 and 1935.

Upon assuming the ATC's chairmanship, Avery had wasted no time putting his stamp on the organization's activities. Besides propelling the trail-building effort forward, Avery also promoted the expansion and professionalization of the ATC's publications efforts. Among those publications was a detailed general-information brochure, identified as ATC "Publication No. 5." This publication included a history of the AT project to date, as written by Avery.

This publication, I believe, has subtly but fatefully colored the early history of Appalachian Trail ever since, to MacKaye's disadvantage. Its publication in 1934 also documented in somewhat cryptic form the personal differences that were developing between the two men.

Avery sent a draft of the historical sections of Publication No. 5 to MacKaye for his review. Avery generously credited MacKaye for his early conception of the Trail; but he went on to state that the project, in the years immediately after the first 1925 Appalachian Trail Conference—that is, until Avery himself came on the scene in 1927 at the side of Arthur Perkins—was "practically moribund" and "was rapidly degenerating into a fireside philosophy." MacKaye, who had been given the title of ATC "Field Organizer" at the 1925 meeting of the ATC, disputed Avery's characterization, which he must surely have taken as a personal slap in the face. "I do not agree with the sentence marked," MacKaye wrote Avery. "Interest in the Appalachian Trail has had its ebbs and flows," MacKaye admitted, "and the big 'flow' came in 1927 with the advent of Judge Perkins and the Potomac A. T. Club. But many workers—notably Raymond Torrey—kept throughout a sustained interest and zeal." In the final version published by the ATC, however, Avery let stand the original language, notwithstanding MacKaye's objections.

"[D]espite the interest shown and the wide-spread representation at the [1925] Conference," read the ATC's "Publication No. 5," "little progress resulted. The project lost momentum; it had failed to enlist sufficient workers and was rapidly degenerating into a fireside philosophy. In 1927, when practically moribund, the Trail project was resurrected by Arthur Perkins . . . and carried to a stage which insured its completion."

This characterization of Appalachian Trail activity in the two-year interval between 1925 and 1927 might have come as a surprise to others besides MacKaye—including, for example, the members of the Blue Mountain Eagle Climbing Club who had initiated their trail work during that period.

In any event, Avery's account of this era of Appalachian Trail history was issued virtually unrevised by the ATC for more than fifty years. It implicitly depicted himself and Perkins as the saviors of the trail project from carefree "fireside philosophers," by whom he could really only have meant MacKaye. Avery in fact had no firsthand knowledge of the Trail's history before 1927, which was when he first became involved in the project. He had no little or no idea of MacKaye's efforts or personal circumstances during the previous years, including the interval between 1925 and 1927.

In my book, I've detailed MacKaye's efforts to promote the Appalachian Trail between 1921 and 1925, when he help to organize the first meeting of the Appalachian Trail Conference. It was there, as noted, that he was given the title of "Field Organizer"—as Avery never failed to point out. According to MacKaye, there were discussions at the 1925 conference to fund his work in the amount of $5,000.

At the time, MacKaye had no regular employment or income. He needed money in order to devote his time to the Appalachian Trail. What little support he had received before then had come from his planning friends and associates, notably the architect Clarence Stein and the writer Lewis Mumford. But MacKaye received no financial support and little direction from the ATC executive committee established in 1925. Shortly after the 1925 meeting, in fact, he had returned to his home in Shirley Center, Massachusetts, partly to provide company and support for his sister Hazel, who was beginning her long descent into mental illness. "Heretofore my basic source of income, as I have told you, consisted in 'not having children'," he wrote his friend Lewis Mumford. "Now all is different: I suddenly find myself 'with child'"— by which he meant his sister. Throughout these years, as Mumford later wrote, MacKaye survived "by tightening his belt and accepting what the ravens brought him."

There's no doubt that MacKaye was an idealist, a visionary, and a self-styled philosopher of outdoor culture. His abstract rhetoric could provide plenty of fuel for caricature. I can't help but feel, though, that the characterization of MacKaye as a mere "fireside philosopher," responsible for somehow allowing the trail effort to "degenerate," is an unfair and exaggerated portrait. MacKaye and the busy William Welch, first chairman of the ATC, had been thrilled and enthusiastic when Arthur Perkins stepped forward to spearhead the Appalachian Trail project in 1927.

The standard, quasi-official history, folklore, and mythology of the AT depicts MacKaye, on the one hand, as a "dreamer," a "visionary," an "impractical" eccentric, who conceived the trail as a utopian "project in housing and community architecture," to use his own phrase from the 1921 article in which he proposed the idea. Avery, on the other hand, was the "doer," the man of action, who actually got the trail built. Harold Anderson, who knew both men well, wrote MacKaye ironically on the eve of the 1935 ATC: "You are a dreamer and a philosopher, inclined to be fanatical, while [Myron] is a practical man, getting things done." Anderson was among those who chose to cast his lot with the dreamer. In fact, MacKaye, in his later years, helped to perpetuate this characterization: he always credited others as the actual builders of the Trail. "I did conceive the thing, the idea, and I named it," he said in a film shown to the ATC in 1975, the year of his death. "Other people did the rest. I dropped it [the idea, that is] and they did it."

The exhibit dedicated today uses selected emblematic artifacts to reflect this handed-down characterization of the two men. MacKaye's typewriter represents his role as a man of ideas, who used the medium of print on paper, both words and maps, to introduce the idea of the Appalachian Trail, to promote its purposes as a vehicle of social change, and to advocate the creation of a network of amateur activists to build it. Avery's measuring wheel touched the ground, as he pushed it along inch by inch, foot by foot, mile by mile, as the trail took physical form.

The standard portrayal of Appalachian Trail history has been most widely and breezily depicted in Bill Bryson's *A Walk in the Woods*. Bryson's book makes for lively reading, but I don't think it's very good history. For instance, here's how he describes the situation immediately after the creation of the Appalachian Trail Conference in 1925. "In fact, however, for the next five years nothing happened, largely because MacKaye occupied himself with refining and expanding his vision until he and it were only tangentially connected to the real world," Bryson writes. In the years immediately after 1925, as I've noted earlier, MacKaye was in fact all too connected to the harsh realities of the real world.

Bryson continues: "Not until 1930, when a young Washington admiralty lawyer and keen hiker named Myron Avery took over the development did work actually begin, but suddenly it moved on apace. . . . He had no patience with MacKaye and his 'quasi-mystical epigrams,' and the two never got along. . . . It was really Avery's trail. . . ."

When the trail was first completed in 1937, Bryson adds, "Remarkably, the building of the longest footpath in the world attracted almost no attention. Avery was not one for publicity, and by this time MacKaye had retired in a funk."

As a talented comic writer, Bryson skillfully employs the rhetoric of hyperbole and exaggeration. But of course he didn't know MacKaye and Avery. And there is little evidence, though he lived only a few steps from MacKaye's voluminous papers at Dartmouth College at the time he wrote his book, that he troubled to consult this rich source for the AT's history. Bryson must have discovered his version of the history of the AT from someplace and somebody else.

Bryson essentially adopted the conventional history of the AT that Myron Avery himself wrote. "To the victor goes the narrative," *New Yorker* editor David Remnick has written in a different context. And Avery in the 1930s won uncontested control of the ATC. So it is his narrative—that is, the version Avery wrote for Publication No. 5—that the ATC continued to distribute until the late 1980s, when the organization, for the first time since the 1930s, revised this official history, first in its *Members Handbook*, written principally by Brian King, and in the 75th anniversary issue of the *Appalachian Trailway News*, published in 2000 under the editorial guidance of Brian King and Robert Rubin.

Bill Bryson said that MacKaye "retired in a funk." At the time, of course, MacKaye did not hold any Appalachian Trail office or position, paid or unpaid, to "retire" from. In fact, what he did do at the time was to serve in 1935 as one of the principal founders of the Wilderness Society, which became an influential national conservation organization and of which he would eventually become president.

Besides MacKaye, the eight founders of the Wilderness Society included others who had been directly involved in the Appalachian Trail effort and the debate over scenic parkways. Harold Anderson, Harvey Broome, and the Wilderness Society's chief organizer and funder, Robert Marshall, had also clashed in one way or other with Avery and the ATC. Shortly after the stormy 1935 meeting of the Appalachian Trail Conference, MacKaye explained the situation in a long letter to his long-time friend Stuart Chase, a popular writer on economic affairs during the 1930s. He also sent copies to Broome and Marshall.

"This situation has just brought on a crisis in Appalachian Trail affairs," he wrote:

It came about at the meeting in June at Skyland, Virginia, in the Shenandoah National Park, of the A. T. Conference, the supposed guardian of the A.T. itself, which Clarence [Stein] and I organized ten years ago. I'll not go into the story but the gist of it was that the Conference forsook the Trail and the whole wilderness concept and went over bag, baggage, and pantaloons to the skyline highway interests. The National Park Service sold out to them about three years ago. This has made a schism in all but one or two of the A.T. clubs from Maine to Georgia—the celluloid outfit going one way and the real folks (the "left wingers") going the other. The latter are looking to me to lead them not out of but *into* the wilderness.

This clash of Trail vs. Highway on the mountain tops is something bigger than it seems. It appears offhand like a humorous squabble among a bunch of picknickers. But you will realize it is something of very different calibre from that. The first strikes must have seemed like petty brawls, and so perhaps of this thing. It is an early skirmish, perhaps the first significant skirmish, in the retention of a humanly balanced world. This is the world that the Wilderness Society was formed to fight for. The current forces, financial and mechanized, are hell bent for urbanism; but the eternal forces, properly integrated, can by skillful strategy hold their own against it.

Raymond Torrey, reporting in his column in September, 1935 on appearance of the first issue of *The Living Wilderness*, magazine of the new Wilderness Society, noted that it included MacKaye's message to the 1935 ATC, titled "Why the Appalachian Trail?" The message was given "very little emphasis" at the conference, according to Torrey. "Those now in control of the conference do not see eye to eye with MacKaye, and his message was hurriedly read and given little circulation and has not been circulated in literature of the conference." MacKaye had been effectively read out of the ATC.

With MacKaye and other dissenters effectively silenced, though, Avery was able to forge ahead, with considerable success. He achieved his dream of a continuous trail, at least for a time, in August 1937, when the last links were finished in Maine. That year, Edward Ballard proposed to the ATC the idea of an Appalachian Trailway, a buffer of protected land encompassing the trail. In 1938, the ATC, the Forest Service, and the Park Service signed a trail maintenance agreement affecting some 875 miles of the AT on federal lands.

Likewise, the Wilderness Society gradually achieved influence as a nationwide voice for the growing wilderness preservation movement. When the Wilderness Society was created in 1935, its founding members insisted on strictly policing its membership ranks, partly as a result of the Appalachian Trail Conference experience. "Above all we do not want in our ranks people whose first instinct is to compromise," their founding statement stated. Robert Marshall put it this way in a letter to Harold Anderson: "We want no straddlers, for in the past they have surrendered too much good wilderness and primeval areas which should never have been lost."

Without naming Avery, MacKaye may well have had him in mind when he wrote Marshall: "My own doctrine of organization is that any body of people coming together for a purpose (whatever it may be) should consist of persons wholly wedded to said purpose and should consist of nobody else. If the purpose is Cannibalism (preference for Ham a la Capitalist) then nobody but a Cannibal should be admitted."

Marshall explained to another of their colleagues the basis for MacKaye's cranky insistence on rigid standards for membership in the Society: "Benton is really a grand fellow but very eccentric," he wrote, "and he has been hurt so badly by the traitorism of his own Appalachian Conference that he naturally is worried about any other organization going bad."

Some of Myron Avery's long-time friends in the PATC, according to Ed Garvey, a legendary AT thru-hiker and trail activist, later spoke bitterly of Avery's exclusion from the 1935 organizational meeting of the Wilderness Society; they assumed, apparently accurately, that his exclusion was deliberate. When Garvey proposed that MacKaye be awarded an honorary membership in the ATC, he "encountered resistance from the Avery group," he recalled. "There was a feeling that MacKaye really hadn't done the pick and shovel work that Avery did and therefore he, MacKaye was not nearly so deserving of the honor. In his own mind," Garvey surmised, "Avery probably shared the same feelings."

The World War II years of course sapped time, energy, manpower, and resources that had previously gone into AT effort. Avery was on active duty as a lawyer in the Navy Reserve. During most of the war years, MacKaye worked for the Rural Electrification Administration, living for those years in St. Louis. But when his sister, then living in a Connecticut sanitarium, died in 1944, MacKaye was at last relieved of the financial burden of her care. He retired on his 66th birthday in 1945. Within only a few months, he had become president of the Wilderness Society, after the death of its first president and executive secretary, long-time conservationist Robert Sterling Yard. The job was unpaid, but MacKaye proved to be the bridge between the founding generation of the Society and a new generation of leaders. It was MacKaye, as Wilderness Society president, who presented offers of employment to the Society's new executive secretary, Howard Zahniser, and to wildlife biologist Olaus Murie, who would hold the new position of director.

In that postwar moment, pent-up private and public energies and ideas burst forth in the conservation movement. As it happens, in 1945 and 1946, the efforts of Avery and MacKaye were once again conjoined through the linked causes of the Appalachian Trail and the growing wilderness-preservation cause. The immediate personal connection was Daniel Hoch, who had participated in those 1931 festivities on Bake Oven Knob. As it happened, Hoch had won election to the United State Congress in 1942 as a Democrat from his Pennsylvania district. At that time, Hoch was also serving as president of the Blue Mountain Eagle Climbing Club. With Avery's support, the long-time trail enthusiast sponsored a federal law to construct a national system of foot trails. Hoch's bill explicitly and exclusively named the Appalachian Trail as a part of the national trail system and called for an initial appropriation of $50,000 for the program. "All trails of such system," the bill said, "shall be constructed, developed, and maintained in a manner which will preserve as far as possible the wilderness values of the areas traversed by the trails of such system." Here, in 1945, the first proposed federal law calling for a national trails program including the Appalachian Trail explicitly linked the program to the preservation of "wilderness values."

Hoch, Avery, L. F. Schmeckebier, then president of the Potomac Appalachian Trail Club, and Harlean James, long-time AT supporter in her role as executive secretary of the American Planning and Civic Association, testified at an October, 1945 hearing for the bill before the House Committee on Roads. Hoch listed the dozens of trail clubs and conservation groups endorsing the bill. Avery was grilled by the doubtful committee chairman, J. W. Robinson of Utah, who expressed his region's skepticism about federal land-use policies. "Isn't it rather a State problem to take care of these local lands within the States, so far as the trail concerned?" Robinson asked. "In other words, the trail is not a national affair, or anything like that; it is a local affair, isn't it?"

"We regard it the other way," the quick-witted Avery responded. "We regard it as a national thing, as one project, rather than 14 separate projects which might have 14 different and varying policies."

The bill was not endorsed by any federal agency. When the administrator of the Federal Works Agency claimed that most federally financed roads made provision for pedestrian traffic, Daniel Hoch could barely restrain his exasperation. The Public Roads Administration, a bureau of the FWA, pursued "activities [that] invade the wilderness," Hoch charged. "[T]hey turn too many trails into roads anyway." The federal bureaucrat had "completely failed to grasp the intent of this project," Hoch sputtered. "The Bureau said it was building on new roads a strip beside the edge of the hard surface to walk on and that ought to suffice! I don't need to labor this point," Hoch added. ". . . We want to walk away from the roads."

The Forest Service did not support the bill, but Assistant Forest Service Chief L. F. Kneipp was at pains to distance his agency from the views expressed by the Federal Works Agency. Indeed, Kneipp said that the testimony of the bill's proponents about the public interest in trails represented "the existence of this interest on the part of a considerable minority of the people, and the expressed desire that provision be made for that type of activity throughout the country."

MacKaye, for his part, remained a leading spokesman for that "considerable minority" of the people in his capacity as president of the Wilderness Society. He learned of Hoch's bill, which he promptly rewrote for a different purpose and with a different title. His bill called for establishment of "a national system of wilderness belts." Such wilderness belts, he imagined, would be "located along the several mountain ranges of the country, including the Appalachian, Rocky Mountain, Sierra and Cascade Ranges, and along other natural resources including river courses."

MacKaye elaborated on this concept in a letter to his old friend Daniel Hoch. "A wilderness belt is merely a linear wilderness area, but the term itself 'wilderness area' (Aldo Leopold's) had not yet sunk into the public mind," he wrote. "People in the 1920's could visualize and Appalachian 'Trail' but not an Appalachian 'Wilderness Belt.'. . . But now I believe they can. . . . The 'belt' is a cross between line and area: it is a wide line and a narrow area; it allows the visualization of a system and it achieves our final object—area. The width would be anything to insure 'insulation'—anywhere from a half mile up." Aldo Leopold, the brilliant forester and conservationist who coined the term "wilderness area," had been acquainted with MacKaye since the mid-1920s. He had been one of the eight co-founders of the Wilderness Society and served as vice-president during part of MacKaye's tenure as president.

In MacKaye's view, Hoch's original trail-system bill, as supported by Avery and the ATC, represented a vision of the Appalachian Trail and of wilderness protection that was literally too narrow, both geographically and conceptually. He called for local groups to nominate interstate wilderness belts to a new federal panel, with representation from the Forest Service, the Park Service, and the Fish and Wildlife Service. It was, in fact, an updated version of a similar legislative scheme for federal wilderness protection he had drafted late in his short-lived tenure at the Tennessee Valley Authority, in the mid-1930s. MacKaye presented his draft wildland belts law to Howard Zahniser, the new Wilderness Society executive secretary, with the idea that the Society might adopt the plan as its own legislative initiative.

Hoch, based on the tepid reaction to the trails bill, was not eager to promote an even more ambitious wilderness law. Zahinser distributed MacKaye's draft, without identifying the author, to leaders of other national conservation organizations—including the ATC's Myron Avery. Zahniser did not reveal the authorship of the wildland belts bill, but Avery, who wrote back to complain about the competition it represented to the trails bill, no doubt had his suspicions. "I shall be interested to learn the origin of this bill and whether the project of the Hoch bill inspired its thought," he pointedly commented. "In any event, I think it well to determine if your controlling principles necessitate our organizations traveling separate paths toward what in many respects is a common objective."

Neither Hoch's bill nor MacKaye's wilderness belts bill went anywhere at the time. The moment was not yet ripe for federal bills to create a national trails system or a national wilderness preservation system. But it is an interesting, entirely understandable coincidence of history that these two smart, determined, forward-looking men, both amateurs working on their own time, on behalf of two important conservation organizations—both of which MacKaye was instrumental in creating, one of which Avery had set securely on its feet—had within a few months promoted arguably the earliest specific versions of the federal trails and wilderness legislative initiatives that would come to fruition with passage of the Wilderness Act in 1964 and the National Scenic Trails Act in 1968.

Avery died in 1952. In writing the official history of the ATC, Avery had been able to shape the story of the AT effort somewhat to his advantage. MacKaye, surviving Avery by several decades, now had the opportunity to regain some control over the narrative. In addition, MacKaye renewed friendly relations with members of the PATC and the ATC in the years after Avery's passing. PATC's bulletin in the 1950s included useful, interesting interviews with and articles by MacKaye about the AT's early history—especially the years of the early 1920s, before Avery's involvement with the AT effort. He always made sure to emphasize the roles of early trail promoters from outside the trail community, such as his friends Clarence Stein and Charles Harris

Whitaker (who, MacKaye noted his diary in May, 1925, had proposed the idea for a federal law in support of the AT.)

MacKaye had stepped down as president of the Wilderness Society in 1950; he served as honorary president until 1975, long enough to witness passage of the Wilderness Act (among many other environmental laws). The world had caught up with his vision, a half century after his lectures on "Outdoor Culture," which Arthur Perkins found amusing and which Avery dismissed as "fireside philosophy." In 1956, a decade after MacKaye had placed on his desk a copy of his wildland belts bill adapted from the Hoch trails bill, Wilderness Society executive secretary Howard Zahniser offered a new approach to federal wilderness legislation, drafting and finding legislative sponsors for the first version of the bill that would be enacted as the Wilderness Act in 1964.

In 1963, one of Avery's successors as ATC chairman, Stanley Murray, while on a hiking trip in Maine, considered whether the time had come to propose national trails legislation. MacKaye followed the progress of the law, monitoring it for signs of weakness on the question of incursions on the wilderness qualities of the Appalachian Trail. In 1966, he was given the Department of the Interior's Conservation Service Award, with an inscription from Secretary of the Interior Stuart Udall, crediting MacKaye for his legacy of "linking action with prophecy," as Udall put it.

When the Park Service officials showed up at Shirley Center to give the award to the 87-year-old, nearly blind MacKaye, he had made sure that several local newspaper reporters were on hand. He ambushed the Park Service representatives with a memo, titled "Of Wilderness Trails and Areas: Steps to Preserve the Original America," and accompanying maps. The memo called for the creation of what he called a "Cordilleran Trail," following the route of what is now the Continental Divide Trail, connecting existing and proposed national parks, national monuments, national forests, and wilderness areas. "The Trails can help the Areas, and the Areas can help the Trails," he explained to his long-time friend and fellow Wilderness Society founder Harvey Broome. "I'm working on a scheme to put these two jobs together."

At the time, MacKaye was corresponding regularly with ATC leaders and activists, including ATC chair Stanley Murray and Ed Garvey, then secretary of the PATC. Garvey shared with MacKaye a copy of a memo he had prepared for the ATC Board of Managers, in which he promoted the idea that ATC should hire its first full-time executive secretary. He noted that the Wilderness Society then had 35,000 members but that the ATC had just 600 individual members—and he drew the connection between the relative political influence of the two groups; the Wilderness Act, after all, had passed, but a trails law had not.

In 1968, the National Trails Systems Act became law (as did another sort of wildland belts law, the Wild and Scenic Rivers Act). The dreams and initiatives of Benton MacKaye, Myron Avery, Daniel Hoch, and so many others, reaching back for decades, had at last converged.

Despite Myron Avery's relatively short life, the energies and efforts he had packed into the quarter-century he devoted to the Appalachian Trail had, whatever his other frustrations and disappointments, enabled him to witness the completion of the AT as a continuous footpath from his beloved Katahdin to Georgia; the establishment of the ATC, though still a volunteer-based group, as a durable, functioning steward of the trail; and the forging of constructive, official agreements with federal and state agencies, which laid the groundwork for passage and implementation of the 1968 trails bill.

"The Appalachian Trail derives much of its strength and appeal from its uninterrupted and practically endless character," Avery wrote in his last report as ATC chairman in 1951. "This is an attribute which must be preserved. I view the existence of this pathway and the opportunity to travel it, day after day without interruption, as a distinct aspect of our American life." He worried, though, that intensifying development on unprotected private lands and growing population "may possibly produce the unavoidable result that, in lieu of a continuous uninterrupted Trail, we shall have to content ourselves with disconnected segments of an extensive length." At the time of his resignation as chair of the ATC and his death shortly thereafter, Avery worried that his vision and his achievement of continuity were under threat.

MacKaye was fortunate to see public and political support grow for the ideas of both a continuous trail and an expanding realm of wildlands surrounding it. The battle to preserve these visions in concrete form continues, but MacKaye and Avery demonstrated through their words and deeds that the Appalachian Trail and all it represents are the product of both philosophy and action.

I first saw the 1931 photo of MacKaye and Avery together on Bake Oven Knob in the excellent 75th anniversary issue of the July/August 2000 *Appalachian Trailway News* produced by Brian King and editor Robert Rubin. At that time, I was nearing the completion my book. I had struggled throughout to treat fairly and accurately the complex and consequential relationship between the two men. And there, at last, was the photographic evidence of one aspect of the relationship that I had been struggling to describe in my own words. But it was really quite simple, and the one picture did indeed count for thousands of words. There were Benton MacKaye and Myron Avery, together, on the Appalachian Trail, celebrating and promoting this unique American institution and their own remarkable accomplishment, the product of prodigious quantities of both inspiration and perspiration. The rest of us, of course, have been following in their big footprints ever since.

A Note on Sources

Portions of this essay rely closely on passages from my book, *Benton MacKaye: Conservationist, Planner, and Creator of the Appalachian Trail* (Baltimore: Johns Hopkins University Press, 2002; paperback, 2008). Readers will find more comprehensive treatment of some of the issues and events discussed here (as well as citations of sources) at pages 143-168, 221-227, 230-231, 235-237, 267-284, and 346-366 of *Benton MacKaye*.

Additional sources include: Lewis Mumford, "Introduction," *The New Exploration: A Philosophy of Regional Planning* (reprint, Harpers Ferry, West Virginia: Appalachian Trail Conservancy, 1991); Raymond Torrey, "Inspired Appalachian Trail Meeting," *New York Evening Post*, October 16, 1931; Raymond Torrey, "Long Brown Path," *New York Post*, September 7, 1935; Edward B. Garvey, "Memorandum to Appalachian Trail Conference Board of Managers," August 5, 1966, p. x, MacKaye Family Papers (MFP); Edward B. Garvey letter to Laura and Guy Waterman, March 16, 1986, David Sherman papers, in author's possession; Bill Bryson, *A Walk in the Woods: Rediscovering America on the Appalachian Trail* (New York: Broadway Books, 1998), pp. 27-28; Harvey Broome letter to Myron Avery, December 18, 1931, Harvey Broome Papers, McClung Historical Collection, East Tennessee Historical Center, Knoxville, Tennessee; Myron Avery letter to Harvey Broome, December 21, 1931, Harvey Broome Papers, McClung Historical Collection, East Tennessee Historical Center, Knoxville, Tennessee; "Myron Avery's Final Report to the Appalachian Trail Conference (excerpt)," in *Trail Years: A History of the Appalachian Trailway Conference, Special 75th Anniversary Issue, Appalachian Trailway News,* July 2000, p. 15; Robert A. Rubin, "The Short, Brilliant Life of Myron Avery," also in *Trail Years,* pp. 22-29; Benton MacKaye, "On the Purpose of the Appalachian Trail," message prepared for Pennsylvania Appalachian Trail conference, May 13, 1927, MFP; Appalachian Trail Conference, "Publication No. 5," 1st edition, January, 1934; Benton MacKaye letter to Myron Avery, July 16, 1933, MFP; David Remnick, "The Seventh Day," *The New Yorker,* May 28, 2007.

(2007)

"Work and Art and Recreation and Living Will All Be One": Benton MacKaye and Henry David Thoreau

Adapted from comments for a panel titled "Influence of Thoreau's *Walden* on Personal Values and Lifestyles" at the 2004 Gathering of the Thoreau Society.

Benton MacKaye attended several of the Thoreau Society's annual Gatherings. He was in Concord for at least the meetings of 1958, 1959, and 1960. What attracted him to those Gatherings was not just his lifelong interest in Thoreau but the fact that two of his closest friends and colleagues at the time, Howard Zahniser and Paul Oehser, were leaders of the Thoreau Society during that era: Zahniser was president in 1956 and 1957, Oehser in 1959 and 1960. Besides their common interest in Thoreau, all three men were also leaders of the Wilderness Society. MacKaye had been a founder of the influential conservation organization in 1935, had served continuously on its governing council, was the organization's president from 1945 through 1950, and then became its honorary president until his death in 1975. Zahniser had been the society's executive secretary since 1945, edited the organization's magazine, *The Living Wilderness*, and was the principal author and promoter of the 1964 Wilderness Act. Oehser, the chief editor at the Smithsonian Institution, was for many years a member of the Wilderness Society's council. During the 1950s and early 1960s, MacKaye usually spent the winter months living at the Cosmos Club in Washington, D.C., where he often joined Zahniser and Oehser for meals and meetings. The three Thoreau enthusiasts were all literary men in their own right, but through their efforts on behalf of the Wilderness Society and other conservation and civic organizations, they were also intensely involved in public affairs.

When MacKaye attended the Gathering in those years, in the company of other Thoreauvians, he could well appreciate the connections between his long, interesting life and that of Thoreau's. The parallels between MacKaye and Thoreau are many, both intellectually and biographically. They both attended Harvard College. They both lived in small Massachusetts towns that came to represent for them places that were at once universal and representative. Like Thoreau in Concord, MacKaye traveled much in Shirley, a town not even 20 miles further west along the Fitchburg Railroad from where that line's tracks nicked the southwest edge of Walden Pond. But both men were, in a literal sense, cosmopolitan, at home in the world. MacKaye, for instance, once described himself as an "amphibian as between urban and rural life."[1] They both traveled far afield, geographically and intellectually, while "referring everything to the meridian of" their home towns, in Emerson's phrase.[2] They both chose careers that offered them the chance to work outdoors and to study the landscape, Thoreau as a surveyor, MacKaye as a forester. They both have had a significant impact on the American conservation movement. Finally, MacKaye spent six of his 96 years as a married man, but for most of his long life he, like Thoreau, lived as a single man in modest circumstances and surroundings.

I also think that they both wouldn't have recognized the word "lifestyle," at least in the sense that we often use it today. I told the organizers of this panel that I would register a mild dissent about applying the notion of "lifestyle" either to Thoreau's influence or to the manner in which Thoreau, MacKaye, and other idealists of their ilk chose to live their lives. At least according to my dictionary, the term "lifestyle" did not enter the language until the mid-1920s or so, an era that saw an explosion of mass culture, mass media, and mass marketing. The term "lifestyle" suggests something you pick off a rack or from a catalog, to suit the changing seasons or the latest fad. For a Thoreau or a MacKaye, the fundamental choices they made about how they would live their lives confronted directly the economic and material realities of day-to-day life. Thoreau did not title his essay "*Lifestyle* Without Principle." The published essay, "Life Without Principle," was based on versions of a lecture Thoreau variously titled, among other things, "Getting a Living," or "What Shall it Profit," or "Life Misspent." He did not, in *Walden*, write that "I went to the woods because I wished to pursue a deliberate *lifestyle*." Instead, He went there "to *live* deliberately." Lifestyle suggests something ephemeral and mutable. Thoreau and MacKaye were interested in pursuing "life" or "living" at its most essential and integral. The challenge of creating a truly integrated life is to balance somehow the means of living with the ends or aims of living, a challenge Thoreau and MacKaye were forced to address practically and pragmatically.

In his 1928 book, *The New Exploration: A Philosophy of Regional Planning*, a one-of-a-kind text that shares many attributes with *Walden*, MacKaye included a central chapter titled "Living vs. Existence." And he began that chapter by invoking Thoreau's ideas. "I am convinced," MacKaye quoted *Walden*, "both by faith and experience, that to maintain one's self on this earth is not a hardship but a pastime. . . . Let not to get a living be thy trade, but thy sport." MacKaye then elaborated on Thoreau's notions in his own words. "We have here the essence of the meaning of *living*: to maintain ourselves on this earth not as a toil and hardship but as a sport and quest," he wrote. "Thoreau was convinced this could be done. Modern engineering proves it can be done."[3]

Paul T. Bryant borrowed directly from *Walden*'s chapter titled "Where I Lived and What I Lived For" to find the title of his pioneering and discerning 1965 dissertation, *The Quality of the Day: The Achievement of Benton MacKaye*. Bryant perceived in MacKaye an exemplar of one who chose "to elevate his life by a conscious endeavor," as Thoreau set forth the human task. "It is something to be able to paint a particular picture, or to carve a statue, and so to make a few objects beautiful," he wrote in *Walden*, "but it is far more glorious to carve and paint the very atmosphere and medium through which we look, which morally we can do. To affect the quality of the day, that is the highest of the arts."[4]

MacKaye's notion of regional planning, as the title of his book implies, was not merely technical, but truly philosophical. He was, as I have written elsewhere, a sort of transcendental engineer. MacKaye was interested in the design of roads, residential communities, open spaces, and the rest of the physical infrastructure of modern society, but only as it served a higher purpose. The goal of regional planning was to "arrange the environment," as he put it, "so that finally work and art and recreation and living will all be one."[5]

I want to suggest briefly how MacKaye applied that precept—"work and art and recreation and living will all be one"—in his own life, especially with regard to his conception of the Appalachian Trail. "The problem of living is at bottom an economic one," MacKaye had written in the 1921 article introducing his idea, which he described as "a series of recreational communities throughout the Appalachian chain of mountains from New England to Georgia, these to be connected by a walking trail."[6] He addressed the fundamental economic problem of living by tackling first not the matter of work and labor—but that of play and leisure.

MacKaye was one of six children born to a literary and high-minded family, whose patriarch, a larger-than-life but profligate playwright, actor, and impresario named Steele MacKaye, was effectively disowned by his wealthy father. Hence, Benton and his siblings were raised with high expectations but limited financial resources. In fact, the family had bought its small cottage in Shirley in the late 1880s partly to secure an inexpensive place to live, at least during the summer months. As an energetic adolescent during the 1880s and 1890s, Benton enjoyed exploring the rural countryside of Shirley. Of course he never met Thoreau, but he had once talked with a Shirley old-timer who had. "I'll mention that I once talked with a man (one Holden) who as a boy had talked with Thoreau, and at Walden," as MacKaye recollected the story in his eighties. "He and some playmates happened on the Pond. The great man took an interest in them and gave them some pointers on fishing. This is almost all that I recall (after half a century). It is my great regret that I did not quiz Holden thoroughly and record something of this first hand contact."[7]

MacKaye was a restless student. He dropped out of Cambridge Latin School in his senior year, returning to Shirley to tutor himself for the Harvard entrance exams. But before that, at age 15, he had read *Walden* while recuperating from a bout of poor health. He may have been prompted to pick up the book by one of his older brothers, James, then enrolled at Harvard himself, who was a lifelong disciple of Thoreau. (In 1930 James published a selection entitled *Thoreau: Philosopher of Freedom.*) James MacKaye was Benton's intellectual and personal mentor, "the rock-bottom foundation," as Benton later put it, and "the *chief source* of inspiration" for his own work and writing.[8]

Benton graduated from Harvard in 1900, but without a clear sense of vocation. He spent several frustrating years in New York City as a private tutor. During another convalescence, in the winter of 1901, he had corresponded with James about his future. James had urged Benton not to be one of those who "lose sight of the end in their effort to attain the means."[9] Benton replied: ". . . [W]hat is the career? . . . What is the problem of the day which I want to tackle? It is the problem of distribution (both of men and of necessities), and embraces the question of transportation, natural resources, of 'Lonesomehurst' [his derogatory codeword for suburban life], of the sacrifice of the country's good soils to the ignorant and the covetous. . . . A career which takes me over the country, out of doors, and into all communities and places, is the one for me, it is a scheme to be developed and difficult to be attained, but one toward which I shall 'hammer, hammer, hammer.' Such are my vague ideas for the future."[10]

A self-styled philosopher, James MacKaye wrote a variety of books promoting his own version of what he sometimes called "pantocracy," or, in what he hoped was a less forbidding phrase, "Americanized Socialism." The most elaborate of these treatises, published in 1906, was titled *The Economy of Happiness.* In that dense and austere book he applied Thoreauvian principles at the scale of the national economy. "Simple tastes are better than any others," he had written. "A nation whose tastes are of the simplest can, other things being equal, dispense in greatest proportion with the most universal of needs—the need of labor. It is for this reason that luxurious tastes are so uneconomic."[11]

James had rehearsed these arguments with Benton during the late summer of 1903, when they traveled up the St. Lawrence and Saguenay rivers by steamer, retracing part of the route of Thoreau's *A Yankee in Canada*. Upon his return from Canada, Benton experienced a severe bout of appendicitis, resulting in emergency surgery performed on the kitchen table in the kerosene-lit Shirley cottage. The health scare shook him out of his vocational lethargy. He decided to become a forester. He returned to Harvard that fall. In 1905, he became the first student to receive a graduate degree from the university's new forestry program. His early career as a forester included work for the U.S. Forest Service in New England and the northeast as well as a stint teaching forestry at Harvard.

MacKaye confronted another career crisis in 1910. He had just become engaged to a recent Radcliffe graduate when he was fired from his Harvard teaching job. A change of leadership at the Forest Service—the inspirational and charismatic Gifford Pinchot had been fired by President William Howard Taft in January 1910—threatened his prospects in that agency. Unemployed, MacKaye worked on a few private forestry projects and struggled to write a forestry textbook that he hoped might establish his standing in the profession; his family worried about his state of mind. Brother James turned toward Concord as a source of therapy, strength, and stability. "I heard he is overworking, . . ." he wrote their mother about Benton's frazzled state. "I wish he would read Thoreau and get his equilibrium."[12]

As it happened, Benton secured a permanent new position with the Forest Service in Washington, D.C. He was headquartered in the nation's capital from 1911 to 1920. In Washington he became associated with a group of liberal and left-wing journalists and activists who referred to themselves as the "Hell Raisers." It was at this time that he met and married in 1915 a militant suffragist and peace activist, Jessie Hardy Stubbs, or "Betty," as she was known to friends. Shortly after their marriage, MacKaye began to grow frustrated with his situation at the Forest Service. Again he articulated the dilemma of balancing one's principles with the demands of earning a living. "Of course I may go right on with the Forest Service," he explained to his sister Hazel, "but unless some big changes in attitude are shown, I want to get out— sooner or later—or that office will make a cave man of me." He and Betty, he continued, were considering "lowering the standard of living and thus gaining independence."[13] By conventional American standards, this formulation made no sense. By the Thoreauvian precepts which MacKaye well understood and which he attempted to apply in his own life, however, reducing one's material needs represented a practical path to self-reliance.

MacKaye left the federal government in 1920, as the political landscape shifted. He soon went to work as an editorial writer for a socialist newspaper in Milwaukee. But he left that job in a dispute over his wife's vocal advocacy of what she called a "bride strike" as a means to control militarism. The equation was simple, if somewhat at odds with human nature: no babies, no soldiers, no wars.

The couple moved to New York City, to search for new careers. But his wife committed suicide in April of 1921. The tragic event left him distraught. He did not, of course, plan to become a widower as a young man, but Betty's unexpected death freed him from conventional expectations about a career, turning him down the path of his greatest social contributions, beginning later that year with the Appalachian Trail.

In the shadow of World War I, he conceived and explicitly promoted the Appalachian Trail as a nonviolent, cooperative alternative to militarism and the conventional politics of reform. MacKaye's first allies in promoting the Appalachian Trail were not members of the trail and conservation community but a group of reform-minded architects and planners. The subversive beauty of his idea, MacKaye confessed to his closest associates among the group, was that his program could be undertaken and its efficacy proved by ordinary citizens, without a political thought in their minds, whose only ambition was to spend some leisure time in the mountains, blazing and walking a hiking trail. A "frontal attack" on the industrial system, involving the construction of the worker-owned industrial communities that were part of his original trail scheme, would meet stiff opposition from "ultra conservatives" and big business, he wrote his new friend, architect Clarence Stein. "If they did not call it 'visionary' they would say it was 'bolshevistic' and 'dangerous.'" By contrast, a project combining a mountain trail and a series of recreational camps and communities "would make a flank attack on the problems of social readjustment," he predicted. "This fact if understood, would lose for the project the support of the ultra conservatives among the recreation group. But it would retain the support of the liberal minded and radicals therein. And these together would form the majority of the recreation group." The Appalachian project, "a flank attack on the problem of social readjustment," would, in other words, provide an indirect route to his conception of the ideal American society—which was, as he wrote, "to live, work, and play on a non-profit basis."[14]

"The camp community is a refuge from the scramble of every-day worldly life," MacKaye concluded in his published 1921 article proposing the AT, which appeared in the *Journal of the American Institute of Architects*. "It is in essence a retreat from profit."[15]

One of MacKaye's closest friends and colleagues was the author Lewis Mumford. The two men first met in 1923, when the idea for the Appalachian Trail was rapidly gaining public recognition and support—and just as Mumford's literary career was beginning to catch fire. In an article published that year, only months after they first became acquainted, Mumford wrote about his new and older friend's approach to social change. "Unlike so many reformers, who urge people to desert their pleasures and recreations and 'consider things seriously,'" Mumford wrote, MacKaye proposed "simply to call people, especially young people, out into this Appalachian region; he asks nothing more, at first, than that the folk who are cribbed, cabined, and confined by the great cities along the coasts should camp out in the open spaces of Appalachia, scramble over its hills, make themselves at home in its woodlands, fight the forest fires when need be and guard against them at all times. In short, he want them to possess the whole landscape, not by act of the legislature, but by the process of use and wont, whereby the people of

England once upon a time acquired their right to the common lands, and to this day keep their title to the common footpaths that run across their fields. In short, he does not propose that this domain should be given to the 'people,' as our national forests are given; he proposed that it should be conquered."[16]

During their more than fifty years of friendship, Mumford had many occasions to compare MacKaye to Thoreau, not only regarding their ideas about the natural environment but also in terms of the choices these men made about how to live their lives. "He lives a very quiet abstemious life: plain living and high thinking: and wastes less of his time on the *means* of living than anyone I know," Mumford said of his friend in 1932, as the nation suffered through economic calamity. "He anticipated the present depression long ago, and is completed unaffected by it personally."[17]

MacKaye once told Mumford that his "basic source of income . . . consisted in 'not having children.'"[18] In reality, of course, MacKaye's frugal way of life was not simply a matter of choice. In practicing and advocating a simpler mode of living, he was, like Thoreau, making a virtue of necessity. Both men had a playful, ironic turn of mind, which they displayed to their respective Harvard classmates in explaining their atypical vocational status. In 1847, upon his 10th class anniversary, Thoreau reported: "I am a Schoolmaster—a private Tutor, a Surveyor—a Gardener, a Farmer—a Painter, I mean a House Painter, a Carpenter, a Mason, a Day-Laborer, a Pencil-Maker, a Glasspaper Maker, a Writer, a sometimes Poetaster."[19] MacKaye, writing to his classmates in 1930 on their 30th anniversary year, could not match the variety of Thoreau's vocational endeavors; he described his life more tersely. "Since 1925," he reported, "I have been working at my chosen job which is also my hobby which is regional planning."[20] In other words, his job and his hobby, his vocation and his avocation, were inseparable.

Throughout the 1920s, MacKaye, while promoting the Appalachian Trail and developing his notions about regional planning, did not hold a permanent, full-time job. He was sometimes supported by his friends Mumford and Stein, who recognized MacKaye's truly unique talents, which could not find their fullest expression in conventional career roles or institutions. Mumford summarized his friend's situation and influence in the spring of 1925, after the creation of the Appalachian Trail Conference, the organization that would carry to completion the work of building the trail. "Benton . . . has been living by the skin of his teeth as usual," he reported to Stein, "and yet without his following the numerous scents he opened during the last four years, we'd be far from where we are now in our conception of regional planning."[21]

I can't relate here the full story of MacKaye's life and accomplishments after these years. But Mumford, writing in 1969 as the environmental movement was rapidly gaining political and popular support, was as usual the most cogent chronicler of his friend's endeavors and influence. "Instead of looking for money and legislation, MacKaye treated the [Appalachian Trail] project as Thoreau might have organized a huckleberrying party," Mumford wrote on the occasion of his friend's 90th birthday. "In old fashioned Yankee style he looked for help from his friends and neighbors, and he found all he needed. . . . The fact that the idea took on, that MacKaye, by correspondence and occasional personal appearance, evoked the spirit needed to build the trail, in little groups from Hanover, New Hampshire to Knoxville, Tennessee, . . . shows the sheer force of personality, as against the current forces of depersonalized power."[22]

Mumford's comment about Thoreau and huckleberry parties was of course an allusion to Emerson's funeral address, upon his younger friend's death in 1863. "Had his genius been only contemplative," Emerson wrote on that occasion, "he had been fitted to his life, but with his energy and practical ability he seemed born for great enterprise and for command; and I so much regret the loss of his rare powers of action, that I cannot help counting it a fault in him that he had no ambition. Wanting this, instead of engineering for all America, he was the captain of a huckle-berry party."[23] When Mumford characterized MacKaye in a similar manner, though, he was offering a profound and sincere compliment. He understood the subversive manner of MacKaye's unconventional variety of leadership.

Another conservation leader, the firebrand Sierra Club executive director David Brower, had come to know MacKaye during tumultuous political battles of the 1950s and 1960s. Years later he succinctly summarized in a phrase the distinctive essence of his friend's influence: he called it "Benton MacKaye's Theory of How to Build Big by Starting Small."[24] Mumford and Brower had learned from their friend's life and example that one could indeed be an engineer for all America precisely by excelling as a captain of huckleberry parties. Lead enough such parties, and before long—especially if you live almost a century, as MacKaye nearly did—you have built a 2,100-mile hiking trail and protected more than 100-million acres of designated wilderness areas. Benton MacKaye largely succeeded in creating a life of genuine and literal integrity, in which, as he had put it, "work and art and recreation and living will all be one."

Throughout MacKaye's long and productive life, Thoreau remained an intellectual and inspirational touchstone. In a 1944 article, "Thoreau on 'Ktaadn,'" MacKaye, after examining the Concord explorer's accounts of his adventures in the Maine woods, declared him "the greatest interpreter perhaps in all time of the wilderness environment."[25] During the early 1970s, when the Appalachian Trail was experiencing a boom in popularity and use, MacKaye regularly warned trail enthusiasts, many of whom were focused on how many miles they could cover and how fast they could so, to slow down and observe closely the surrounding trail environment. In 1975, the year of his death at age 96, he wrote a letter to a trail activist about the history and philosophy of the Appalachian Trail. He noted that the publication of the venerable and important New York-New Jersey Trail Conference, to which his correspondent belonged, was titled "Trail Walker." MacKaye endorsed the spirit embodied in that title by invoking Thoreau's perambulatory perspective. "I have always liked to walk, but I have refused to hike unless I needed to catch a train," he observed. "The word 'hike' to me suggested hurry, the need to 'get there' and to get it over with. . . . Thoreau wrote a famous piece called 'Walking.' It is hard to think of him 'hiking.'"[26]

Though separated in time by several generations, Henry David Thoreau and Benton MacKaye walked side by side in experiencing and sharing some of the same geographic, intellectual, and spiritual landscapes.

Notes

[1] Benton MacKaye (hereafter cited as BMK) letter to Harvey Broome, Sept. 5, 1932. (All unpublished letters and manuscript materials cited in these notes are from the MacKaye Family Papers, Dartmouth College Library.)

[2] Ralph Waldo Emerson, "Thoreau," in *The Selected Writings of Ralph Waldo Emerson*, ed. Brooks Atkinson (New York: Modern Library, 1968), 904.

[3] BMK, *The New Exploration A Philosophy of Regional Planning* (1928; reprint, with an introduction by Lewis Mumford and a foreword by David N. Startzell, Harpers Ferry, West Virginia: Appalachian Trail Conference, 1991), 120. In quoting *Walden*, MacKaye is conflating passages from the chapters "Economy" and "Baker Farm."

[4] Paul T. Bryant, *The Quality of the Day: The Achievement of Benton MacKaye* (Ann Arbor: University Microfilms, 1981), v. The quotation, which Bryant uses as an epigraph for his dissertation, is from the "Where I Lived, and What I Lived For" chapter of *Walden*.

[5] BMK, *New Exploration*, 133.

[6] BMK, "An Appalachian Trail: A Project in Regional Planning," *Journal of the American Institute of Architects* 9 (October 1921), 325-330; reprinted in Anderson, *Benton MacKaye*, 371-379.

[7] BMK letter to Sherman Paul, June 29, 1961.

[8] BMK letter to Paul Bryant, July 25, 1964.

[9] James Medbery MacKaye letter to BMK, March 5, 1901.

[10] BMK letter to James Medbery MacKaye, April 7, 1901.

[11] James Medbery MacKaye, *The Economy of Happiness* (Boston: Little, Brown,1906), 326-327.

[12] James Medbery MacKaye letter to Mary Medbery MacKaye, Jan. 11, 1911.

[13] BMK letter to Hazel MacKaye, Aug. 16, 1915.

[14] BMK, "Regional Planning and Social Readjustment," 1921, 12-14, 18.

[15] BMK, "An Appalachian Trail," 329.

[16] Lewis Mumford, "New Trails for Old," *The Freeman*, July 4, 1923, 396-397.

[17] Lewis Mumford letter to Harvey Broome, April 24, 1932.

[18] BMK letter to Lewis Mumford, Nov. 13, 1927.

[19] Henry David Thoreau letter to Henry Williams, Jr., in *The Correspondence of Henry David Thoreau*, ed. Walter Harding and Carol Bode (New York: New York University Press, 1958), 185-186.

[20] BMK, Harvard class of 1930 draft biography, 1930.

[21] Lewis Mumford to Clarence S. Stein, May 18, 1925, Clarence S. Stein Papers, Rare Books and Manuscript Collections, Carl A. Kroch Library, Cornell University, Ithaca, New York.

[21] Lewis Mumford, typescript, "Benton MacKaye," March 24, 1969, attached to Lewis Mumford letter to BMK, March 6, 1974.

[23] Emerson, "Thoreau," 911.

[24] David R. Brower and Steve Chapple, *Let the Mountains Talk, Let the Rivers Run* (New York: HarperCollins West, 1995), 179.

[25] BMK, "Thoreau on Ktaadn," *The Living Wilderness*, Sept., 1944, 3-6.

[26] BMK letter to Alfred Smalley, March 31, 1975.

(2004)

Lewis Mumford: An Early Trail Champion

When the eminent author Lewis Mumford died on January 26, 1990, at his home in Amenia, New York, the Appalachian Trail community lost one of its most venerable and renowned members. Mumford, until his death at the age of 94, was one of the last living links with the earliest days of the Appalachian Trail.

Mumford spent only a few days on the Appalachian Trail during his long lifetime. He probably never painted a blaze or sawed a limb along the Trail's route. Nor did he claim any credit for his involvement with the Trail effort. Nonetheless, he had a significant role in establishing the Appalachian Trail—both on the landscape and the public's imagination—as a unique and durable American institution.

Mumford read an article in the October 1921 issue of the *Journal of the American Institute of Architects* (JAIA), entitled "An Appalachian Trail: A Project in Regional Planning," in which Benton MacKaye described his vision of "a series of recreational communities throughout the Appalachian chain of mountains from New England to Georgia, these to be connected by walking trail."

"I well remember the shock of astonishment and pleasure that came over me when I first read this proposal," Mumford recalled many years later. "But even the most sanguine backer of MacKaye's idea could hardly have guessed that this was such an *idée-force*—to use a French term—that MacKaye would live to see the trail itself and some of the park area, as in the Great Smokies, finished before another 20 years had passed."

Mumford and MacKaye were introduced in February 1923 by their mutual friends, the *JAIA*'s iconoclastic editor Charles Harris Whitaker and the reform-minded New York architect Clarence Stein, chairman of the AIA's Committee on Community Planning. It had been Whitaker and Stein, during a talk at the Hudson Guild Farm in Netcong, New Jersey, in July 1921, who encouraged MacKaye to write up his Appalachian Trail idea. And Stein's committee became the Trail project's first informal sponsor, reprinting copies of MacKaye's article and distributing them to trail clubs, public officials, and social activists.

In April 1923, this intellectually high-powered quartet organized the Regional Planning Association of America (RPAA), a small, tight-knit, informal group that, for a decade, spewed out innovative ideas about housing, land-use, transportation, and regional development. The Appalachian Trail, according to RPAA historian Carl Sussman, "became the [RPAA's] first rallying point."

Mumford, 16 years MacKaye's junior, was then on the threshold of his career as one of America's most penetrating and influential 20th-century commentators on architecture, urban affairs, technology, culture, and literature. The first of his almost 30 books, *The Story of Utopias*, appeared in 1922. In the Appalachian Trail, and in its conceptualizer, Benton MacKaye, Mumford discovered the embodiment of the communal and regionalist ideas that he advocated throughout his prolific writings.

Mumford and MacKaye became close friends and were productive professional collaborators until MacKaye's death in 1975. Mumford's influence and substantial editorial work made possible publication of MacKaye's own pioneering book, *The New Exploration: A Philosophy of Regional Planning* (1928). And, throughout the years, he sometimes contributed directly to the financial support of the high-minded MacKaye, who, as Mumford put it, often subsisted "by tightening his belt and accepting with the ravens brought him."

Lewis Mumford and Benton MacKaye, in May 1923, at the Hudson Guild Farm, Andover, New Jersey. (Courtesy of the Division of Rare and Manuscript Collections, Cornell University Library, and Robert McCullough.)

Mumford was on hand in October 1923 for the first major gathering dedicated exclusively to the Appalachian Trail, a three-day gathering at the Bear Mountain Inn in the Palisades Interstate Park along the Hudson River. But his most important contribution to the Appalachian Trail was his instant recognition of the project as "one of the fine imaginative works of our generation," as he wrote in 1927, when the trail's prospects were still tenuous and uncertain.

In the string of popular and pathbreaking books, including *Sticks and Stones* (1924), *The Golden Day* (1926), *The Brown Decades* (1931), and *The Culture of Cities* (1938), Mumford routinely described the Appalachian Trail in glowing terms and cited the "bold," "fundamental," "indispensable" ideas of MacKaye. During the trail's formative years, Mumford's widely read writings and growing reputation gave the project a measure of intellectual respectability and cultural significance.

In March 1925, the RPAA turned over leadership of the Trail effort to the newly founded Appalachian Trail Conference. Thereafter, under the leadership of early ATC chairmen William A. Welch, Arthur Perkins, and Myron Avery, the project was in the hands of experienced outdoors activists who knew the mountain terrain and could mobilize volunteers to undertake the hard, tedious, but rewarding work of trail-building.

Mumford, MacKaye, and the other intellectuals and social reformers who helped launch the A.T. in the early 1920s were committed to more than simply the creation of a footpath through the wilderness. They also yearned to develop healthy, inspiring human communities, in which, as MacKaye wrote in his 1921 article, "cooperation replaces antagonism, trust replaces suspicion, emulation replaces competition."

Those qualities, as Mumford later wrote, were essential to the RPAA's endeavors. "Actually it was the providential conjuncture at the right moment of Whitaker, MacKaye, Stein, and—I must add—myself that produced a fusion reaction that released energy and light. Where two or three are gathered together something happens that no individual ego, however inspired, knowledgeable, constructive, or imperious, can bring into existence."

Lewis Mumford's words apply just as well to the Appalachian Trail, which still exemplifies the communal values he, MacKaye, and thousands of other trailworkers and hikers have nurtured for almost 70 [now more than 90] years.

(1990)

"Hiking the Appalachian Trail": Mark Sanford's Great Adventures

South Carolina Governor Mark Sanford's dubious legacy will forever be linked to the phrase "hiking the Appalachian Trail," now securely established as a euphemism for an adulterous tryst. I was interested to learn, though, that Sanford is, in fact, a long-time Appalachian Trail (AT) hiker.

Sanford confessed his "love of the Appalachian Trail" at the mawkish June 24, 2009, press conference when he described his Buenos Aires rendezvous with a woman other than his wife. "I used to organize hiking trips, actually, when I was in high school," he reminisced. "I would get a soccer coach or football coach to act as chaperone, and then I'd get folks to pay me 60 bucks each, or whatever it was, to take the trip, and off we'd go and have these great adventures on the Appalachian Trail."

Sanford's exploitation of the AT as an alibi for his recent misadventure assumes sharply ironic significance, especially in light of his unsuccessful attempt to reject $700 million in federal stimulus funds allocated to South Carolina. The Appalachian Trail, after all, exemplifies an array of inspirational American values directly at odds with the free-market, individualistic, and anti-government dogmas on which the wayward governor built his political career.

The Appalachian Trail originated as a grassroots, volunteer project in the early 1920s. Today, much of the work and expense of maintaining the Trail is undertaken by the 74-year-old, nonprofit Appalachian Trail Conservancy and its 30 affiliated outdoor clubs.

But the AT's existence and survival have always depended upon extensive government support. With the passage of the 1968 National Trails System Act, the AT was designated the first National Scenic Trail and became a unit of the National Park Service. The 2,178-mile hiking path links 14 states along its ridgeline route from Springer Mountain, in Georgia, to Katahdin, in Maine. Virtually its entire route is publicly owned. The government-protected trail corridor traverses six National Parks and eight National Forests, as well as numerous state parks, forests, and wildlife areas. Public access to the Appalachian Trail is available to any hiker, without charge. When the trail was first completed in 1937, much of the trail-making and shelter-building labor was then being undertaken by federal employees of the Civilian Conservation Corps, a New Deal economic-stimulus and relief program.

And the original conceptualizer of the trail was a visionary forester, writer, and left-wing activist named Benton MacKaye, who spent more than a decade as a federal employee with the U.S. Forest Service and the Labor Department. During the year before publishing the article proposing creation of the AT, though, MacKaye was writing editorials for a Socialist daily newspaper in Milwaukee.

MacKaye's article in the October 1921 issue of the *Journal of the American Institute of Architects*, titled "An Appalachian Trail: A Project in Regional Planning," promoted the AT as a utopian alternative to the era's accelerating pace of urbanization and industrialization. "The camp community is a sanctuary and a refuge from the scramble of every-day worldly commercial life," MacKaye wrote. "It is in essence a retreat from profit. Cooperation replaces antagonism, trust replaces suspicion, emulation replaces competition."

In addition to the challenging mountain trail and the rustic shelters that characterize the AT as we know it today, MacKaye also proposed the creation of "community camps" along the route, "for recreation, for recuperation, and for study," as well as "food and farm camps," to provide "permanent, steady, healthy employment in the open."

Such camps never won much support from the outdoor enthusiasts and government officials who were the driving force behind the AT's creation. But the spirit of MacKaye's original conception of the project as "a base for a more extensive and systematic development of outdoor community life" still thrives.

As an ambitious teenager, Mark Sanford was at least consistent with his free-market ideas in finding ways to make a few dollars organizing AT hikes. But the public's significant investment in the Appalachian Trail made possible his youthful enterprises and exploits.

Governor Sanford, self-described lover of the AT, should take a hike—a real one. While confronting the trail's rigors, he can contemplate the shambles of his political career and personal life. At the same time, perhaps he can reflect on Benton MacKaye's original vision of the AT as a "camp community," the efforts of the thousands of volunteers who built and still maintain the trail, and the legacy of the government-paid CCC workers who devoted their labor to its completion.

The Appalachian Trail, as Sanford has comically and clumsily revealed, remains a treasured public resource that continues to provide a rugged and inspiring setting for great adventures.

(2009)

The Spectatorium: Steele MacKaye's Epic Failure

During the World's Columbian Exposition of 1893, Chicago was a showcase for the era's kaleidoscopic variety of popular entertainment. The art, architecture, and technological marvels on display at the White City represented a high-minded exercise in the cultural betterment of the American people. The nearby Midway Plaisance, on the other hand, "distinctly exotic, polyglot, cosmopolitan, festal,"[1] drew crowds with such attractions as hootchy-kootchy dancers, the original Ferris Wheel, and dozens of other sensational acts and spectacles. And throughout Chicago, entrepreneurs sought to profit from the visitors, all eager to be entertained, who flocked to the city during the world's fair. Theaters, music halls, vaudeville shows, Buffalo Bill's Wild West Show, dime museums, and other attractions—as well as brothels, saloons, and gambling parlors—all vied for the tourist business.[2]

On paper, Steele MacKaye's Spectatorium, a colossal theatrical enterprise planned for the Columbian Exposition, seem to epitomize this entertainment frenzy. In reality it ranked among the great disasters of American show business. In its grandiose, eccentric conception and ultimate failure, the Spectatorium mirrored MacKaye's career in American popular entertainment. All who have attempted to describe his quixotic personality and colorful career, be they contemporaries or historians, have resorted to superlatives. Called the "era's great erratic genius,"[3] and the "master spectacle-maker of the American theatre,"[4] MacKaye was born in Buffalo, New York, in 1842. As an actor, director, teacher, playwright, inventor, producer, and free-spender, he had achieved a substantial measure of fame and notoriety during the 1870s and 1880s.

Despite his prodigious talents, MacKaye lacked any business acumen. Indeed, his acquaintance Thomas Edison once commented that MacKaye "had all the charm of those peculiar men who give no thought to commercialism."[5] But the venturesome dramatist possessed a sure sense of America's appetite for grandiose diversions. For the Chicago fair, MacKaye conceived his theatrical pleasure dome as a hybrid of the most popular amusements of his time. The gigantic 10,000-seat theater that MacKaye named the "Spectatorium" would be an entire building full of his mechanical inventions. The entertainment there would include elements of panoramas and cycloramas, musical drama on a Wagnerian scale, and elaborate scenic techniques prefiguring those soon to be employed in the nascent medium of motion pictures—all combined with a generous measure of pure Barnumesque hokum. The theme of the world's fair—the 400th anniversary of Christopher Columbus's discovery of the Americas—was the basis for the story that MacKaye intended to depict. His dramatization of the epic quest, which he titled variously *The Great Discovery* and *The World Finder*, would take the form of a "spectatorio," a performance genre that MacKaye had developed (the name presumably an amalgam of "spectacle" and "oratorio"). The six-act "metaphysical musical poem"[6] would be staged as a giant pantomime involving 1,200 actors, 500 singers, a huge troupe of dancers, an orchestra, and MacKaye's remarkable collection of mechanical and lighting devices.

Part of MacKaye's inspiration for the Spectatorium came from the panoramas, cycloramas, dioramas, and cosmoramas that had attracted crowds throughout the century. Americans were thrilled by the famous battles, landscapes, and other scenes and events depicted on these huge painted murals displayed in various ingenious formats.[7] MacKaye himself had once prepared an oration for a popular twelve-panel Civil

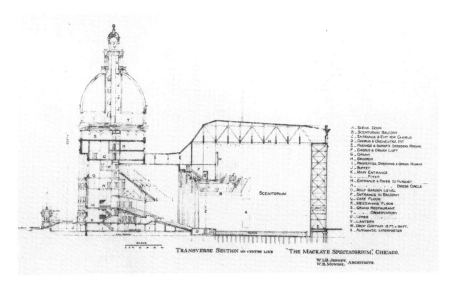

Section view of Steel MacKaye's Spectatorium.
(Courtesy of Dartmouth College Library.)

War panorama that traveled the country in the mid-1880s.[8] And in something of a last gasp for the genre, several panoramas portraying scenes such as the Battle of Gettysburg, Niagara Falls, the Chicago Fire, the Kilauea Volcano, and the Bernese Alps were on display throughout Chicago during the Columbian Exposition.[9]

The Spectatorium, as it took shape in MacKaye's fervid imagination, was to incorporate all the dramatic and mechanical ideas he had conceived since bursting onto the American theatrical scene in the early 1870s. MacKaye had been a vigorous proponent of the "Delsarte Method," an acting technique that involved a rigorous battery of exercises in physical movement, facial expression, pantomime, and other "harmonic gymnastics." MacKaye's technical discipline was combined with a genuine, if sometimes eccentric, talent for mechanical invention that he developed during the reconstruction of several New York theaters. He took credit for being the first to introduce electric lighting to the city's stage. His "double stage," a two-story elevator operated by four men, was designed to speed set changes and to raise the orchestra from stage level to a position above the proscenium arch. And he patented a folding theater seat—an invention that, when first introduced, caused him no small embarrassment when some unoccupied seats snapped shut like rifle-fire during performances.

In 1880 MacKaye wrote and produced one of the most popular plays of his era, the melodramatic *Hazel Kirke*. (Characteristically, he allowed himself to be duped out of the play's huge profits.) He was equally well known for his skill in staging the realistic and elaborate scenic effects that were then the staple of American theater. His 1887 play *Paul Kauvar*, set during the French Revolution, won renown for a terrifying mob scene of "indescribable carnage"[10] and a haunting tableau of the guillotine. Perhaps the best showcase for MacKaye's unique talents was his collaboration with Buffalo Bill Cody and Nate Salsbury. In 1886 MacKaye restaged Cody's Wild West Show in New York's Madison Square Garden. The Wild West Show had previously been staged as a series of unrelated skits and exhibitions. MacKaye, as designer and director, transformed it into the *Drama of Civilization*, depicting the exploration and settlement of the West. The show's popularity was magnified by exciting and lifelike (if sometimes malfunctioning) special effects such as a stampede of live cattle, a herd of grazing elk, the attack of a wagon train by authentic Indians on horseback, a prairie fire, and a dust storm, all set against a series of huge, movable panoramic murals.[11]

MacKaye's pioneering technical innovations for the theater reflected his impatience with the limitations and imperfectibility of the actor. *The World Finder* would include no dialogue or spoken parts. The awe-inspiring "stage pictures" MacKaye planned to create in his Spectatorium represented the culmination of his desire to control every aspect of his productions. His aim, one scholar has suggested, was to create "a theater without people, a theater of machines."[12]

MacKaye first proposed his project for the Chicago fair in late 1891 and eventually won the support and the financial backing of some of the city's leading citizens and businessmen. Landscape architect Frederick Law Olmsted, who attended one of MacKaye's inspiring presentations, called the dramatist's plan "the noblest artistic scheme I have ever heard of."[13] After observing MacKaye's demonstration of a small working model of the Spectatorium, prominent, wealthy figures such as George Pullman and banker and future secretary of the treasury Lyman

Gage saw an opportunity to support MacKaye's artistic vision—and also the profit potential of a ground-floor investment in the Spectatorium. MacKaye assured Chicago's shrewdest men of finance that the theater might attract as many as 45,000 patrons a day to its continuous performances, producing as much as a $5 million profit within six months.[14]

In July 1892 MacKaye was named director-general of the newly formed Columbian Celebration Company. The elaborate legal and financial structure of the company was based primarily on the inflated value of MacKaye's theatrical inventions, which he had pledged in lieu of cash for his stock in the company. With the sale of more than $500,000 in bonds to finance the enterprise, MacKaye began constructing his grand and complex Spectatorium in September.

The company leased a lakeshore site just outside the fairgrounds at the north end of Jackson Park on the corner of East 56th Street and Everett Avenue. The exposition managers had rejected MacKaye's appeal for site on the fairgrounds proper because the proposal was late, and also because they were understandably wary of the final outcome of the strange building: would it be a high-minded artistic endeavor or a frankly commercial amusement? The exposition relegated lowbrow popular entertainment to the Midway Plaisance while attempting to maintain the architectural, economic, and "spiritual" integrity of the White City. The Spectatorium, which attempted to be all of these things, was too enigmatic for exposition managers to agree upon or to approve.

The Chicago architectural firm of Jenney and Mundie, which had pioneered the steel-frame construction techniques used to build the first skyscrapers, was commissioned to design the Spectatorium. The structure itself— the "largest building ever erected in the world for amusement purposes," its promoters claimed[15]—was to be 480 feet long, 380 feet wide, and 270 feet high at the top of its crowning dome. Roof gardens, restaurants, vast lobbies, observation floors, a Turkish bath, a barbershop, and an array of elevators were among the attractions included in the building's design.[16]

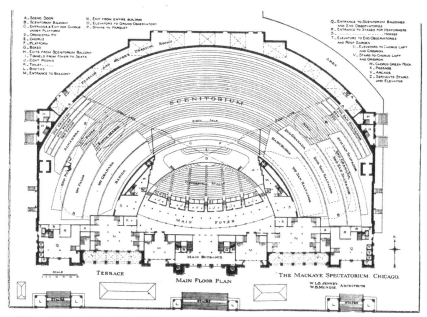

Plan of Steele MacKaye's Spectatorium. (Courtesy of Dartmouth College Library.)

MacKaye hoped to achieve in the Spectatorium a degree of visual and aural verisimilitude—the "mechanical duplication of Nature," as another critic put it—the like of which no other American showman had ever dared to attempt on a comparable scale.[17] "The rear of the building was a vast semi-circular reservoir, the surface dimensions of which were over 100,000 square feet," MacKaye explained.[18] The reservoir was designed to accommodate a moving, fully manned replica of Columbus's three-ship fleet. What MacKaye described as the theater's "scenic department" or "scenitorium" was a 17-million-cubic-foot space rising 170 feet from its foundation to the iron framework supporting the building's roof.

The scenitorium would include twenty-five "telescopic stages" carrying sets and scenery "of an entirely new species devised by myself," MacKaye proclaimed.[19] The floating and sliding stages accommodating the three-dimensional sets would ride on more than six miles of railroad track. His "proscenium-adjuster," a sort of enormous adjustable lens aperture, consisted of a series of wall panels surrounding the theater's stage. "The frame of the stage pictures was 150 by 70 feet," MacKaye said, "and the full range of the vision of the public, at the horizon of the picture, would have been over 400 feet."[20] All of this equipment was to be powered by the building's own 1,200-horsepower generator; the "cyclone" machinery alone would require 400 horsepower.

MacKaye also aimed to reproduce a breathtaking variety of lighting effects. His opaque screen of light in front of the stage, or "lux-auleator," would replace a fabric curtain. His "nebulator" would produce the effects of clouds and their shadows. His "illumiscope" or "colourator" would simulate the different shades of light throughout the day. He planned other devices to replicate the constellations and other phenomena of the nighttime sky.[21] And MacKaye's "silent unfolding announcer," two huge shields on either side of the proscenium, would narrate the stories "in letters of fire a foot-long, a sentence at a time."[22]

By December the structural framework of the Spectatorium had reached the roof garden. But despite indications of progress as the May opening approached, MacKaye's project seemed headed for disaster. By February the company had already committed itself to more than $800,000 in expenses; but it had not raised any additional capital since the original sale of bonds, and construction of the theater was only half completed. Labor shortages, strikes, and severe late winter weather hindered the work. The company's directors and stockholders had left most of the details and responsibilities for the building's construction in MacKaye's hands, believing him to be the only person who fully comprehended its scope and operation. But the financiers realized too late that while their director-general may have been a man of vast ambition and vision, he was inept as an administrator. The national financial crisis of 1893 finally finished off the Spectatorium, as nervous investors refused to pour more money into the project. Despite Mac-Kaye's last-ditch efforts to salvage his dream, now so close to realization, creditors pressed for payment. On May 31, 1893, work on the Spectatorium ended; the Columbian Celebration Company was declared bankrupt.

Exhausted from his exertions and gravely ill with cancer, MacKaye watched helplessly as bankruptcy receivers sold the Spectatorium to a wrecking company for $2,250. But the entertainer did not give up the hope of producing a vision of his spectatorio. MacKaye, using funds promised by long-standing financial backers such as Lyman Gage and Albert Spalding, formed a new Chicago Historical Entertainment Co., and managed to raise enough money to lease the Chicago Fire Cyclorama Theater at 130 N. Michigan Ave. He renamed it the MacKaye Scenitorium and set to work constructing new copies of his inventions for a scaled-down adaptation of *The World Finder*.

MacKaye opened the Scenitorium on February 5, 1894. From his seat on the stage, the ailing dramatist summoned up his remaining strength and his formidable oratorical talents. To the accompaniment of a chorus and orchestra—he could not afford to use actors, as he had planned—he narrated the events displayed in his mobile panoramas. Those in attendance, one critic wrote, "saw no actors, they heard no poet; but they were gorged with scenery and nothing but scenery. The eye was feasted and the imagination was starved."[23]

Lukewarm reviews, insufficient attendance, and MacKaye's poor health combined to doom the Scenitorium. Several faithful benefactors, including George Pullman, provided the impecunious but proud dramatist with a private railroad car for a trip to California, where MacKaye hoped to recover from his illness. But he died en route on February 25, 1894. MacKaye's funeral service was held in the Scenitorium, which thereupon closed its doors, a total financial loss for its investors.[24]

Part of MacKaye's final failure is explained by the untimeliness of his vision. He was caught between two eras of popular theatrical entertainment—a newly emerging stagecraft for the theater and the realistic illusion of the cinema. He imagined that his Spectatorium would represent a revolution in dramatic art. But the most successful dramatic impresarios of his era, such as MacKaye's shrewd rival David Belasco, continued to attract audiences into the 1920s by producing conventional melodramas and comedies that they staged with extravagant scenic effects.[25] During the early years of the twentieth century, moreover, a new generation of American and European stage designers and directors including Adolphe Appia, Edward Gordon Craig, Max Reinhardt, and Norman Bel Geddes mastered the potential of electric lighting and ever-improving stage technology. These practitioners of the "new stagecraft," while surpassing many of the complicated and impressive visual effects that MacKaye had envisioned, did not share his slavish devotion to scenic realism. Reflecting changing theatrical ideals, they used their technical capabilities in a more sparing and suggestive fashion, leaving panoramic realism to the cinema.[26]

There was, at the White City, one genuine harbinger of the momentous change about to take place on the American entertainment scene. At the Electricity Building, Thomas Edison displayed, among many other inventions, his newly patented "Kinetoscope," the peepshow motion picture machine that quickly became a popular arcade attraction. And within a year after MacKaye's death, the first projected motion picture was exhibited to the public. Before 1910 more than 5,000 "nickelodeon" movie theaters were operating across the country.[27] On the eve of the age of cinema, MacKaye had attempted, with his array of electromechanical devices, to create the lifelike effects and larger-than-life images that would make motion pictures so successful. "All he needed at the time would have been a motion picture camera and a sensitized piece of celluloid. Everything else he had provided," one cinematographer wrote during the 1920s. "It is evident to any one familiar with the art of motion picture that [he] was attempting to produce the same effects that pictures rather than the stage can give, and in practically the same manner."[28] But unlike Edison and other cinematic pioneers, MacKaye had not yet comprehended the entertainment possibilities inherent in projected photographic images.

If Steele MacKaye was, in certain respects, ahead of his time, his failed Spectatorium was nonetheless a product and a symbol of his era. The attributes displayed by the effervescent dramatist and his unique theater—ingenious invention, ostentatious excess, extraordinary ambition, and romantic spectacle—reflected the spirit of nineteenth-century American popular entertainment, and perhaps of the American people, as one century gave way to the next.

Notes

This account is based substantially on the MacKaye Family Papers at the Rauner Special Collections Library, Dartmouth College, Hanover, New Hampshire, and on Percy MacKaye's two-volume biography of his father, *Epoch: The Life of Steele MacKaye, Genius of the Theatre, In Relation to His Times & Contemporaries* (New York: Boni and Liveright, 1927; rpt. Grosse Pointe, MI: Scholarly Press, 1968). As the biography's subtitle perhaps suggests, *Epoch* was an attempt by a devoted son to vindicate his father's uneven career and checkered reputation. Despite its manifest prejudices, the book is substantially reliable in its quotation of other sources. Percy's account of the Spectatorium comprises pages 292 through 462 of the second volume of *Epoch*.

[1] David F. Burg, *Chicago's White City of 1893* (Lexington: University Press of Kentucky, 1976), p. 216.

[2] Ibid., pp. 229-233.

[3] Ibid., p. 25.

[4] Richard Moody, *America Takes the Stage: Romanticism in American Drama and Theatre, 1750-1900* (Bloomington: Indiana University Press, 1955), p. 228.

[5] Thomas A. Edison, quoted in *Epoch*, vol. 1, p. 9.

[6] Steele MacKaye ms., "The Great Discovery," quoted in Wade Chester Curry, "Steele MacKaye: Producer and Director," (Ph.D. diss., University of Illinois, Urbana, 1958), p. 154.

[7] On panoramas in the nineteenth century: Moody, *America Takes the Stage*, pp. 205-238; Robert Wernick, "Getting a Glimpse of History from a Grandstand Seat," *Smithsonian*, Aug. 1985, pp. 66-84.

[8] *Epoch*, vol. 2, pp. 72-74.

[9] On panoramas in Chicago during the World's Fair: Burg, *Chicago's White City of 1893*, p. 229-230.

[10] Ibid., p. 25.

[11] On the *Drama of Civilization*: *Epoch*, vol. 2, pp. 74-93.

[12] Curry, "Steel MacKaye," p. 169.

[13] Frederick Law Olmsted, Sr., quoted in *Epoch*, vol. 2, p. 314.

[14] *Epoch*, vol. 2, p. 328; Steele MacKaye ms., "The Columbian Celebration Company," MacKaye Family Papers, Rauner Special Collections Library, Dartmouth College.

[15] Columbian Celebration Co., March 12, 1893 press release, quoted in *Epoch*, vol. 2, pp. 379-380.

[16] Description of Spectatorium features: Steele MacKaye statement, February 5, 1894, quoted in *Epoch*, vol. 2, pp. 346-348; *New York Daily Mirror*, May 6, 1893, quoted in *Epoch*, vol. 2, pp. 401-402.

[17] Monroe J. Moses, *The American Dramatist*, (Boston: Little Brown, 1911), p. 152.

[18] *Epoch*, vol. 2, pp. 346-348.

[19] Ibid.

[20] Ibid.

[21] *Epoch*, vol. 2, pp. lxxiii-c.

[22] March 12, 1893, *New York Daily News* article, quoted in *Epoch*, vol. 2, pp. 385-386.

[23] February 6, 1894, *Chicago Times* article, quoted in Curry, "Steele Mac-Kaye," p. 168.

[24] Ibid.

[25] On David Belasco: Garff B. Wilson, *Three Hundred Years of American Drama and Theatre* (Englewood Cliffs, NJ: Prentice-Hall, 1973), pp. 251-256.

[26] On the "new stagecraft": Kenneth Macgowan and William Melnitz, *The Living Stage: A History of the World Theater* (New York: Prentice-Hall, 1955), pp. 433-458.

[27] On the early history of motion pictures: Gerald Mast, *A Short History of the Movies*, 4th ed. (New York: MacMillan, 1986), pp. 9-48.

[28] A. F. Victor letter to Percy MacKaye, quoted in *Epoch*, vol. 2, pp. ci-ciii.

(1987/1988)

Peculiar Work:
Edward G. Chamberlain's Concentric Cartography

"All this lifetime of peculiar work will be lost when I am gone," lamented Appalachian Mountain Club (AMC) member Edward G. Chamberlain in *Appalachia* in 1922, "for no one else understands just how to use it or would have patience to do it."

A self-trained surveyor who died in 1935 at the age of 90, Chamberlain compiled and drew meticulous panoramas from some of New England's best-known elevations—whether the Custom House Tower and State House in Boston or the summits of such mountains as Washington and Monadnock. His aim over the course of more than 50 years of this careful, solitary, unpaid work was to chart accurately the hills, mountains, large buildings, and other prominent features visible from dozens of observation points throughout the region.

In Chamberlain's orderly mind's eye, the landscape of New England was covered with a spider web of sightlines. Over the years he filled 200 field notebooks with 10,000 angles from 200 lookout points in the six New England states. "My instruments, method, formulas and tables, modified from Coast Survey data, I have invented for my special work," he once explained. "A great deal of data and of geodesic corrections is carried in my head." By the time of his death, Chamberlain—"a man of remarkable patience and perseverance," in the words of AMC leader

Harvey N. Shepard—had completed 52 panoramic maps and gathered the measurements for 18 more. Only eleven of the panoramas were published in the AMC's journal, *Appalachia*; the rest, along with other maps created by Chamberlain, are filed in the AMC library.

Chamberlain's work came to mind when I gave a talk about Benton MacKaye, who first proposed the Appalachian Trail. A member of the audience asked whether Maine's Katahdin could be seen from the summit of New Hampshire's Mount Monadnock, well over 200 miles distant. My interrogator cited a 1949 article by MacKaye as the source of this assertion. MacKaye was a long-time resident of Shirley, Massachusetts, from which Monadnock is visible to the northwest.

In fact, MacKaye had made no such claim, but had written that points in each of the six New England states were visible from Monadnock, which he called "the symbol and watch-tower of New England." And I suspect he may have relied, at least indirectly, on Chamberlain's scrupulous work to support his statement: *Annals of the Grand Monadnock* (1936), a book MacKaye owned and often consulted, used one of Chamberlain's maps to support the conclusion that Monadnock offered that sweeping six-state regional prospect. The book, written by Massachusetts conservationist and longtime AMC leader Allen Chamberlain (a friend, but no relation, of Edward), confirmed that the visible point in Maine was not Katahdin, but the modest, much more southern 692-foot Mount Agamenticus, just inland of Ogunquit, "north of east . . . 76 miles off."

Edward Chamberlain's panoramic maps represented only one aspect of his cartographic interests. He had shown up at an 1879 walk to Prospect Hill in Waltham, Massachusetts, sponsored by the three-year-old AMC. He joined the club in 1881, at the invitation of club leaders J. Rayner Edmands and Charles E. Fay. During his more than half-century with AMC, he compiled detailed maps of the almost all of the estimated 1,000 club "Saturday walks" in which he participated, mostly in the greater Boston area. The process entailed the creation of five drafts of each map and five full days of work. "These maps are not sketch maps nor souvenir maps," he explained in an essay written in the early 1920s. "The author tries to make a precise meander survey of every rod of the

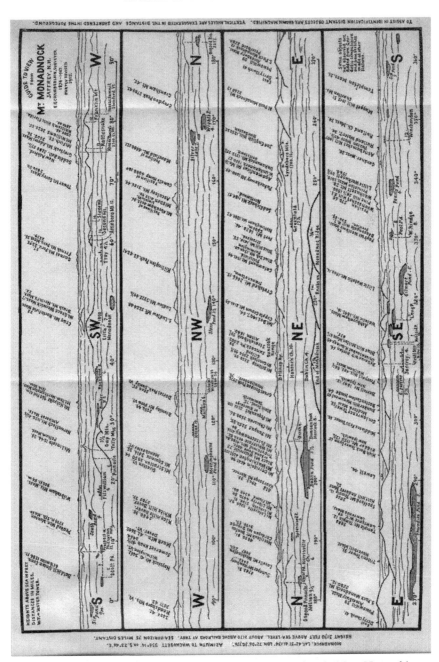

Edward Chamberlain's panoramic map from Mt. Monadnock, New Hampshire,
prepared between 1874 and 1907, "partly revised" in 1915, and published in
Appalachia, April, 1924. (Courtesy of the Appalachian Mountain Club.)

route, to locate accurately those interesting objects that commercial map makers cannot afford to locate. Also they are intended to preserve old names and historical sites, and are got up with great care." Chamberlain claimed that he had distributed 35,000 copies of his reproduced blueprint maps and panoramas to his fellow club members.

Allen Chamberlain once asserted that the Saturday walk maps compiled by his friend "possess an unquestioned historic value. Already [he was writing in 1933] some of the earlier maps reveal the cultural changes that have come over sundry portions of the metropolitan area in the past few years, and they will become increasingly valuable as time goes on."

Since boyhood, Chamberlain had taught himself the tenets and techniques of geodesy, the science of measuring and depicting Earth. During his years as a student at Boston's English High School, he had been inspired by the work of another legendary Massachusetts surveyor, Simeon Borden, whose triangulation map of the state provided a benchmark for the extension of similar triangular surveys across the United States. Without a professional education or degree, Chamberlain spent most of his early career as a clerk and bookkeeper, while pursuing his mapmaking obsession as a hobby. Among his early projects were extensive observations from the cupola of the Massachusetts State House; a map of the route of the Middlesex Canal, from Lowell to Boston Harbor; and a careful survey of the lower stretches of the Charles River, a project comprising 30 maps.

Chamberlain's surveying skills were well regarded outside of hiking circles. Eventually, the Massachusetts Topographical Commission employed him during the 1880s and early 1890s to complete an ongoing survey of town boundaries—the only time during his long life that he actually earned his living as a surveyor. Virtually singlehanded, he established the corners of 52 towns. "To the amazement of other surveyors," Allen Chamberlain recalled at the time of his friend's death, "and to some extent to their amusement, Mr. Chamberlain was accustomed to carry his transit about in a water pail, the tripod over one shoulder, an axe in his belt, and a one-hundred foot steel tape in his pocket. As he was allowed nothing for horse hire he traveled by foot."

Chamberlain's self-discipline and his eccentric, solitary habits were partly the product of his extreme hearing loss; the disability frustrated easy communication and conversation with his fellow AMC members, some of whom regarded their hiking companion as gruff and unapproachable. Describing his procedure for developing the first draft of one of his outing maps, he provided a wry, poignant self-portrait of his sense of isolation among the AMC members to whom his work was devoted. "In the field, from the depot, author records compass direction, counts steps to first bend. Another stop at each little bend, then run to catch up, for party don't wait, counting paces all the way. Records are made in ½ mile sections," he wrote. "The author must keep his mind fixed constantly on the survey, never see or speak to anyone, never get acquainted. A slight error, a missing path, and somebody gets lost in a swamp some Sunday afternoon."

At least some of his tramping companions appreciated his company and efforts, though. To most, he was known as "the active and silent elderly man . . . who accompanied many of the walking parties, mapping in detail the routes of the excursions as he went along," Allen Chamberlain wrote. "Those who enjoyed his intimacy knew him to be a genial companion and a wittily entertaining talker."

Chamberlain's panoramas were distinctive, though. His dedication to panoramic mapmaking reflected a popular approach to the depiction of the recreational and scenic mountain landscapes of New England in the latter half of the nineteenth century. Early guidebook writers, such as Thomas Starr King and Moses Foster Sweetser, included in their publications detailed, sometimes florid descriptions of summit views. "The early guidebooks devoted little time to describing the trail, evidently assuming that the hikers of that day could find their way once they knew where the trail started—or that they would hire a guide," according to mountain historians Laura and Guy Waterman. "The view from the summit, on the other hand, received lavish attention, reflecting the continuing influence of the Starr King era's absorption with sublime scenery."

Before venturing out with his AMC companions to a New England summit, Chamberlain would spend days computing angles, making sketches, and studying photographs and even ads published by hotels and railroads. No wonder, then, his frustration if he wasn't able to carry out his work: on one AMC trip to Moosilauke in 1890, "it rained every day, and I saw nothing. . . . Others went for a good time and had a good time, rain or shine. To me it was a dead loss."

On a successful outing, Chamberlain submitted his observations to three tests: "Is the angle correct? Is the description correct? Is there any similar object nearly in line that might be mistaken for it?" He usually repeated this creed in the terse articles in *Appalachia* that accompanied his panoramic maps, which were drawn in an exacting and unique pen-and-ink style. Four horizontal panels, stacked one atop the other, depict the full 360 degrees of the horizon, with outlines of dozens of features sketched in. His panoramas, he observed, "are not based on photographs, and, intentionally, are not even accurate sketches of the views. They are intended as guides to views, and are purposely distorted in order to better enable visitors to identify the points shown."

"Many a case of mistaken identity has been rectified through his careful observations," Allen Chamberlain wrote of his friend's labors. Indeed, some of his panoramic maps were undertaken to settle longstanding claims about the visibility of one mountain from another; he took a certain wry satisfaction in debunking conventional legends and lore about the region's geography. In response to an AMC member who asked if Mt. Washington "could be seen from any other point in Massachusetts besides Mount Greylock," Chamberlain wrote a long, detailed 1922 *Appalachia* article documenting his claim that Washington "was not visible from Greylock, and that I had seen it only from two Massachusetts points, Wachusett Mountain and Powow Hill in Amesbury." (The mountain mistaken for Washington from Greylock's vantage, Chamberlain asserted, was southwestern New Hampshire's Croydon Peak.)

He also enjoyed telling the story of how he set straight no less august a personage than U.S. Senator George Hoar. The venerable politician had faulted Chamberlain for not including Lafayette and Washington, in the White Mountains, in his published panorama from Asnebumsket Hill, just outside Worcester. Hoar, a resident of that city, "said they had been identified for him by a prominent civil engineer from New Hampshire, and offered to take me up and point them out," Chamberlain laconically related. "[Hoar] showed me the two Uncanoonucs for Washington and Lafayette, and a New Ipswich [New Hampshire] hill for Kearsage." Senator Hoar, we are left to assume, accepted Chamberlain's corrections with equanimity and raised no further objections to the panoramist's geographical claims or qualifications.

Chamberlain's panoramas constitute one man's punctilious, obsessive form of landscape art. Today his panoramas still provide an accurate, entertaining, and informative tool for taking the measure of the landscape, as I have learned while using them on such open summits as Monadnock and Chocorua. A careful observer could, with compass or GPS, some experience, and a dose of intuition, match the silhouettes of mountains and other landscape features with the names and contour lines on a modern trail map or a USGS topographic map. But Chamberlain's panoramas are considerably more fun to use. They place the observer at the center of a local geographic universe.

Looking outward, over New England ridge and range, as far as the eye could see, Edward Chamberlain carried an idiosyncratic mountainscape in his well-trained mind. In an 1883 article meticulously describing his observations from the Blue Hills just west of Boston, he commented on the view from the highest summit of that range, which he measured at 635 feet. "For extent and variety combined," he wrote, "the view is unequalled in this State, except by that from Wachusett, embracing as it does city and country, sea and mountain, pond and river, and all in large measure." From that vantage point, he noted, he had "identified some prominent building in one hundred and twenty-five villages."

Is there a lesson in Chamberlain's almost Zen-like patience, his assiduousness, his evenhanded respect for the gentlest suburban hill as well as the most rugged White Mountain peak? Edward Chamberlain's endeavors were both solitary and sociable. His fastidious maps were his gift to fellow AMC members, representing the amateur spirit in its essential form. Chamberlain's concentric cartography—a "lifetime of peculiar work"—was truly a labor of love.

(2002)

A Note on Sources

This is a revised and somewhat expanded version of an article that appeared in the May, 2002 edition of *AMC Outdoors*, magazine of the Appalachian Mountain Club, p. 18.

Five bound volumes and many looseleaf copies of Edward Chamberlain's outing maps and panoramas are held by the AMC Archives and Library, at 5 Joy Street in Boston.

Writer and long-time AMC leader Allen Chamberlain provided two sensitive appreciations of Edward Chamberlain and his mapmaking endeavors: "The Club's Unofficial Geographer," *Appalachia*, June, 1933, pp. 490-492; and an extensive obituary, *Appalachia*, June, 1936, pp. 84-86.

Edward Chamberlain offered a comprehensive discussion of his methods and findings in an article, "Seeing Mt. Washington from Massachusetts," which appeared in *Appalachia*, December, 1922, pp. 293-300; the article is accompanied by a panorama from Powow Hill, in Amesbury, Mass., which he described as "the Northeastern Watch-tower" of the state. Some of his others maps and panoramas, with accompanying commentary, were also published in *Appalachia*. These include (but are not limited to): "The Blue Hills," April, 1883, pp. 122-129; "Altitudes in Massachusetts," July, 1885, pp. 132-145; "The Panorama from Bunker Hill Monument," May, 1902, pp. 50-52; "The Panoramas from Ram's Head and Prospect Hills," April, 1901, pp. 334-336; "Panorama from Monadnock," April, 1924, pp. 446-447; "Panorama from Chocorua," December, 1924, pp. 75-77; "Panorama from Pleasant Mountain," June, 1925, pp. 167-168; "Panorama from Asnebumsket Hill," December, 1926, pp. 497-498; "Panorama from Bellevue Hill," June, 1928, pp. 51-51; and "Panorama from the Custom House Tower," December, 1928, pp. 151-152;

Allen Chamberlain, in the original edition of his 1936 book, *Annals of the Grand Monadnock* (Concord, N.H.: Society for the Protection of New Hampshire Forests), included a copy and description of Edward Chamberlain's panorama from that mountain's summit in a chapter titled "The View" (pp. 108-111). Benton MacKaye's comments about Monadnock, including the statement that it "is the one and only point in sight of every New England state," are from a letter to the editor, titled "A Mountain and a Man," in *The Fitchburg Sentinel*, dated February 2, 1949. Laura and Guy Waterman, in *Forest and Crag: A History of Hiking, Trail Blazing, and Adventure in the Northeast Mountains* (Boston: Appalachian Mountain Club, 1989), pp. 195-198, provide a characteristically thorough, thoughtful discussion of nineteenth-century mountain guidebooks, including the era's emphasis on detailed descriptions of summit views.

Preserving the East's Wild Spirit

A springtime visitor to the Vermont homestead of Laura and Guy Waterman is straightaway issued a pair of snowshoes and two buckets—and then set to work gathering maple sap. Guy, his pants cinched with a piece of climbing rope, wearing the plaid tam-o'-shanter that is emblematic of his Scottish heritage, describes carefully the lay of the landscape the two have shaped for the past 15 years. He leads the way from their cabin and sheds, down the slope past gardens and compost heaps, across the stream that supplies their water, and into the grove of maple trees and other hardwoods from which they harvest both sweetness and warmth. Laura, who has short, auburn hair, is less voluble than her husband but just as observant and articulate. She pauses along the snow-covered path to check the temperature at one of the "weather stations" that dot the property. Fifty feet farther, after descending from the open field to a tree-shrouded stream-crossing, she notes an abrupt drop in temperature, which she confirms at the next station.

On a circuit of their sugar bush, the Watermans refer by name to each of the 90 maple trees they tap: Everest, K2, Gawain, the Musketeers, Venus, Swamp Fox, Mad Dog. They check the sap buckets several times a day, always hoping for the below-freezing nights and above-freezing days that lead to a successful run. On charts posted in their hand-built log sugarhouse, they record the sap production of each tree, ounce by ounce, day by day, year by year.

The production of maple syrup is just one fixed point in a tightly organized round of subsistence activities the Watermans perform each year at their homestead. Not long after the last gallon of sap is boiled down, they begin turning over their garden (which is surrounded by a high wire fence to discourage deer) and planting the 31 vegetable varieties that provide most of their food. Laura cans hundreds of containers of fruits and vegetables during harvest season and stores root crops in the cool cellar beneath their living room floor. They cut and gather seven cords of wood to warm their house, cook their food, and fuel their maple-sap evaporator. Although they never resort to internal-combustion engines or electricity on their property of just under 30 acres, their home (reachable only by foot) is cozy and comfortable: A grand piano occupies one corner of their book-lined, kerosene-lit living room.

The meticulous attention the Watermans give to their homestead is only one measure of their purposeful lives. Garden schedules, wildlife sightings, visitors, hikes and climbs, weather data, the progress of their writing—they record everything. In fact, the Watermans bring the same zest, discipline, and thoroughness to all their endeavors, whether operating their homestead or working to preserve what they call the "spirit of wildness" in the mountains of the Northeast.

"The single cause that motivates us is to preserve the wildness of the country," Guy says. A decade ago, he and Laura wrote, in a characteristically single voice, that they use the phrase "spirit of wildness" to refer to "a wide spectrum of loosely connected elements of the backcountry experience: to solitude, to difficulty and challenge, to that indefinable but intensely real feeling that grips the hiker buffeted by wind on the rocky heights, or held in fascination by the silence and greenness of deep woods."

That spirit is certainly essential to the Watermans. Guy, a 56-year-old man of compact yet sinewy stature, last winter led a climb up icy Pinnacle Gully in Mt. Washington's Huntington Ravine on a raw, windblown New Hampshire day when climbers several decades younger dared not venture out. Laura, at 48, is just as fit, rugged, and energetic. Eleven years ago she led a winter climb up the same route and was quite possibly the first woman to do so.

Laura and Guy met in 1969 at the Shawangunk Mountains, an escarpment northwest of New York City that has become a mecca for rockclimbers throughout the East. In that culturally and politically tumultuous era—marked by a burst of environmentalism, a boom in outdoor activities such as backpacking and rockclimbing, and widespread interest in getting "back to the land"—the couple soon found they had more in common than simply a passion for climbing. Since then they have built from scratch their modest subsistence homestead and established a reputation as determined, articulate defenders of the wild northeastern landscape.

"They are *the* most effective spokespeople for backcountry users in the White Mountains," says Ned Therrien, public-information officer for New Hampshire's White Mountain National Forest. Even when the Watermans are critical of Forest Service policies and public-resource managers, he adds, their opinions command respect—on matters ranging from the nuts and bolts of trail maintenance and low-impact camping to the complex politics and philosophy of public-land management. "Laura and Guy bring out their points in a way that is not confrontational. You come away feeling that you've been approached in a rational, honest way," Therrien says.

In fact, the Watermans know the region's backcountry terrain as well as anyone. They wander the hills of New York, Vermont, New Hampshire, and Maine relentlessly, keeping a protective eye on the peaks and trails, sometimes discovering old climbing routes long since abandoned. "Guy is an incredible map-and-compass man who can walk anywhere," says Walter Graff, director of education for the Appalachian Mountain Club (AMC). "He's been up every trail in the White Mountains and a lot of places without trails, in all seasons and all conditions."

"Unreconstructed peakbaggers" by their own description, the Watermans have demolished many of the records and milestones available to northeastern hikers. Laura has been up 47 White Mountain

4,000-footers half a dozen times, Guy 15 times—about half during the winter, their favorite mountaineering season. (They've also climbed all 46 of the Adirondacks' 4,000-foot mountains in winter.) Guy, ever on the lookout for a new challenge, recently tackled each of the White Mountain high peaks from all four points of the compass in winter, an endeavor, he notes, that often involved "ferocious bushwhacking." Laura was a member of the first all-woman parties to complete a winter climb of Maine's Katahdin and a winter traverse of New Hampshire's Presidential Range.

At the time they met, Laura worked in New York on the staff of *Backpacker* magazine, and Guy was a corporate speechwriter—following stints as a professional jazz pianist, a writer for jazz magazines, and a Capitol Hill committee staffer, speechwriter, and campaign operative. Both had grown up in families that encouraged scholarship and a love for the outdoors. Laura's father, a distinguished writer and an authority on Emily Dickinson, brought his family to rustic New England cottages during his daughter's childhood summers. Guy's father, a Yale University physicist and the first director of the National Science Foundation, was an avid outdoorsman who led canoe trips through Maine's North Woods every summer.

While many people fantasized about living a simple life in the country, Laura and Guy, who married in 1972, actually began making plans for their move to Vermont. Inspired in part by Helen and Scott Nearing, who described their own experiences as Vermont homesteaders during the 1930s in *Living the Good Life*, the Watermans were convinced they could "live a very simple homesteading life only half the time and have the other half free for other pursuits," as Guy puts it.

Even as they prepared to move, they became involved in protecting New York's Shawangunk Cliffs—the first of many environmental causes to which they would devote their combined talents and energies. Use of the "Gunks" was increasing rapidly by the late 1960s—as was the destructive impact of piton-pounding climbers.

The Mohonk Preserve, the private organization that owns the property including the cliffs, invited Guy to join its board as a representative of the climbing community; later Laura served on the group's publications and land-stewardship committees. Involvement with the preserve permitted the couple to test their belief that the key to protecting outdoor recreation resources is public education, not strict regulation.

"It couldn't be done by edict," Guy recalls of the effort to convince members of the notoriously independent rockclimbing community to change their carefree habits. "It had to be done by education." Through peer pressure and cliffside conversation, they helped convince climbers to begin using one main path instead of several. In just three years during the early 1970s, Shawangunk climbers gave up pitons and started using less-destructive nuts and other "clean climbing" techniques.

When the Watermans moved to Vermont in 1973, writing was a tentative part of their scheme for an independent livelihood; but it was also a way to express their growing sense of personal responsibility for the mountains. Assignments from Laura's former boss at *Backpacker* soon led to other writing opportunities. In the mid-1970s they begin a regular column in a New England outdoor magazine, a forum in which they could write whatever they wanted, Guy recalls.

The column also served as the basis for *Backwoods Ethics: Environmental Concerns for Hikers and Campers*, first published in 1979. The style and tone of that first book is "humorous, intelligent, thoughtful, and kindly"—also attributes of the authors, says long-time climbing friend Lou Cornell. Anecdotal and analytical, *Backwoods Ethics* is a down-to-earth guide to low-impact camping practices. But it also addresses a fundamental question that the Watermans pose for themselves and others: "What backwoods environment do we want?" The answer, they believe, includes both protected physical resources—such as soil, water, and vegetation—and the harder-to-define psychological and experiential qualities of wilderness.

While writing has provided one public platform for their views, the Watermans have also been active with the AMC and a number of other outdoor groups. As a member of the AMC's north country board, Guy vociferously opposed a plan supported by many AMC and Forest Service officials to build a helicopter pad adjacent to the club's White Mountain hut at Carter Notch. Easier helicopter access, proponents claimed, would help supply the hut and support search-and-rescue missions. Guy persuaded the board to squelch the project, however, by arguing that the blasting, damage to the vegetation, and other environmental alterations would be out of proportion to the perceived need.

Laura and Guy again locked horns with the Forest Service in the late 1970s, this time over the fate of five popular hiking trails in the Great Gulf Wilderness of Mt. Washington. The Forest Service, hoping to discourage backpackers from crossing the area to gain access to the summits of the Presidential Range, proposed closing the trails. The Watermans argued that the wilderness area could not be managed as an island separate from the surrounding terrain and its traditional use by hikers. In the end the Forest Service kept the trails open.

Most recently the Watermans have been involved in an effort to protect a stretch of trail along Franconia Ridge, one of the most popular White Mountain hiking destinations. The effort, Guy observes, involves "reconciling a large number of people who want to be in the mountains with a very fragile environment." Above tree line, the 1.7-mile trail section from Mt. Lafayette to Little Haystack is part of a favorite day hiking circuit because of its accessibility from the highway through Franconia Notch; it also serves as a link in the Appalachian Trail and is close to the AMC's busy Greenleaf Hut.

During the late 1970s the Watermans had been outspoken critics of an AMC attempt to protect the ridge by building scree walls alongside the trail. "The first impression was of a sidewalk," says Guy. "You could accomplish so much more if you could educate users to appreciate the resource. If they're asked, rather than told, people appreciate the spirit of the effort."

When the AMC initiated an Adopt-a-Trail program in 1980, the Watermans volunteered to work on Franconia Ridge. "It's now the focus of our summer activities in the mountains," says Guy. "We try not to let three weeks go by in the summer without checking on the trail." The goal, he adds, is not only to preserve the alpine vegetation but to soften the visual impact of human intervention above treeline. "The ideal is that people walking the trail will think that's the way it was naturally."

The Watermans schedule trail work on weekends, when they can most easily observe patterns of trail use and hiker behavior, and when they can talk directly with the hikers who stop to inquire about their activities. They estimate that they have reached hundreds of hikers with their trailside message about the prospects for the vulnerable alpine zone. "It's a fundamentally optimistic message, but it requires that everybody do their part," says Guy.

Indeed, the Watermans' efforts as backcountry educators are unceasing. During their trail-tending trips they often stay at Greenleaf Hut, where they give after-dinner talks about White Mountain history and the purposes of their trail work; this past summer they lectured at each of the AMC's eight huts. Until last winter, they had also been long-time instructors at the winter-mountaineering school operated jointly by the AMC and the Adirondack Mountain Club.

In their new book, *Forest and Crag: A History of Hiking, Trail Blazing, and Adventure in the Northeast Mountains* (1989), the Watermans trace the evolving uses and perceptions of the region's mountain landscape. With their characteristic attention to detail, they spent eight years researching the area in preparation for the work: they visited more than 60 libraries and archives between Maine and Washington, D.C.; talked with more than 250 hikers, climbers, and trail builders; and corresponded with at least a thousand individuals. Adding their personal experiences to their findings, they compiled the stories of scores of men and women who have shaped the public forests and parks today's backcountry users sometimes take for granted.

The Watermans' next writing project, a companion volume to *Forest and Crag*, will focus exclusively on the history of technical climbing in the region. After that they hope to tackle a sequel to *Backwoods Ethics*, aimed at a new generation of hikers. They worry that the recent level of education about wilderness camping practices has declined, even though new people are coming to the mountains all the time, and they believe there is a need for more books and magazine articles on the subject.

In the eyes of some, the unconventional, highly disciplined life that Laura and Guy have set for themselves might seem full of hardship and tedium. From their perspective, though, they have found the freedom, independence, and peace of mind to pursue their varied and public-spirited interests.

"In this push-button age, humanity needs recourse to difficulty," they once wrote. "We need to encounter nature in ways that fully impress on us its enormous power, and set our own efforts in perspective. . . . While there is still difficulty, there is still opportunity to test what a person is made of. The hunter and fisherman know this. The birdwatcher knows it. All lovers of the outdoors tend to respond to the zest of challenge."

(1988)

POSTSCRIPT: For reasons of format, length, the Watermans' careful protection of the image they wished to project, and my own journalistic reticence, this 1988 *Sierra* article did not address certain darker elements of the couple's story. Life at Barra was not necessarily as idyllic and tranquil as my upbeat profile suggested. I didn't mention Guy's struggles with alcoholism. I did not disclose his first troubled marriage, which ended in divorce. Nor did I acknowledge Guy's three sons from that first marriage, two of whom had disappeared in dramatic, unusual circumstances in Alaska. In 1973, his oldest son, Bill, wrote a note to his father that read: "Going off on a trip. Not in Alaska. Will be in touch when I get back." Bill was never seen or heard from again. The next oldest son, Johnny, achieved a considerable reputation as an ambitious, daring mountain climber. His solo 145-day climb and traverse of Alaska's Mt. Hunter in 1978 immediately became a staple of mountaineering history and lore. But Johnny's increasingly unpredictable behavior and state of mind impelled him to pursue ever-riskier adventures. In April 1981, he disappeared during a planned solo ascent of Mt. McKinley. Family members, friends, acquaintances, and anyone else with an opinion were left to speculate that the two young men had consciously sought their demise. Guy Watermen, even as he built a structured, productive life and career with Laura in Vermont, also carried an increasingly heavy burden of grief and guilt over the enigmatic fate of his two sons.

Indeed, during one of my visits to the Watermans in the late 1980s, as we conversed across their small table during dinner, our conversation took a swift, emotional turn, as Guy shared some of these unhappy events and I described the suicide of my youngest brother. Somehow, during that conversation, we ended up talking, at least briefly, about the Hemlock Society. So, though our modest correspondence dwindled in the subsequent decade, I was not altogether surprised to learn in 2000 that Guy had ended his own life. On a cold February morning, Guy walked out of Barra for what both he and Laura knew would be the last time. By the end of that day, he had climbed to the Franconia Ridge, where he sat down near the peak of Mt. Lafayette and waited for the frigid wind to draw the heat of life from his body. The calculated circumstances and setting of his disquieting suicide were widely publicized and debated in climbing and outdoor publications. Two notable, if unsettling, books, have also chronicled and closely analyzed Guy's strenuous passage through life: *Good Morning Midnight: Life and Death in the Wild* (2003), by journalist Chip Brown; and *Losing the Garden: The Story of a Marriage* (2005), by Laura Waterman.

In addition to revealing details of the dark depths of her husband's troubles—and some of her own—Laura's intense memoir also documents how much additional work the two completed even as Guy planned his escape from life. In addition to their books *Backwoods Ethics* and *Forest and Crag*, they went on to publish *Yankee Rock & Ice: A History of Climbing in the Northeastern United States*; *Wilderness Ethics: Preserving the Spirit of Wilderness*; and *A Fine Kind of Madness: Mountain Adventures Tall and True*.

After Guy's death, Laura and others established a small, focused foundation, The Waterman Fund, which awards grants to organizations and individuals researching and working to preserve the alpine habitat of the northeast (The Waterman Fund, Box 1064, East Corinth, Vermont 05040; www.watermanfund.org). Laura donated Barra to The Good Life Center, also the custodian of the Maine homestead of Scott and Helen Nearing. Today, Barra is maintained and cultivated by stewards seeking to pursue a homesteading life.

The View from Breadloaf:
Fostering a Spirit of Wilderness
in the Heart of the Green Mountains

If the Green Mountains of Vermont have a geographic and spiritual center, it may be a point amid the red spruce and balsam fir on the long, level ridge of 3,835-foot Bread Loaf Mountain. A hiker following the Long Trail down the main spine of the Green Mountain range encounters a modest wooden sign here, marking the mid-point of this venerable "footpath in the wilderness." Stopping for breath, the tramper learns that the Long Trail stretches due north 130.4 miles to the Québec border, due south 130.4 miles to Massachusetts.

Bread Loaf Mountain also lies at the heart of the largest designated wilderness area in Vermont's Green Mountain National Forest (GMNF). Lovers of the state's wilder terrain could claim a victory in 1984 when Congress passed the Vermont Wilderness Act, designating the 21,480-acre Breadloaf Wilderness (the law and the Forest Service distinguish between the two-word mountain—"Bread Loaf"—and the one-word wilderness area—"Breadloaf") and three other new wilderness areas farther south, including Big Branch, Peru Peak, and George D. Aiken. Until that year, the only two wilderness areas in the Green Mountain National Forest, both designated in the Eastern Wilderness Act of 1975, had been Bristol Cliffs and Lye Brook (which was expanded in the 1984 law). Together, the six wilderness areas now comprise 59,600 of the national Forest's 340,000 acres.

As in other states, the immediate outcome of the fierce political battle for wilderness designation in Vermont seemed refreshingly clear. The 1984 law defined distinct tracts of protected wildland, measurable in precise acreages, delineated by crisp boundaries on official maps. In the aftermath of the political fray, however, public officials and private citizens faced a new, more ambiguous, and more enduring set of issues about the purposes, uses, and management of this public resource we call "wilderness." Indeed, the well-publicized activities of the "Wise Use" movement, property-rights advocates, and inholders' organizations lend renewed importance to questions about the nature of our responsibility—collectively and as individuals—for public lands, including the National Wilderness Preservation System. Just how far have we progressed in nurturing the principles that should govern the use of commonly owned landscapes like Vermont's Breadloaf Wilderness—where, in the words of the Wilderness Act, "man himself is a visitor who does not remain"? Does that perfect oxymoron, "wilderness management," allow for the personal knowledge and sense of concern inspired by intense familiarity with a particular piece of landscape over time—and not only over individual lifetimes but over generations? Can the public passion that has resulted in wilderness designation for 95 million acres be sustained to provide for the subtle, long-term attention these lands will require if they are to remain "unimpaired for future use and enjoyment as wilderness," as the Wilderness Act demands?

The Breadloaf Wilderness, and the people who are coping with such questions about this rugged piece of Vermont terrain, may hold some answers.

Not until 1990, six years after passage of the Vermont wilderness bill, did the staff of the Green Mountain National Forest begin to prepare individual management plans—Wilderness Implementation Schedules (WIS), in agency parlance—for the six wilderness areas in their charge. The Wilderness Implementation Schedules represent only one gear in the Forest Service's complex legal and regulatory clockworks, which includes a variety of federal wilderness and environmental laws, as well as the agency's own body of regulations. The Forest Service must also take into account the natural condition and human influences unique to each wilderness area. As a bureaucratic instrument, the resulting WIS contains not only precise wilderness-management policies, but the timetables, budgets, and staffing requirements needed to implement and monitor those policies.

Though wilderness areas comprise about eighteen percent of the Green Mountain National Forest, no one on the forest staff, whether in the Forest Supervisor's Office in Rutland or in its three Ranger Districts, is assigned exclusively to wilderness-management duties. The job of developing a Breadloaf WIS fell primarily to Russ Eastwood, a recreation technician in the forest's Middlebury Ranger District. The task has not gone smoothly or quickly. "It's just a classic sample of people being spread too thin," admits the 43-year-old Eastwood, who oversees "non-developed" recreation facilities and activities throughout the district's 65,000 acres, including the western half of Breadloaf Wilderness.

A February 1990 memo pleaded inadequate wilderness-management funding and an overloaded staff as principal reasons for the sluggish progress in developing the Wilderness Implementation Schedules. Later that year, Eastwood's boss, Middlebury District Ranger Paul Lundberg, identified other gaps in the agency's wilderness-management capabilities in the aftermath of the 1984 Vermont wilderness bill. "Many of the key 'players,' both Forest Service and public, have since left the area," he wrote in a letter seeking public comment on the proposed Breadloaf WIS, "and with them some of the historical background as to how Breadloaf should be managed in the future." He also acknowledged "a lack of Wilderness management expertise/experience among Forest Service employees with Wilderness responsibilities"—some of whom, Lundberg added, "have little understanding of what Wilderness is."

Some local observers and critics take a more skeptical view of such rationalizations, however. "It seems to me that wilderness is an easy resource to ignore," says Jim Northup, who worked as a forest planner here from 1979 to 1987. "And that's what has been done." Now a planning consultant, Northup helped to draft the 1987 Green Mountain National Forest Plan, which won unanimous praise from environmental groups for emphasizing priorities such as wildlife habitat protection and backcountry recreation instead of aggressive timber production. The Wilderness Society joined with other state and federal organizations at the time to declare the plan "philosophically the best in the country." Now, as a private citizen "trying to keep the Forest Service honest," Northup worries that the agency's actions are not matching the objectives he helped to formulate.

"Wilderness is just not a priority," declares another Vermont activist, Bettina Mattesen. "They are being pulled into it kicking and screaming." Mattesen was awakened to the need for constant vigilance concerning Forest Service activities when, for a student project, she drafted a management plan for the vestpocket-sized Bristol Cliffs Wilderness Area, which lies less than five miles to the northwest of Breadloaf. During the course of her work in 1988 and 1989, she learned that she had not been the first to labor over wilderness-management policy for that 3,738-acre area, which looms directly behind her home. Forest Service staffers and other volunteers like herself "have done a lot of work and then it just never goes anywhere," asserts Mattesen. Now, she says, "I see my role as reminding them of the Forest Plan's standards and guidelines."

Whatever the reasons and motives for the agency's halting progress in addressing its wilderness-management responsibilities in Vermont, the fact remains: Designated wilderness is still a relatively fresh feature of Vermont's natural and social landscape. It takes some getting used to. Wilderness designation for Breadloaf in 1984 resulted largely from the unrelenting efforts of the Vermont Wilderness Association (VWA). A small, tenacious fellowship of activists loosely affiliated with the Wilderness Society, Sierra Club, and other state and national conservation groups, the VWA spent the late 1970s and early 1980s battling and compromising with an array of wilderness opponents that included timber companies, snowmobile clubs, sportsmen, property-rights advocates—and a Reagan Administration determined to accelerate resource exploitation in national forests. Dick Andrews, one of the group's most persistent and zealous members, describes the tight-knit VWA as "a conspiracy in the literal, original meaning of the word—a breathing together." During the Forest Service's botched RARE II (Roadless Area Review and Evaluation) process, the VWA conspirators identified 100,000 acres in the Green Mountain National Forest they believe qualified as wilderness; but the Forest Service's RARE II recommendations did not include a single acre of additional Vermont wilderness. Nonetheless, the agency gave Breadloaf the highest rating of any of the potential wilderness areas reviewed. It's easy to understand why.

"Basically, Breadloaf is the closest we have to rocks and ice," says Andrews, a freelance journalist. Breadloaf is indeed a landscape with backbone, "the most rugged and wildest seeming of our Vermont wildernesses," adds one of Andrews's VWA colleagues, Wally Elton, public relations director for the Student Conservation Association. Breadloaf bestrides the main ridgeline of the Green Mountains from Middlebury Gap north to Lincoln Gap. The ridge lies mostly above 3,000 feet—high country by Vermont's modest standard—dividing the headwaters of the White and Mad rivers to the east from those of the New Haven and Middlebury rivers to the west. North of Bread Loaf Mountain rises Vermont's Presidential Range, the humble counterpart of its grander New Hampshire neighbor, including Mounts Wilson, Roosevelt, Cleveland, and Grant. Almost the entire area is cloaked with trees, from hardwoods like maple, beech, and birch at lower elevations, to the fir and spruce nearer the ridge. All of this provides attractive habitat for black bear, deer, moose, beaver, and other wildlife. And the area remains perhaps the greatest expanse of Vermont's mountain terrain untouched by the ski developments that have transformed many of the state's other major summits.

Russ Eastwood, a tall, robust Connecticut native, is pleased to get out of the office and into the Breadloaf Wilderness. The personable Eastwood has worked in the Middlebury district since 1980, a long tenure in one place by usual Forest Service standards. His responsibilities have provided him ample experience in reconciling the high-minded language and aims of federal wilderness legislation with the mundane and tangible realities on the ground.

We hike up Burnt Hill Trail to its junction with the Long Trail. Near the gentle rise marking the summit of Boyce Mountain, Eastwood searches for the remains of the moose he had come across the year before. Now the carcass has been reduced by insects, rodents, microbes, and other predators to a dusting of tawny hair and a single six-inch sliver of bone. This organic, evanescent landmark becomes a permanent addition to Eastwood's personal archive of changes and conditions on this landscape.

Other landmarks are emblematic of the human influence that shaped the history and destiny of this wilderness area. Our route north takes us over Battell Mountain, which memorializes the remarkable and eccentric man responsible for preserving most of the southern portion of Breadloaf. Joseph Battell, a one-man wilderness movement, collected mountains the way other connoisseurs acquire fine art. The wealthy bachelor began buying lands along the high central ridge of the Green Mountains in the 1860s. By the time he was done, Battell had acquired more than 30,000 acres encompassing some of the highest and wildest country in Vermont. After his death in 1915, Battell left most of his forest domain in trust to his alma mater, nearby Middlebury College. His mountain headquarters, the rambling Bread Loaf Inn in the town of Ripton, became the summer campus of Middlebury's graduate English program and the celebrated Bread Loaf Writer's Conference. (The poet Robert Frost, who was associated with the summer programs from the early 1920s until the time of his death in 1963, remains the region's literary godfather.) The college set aside as "Battell Park" the high land along the ridge between Middlebury Gap and Bread Loaf Mountain. The remaining property, generally at lower elevations, was termed the "Battell Forest," which the college's staff of foresters managed according to the gospel of sustained-yield. With the arrival of the New Deal in the 1930s, however, the college was an eager seller when the federal government began purchasing land for the Green Mountain National Force. Though the Forest Service carried on logging operations in the area until the early 1980s, Battell's remarkable collection of mountains remained intact and relatively undisturbed.

"We have a kind of providential, inadvertent wilderness in Vermont that's very fragile now," observes John Elder, a professor of English and environmental studies at Middlebury College. Elder, co-editor of *The Norton Book of Nature Writing* (1990), sometimes leads students into the Breadloaf Wilderness to investigate what he calls the "cultural context" in which such a landscape evolves. Loggers, farmers, and the singular Joseph Battell are part of that context, as Congress acknowledged when it stipulated that in the state's designated wilderness areas "man's works may have been present in the past."

Today, recreational varieties of "man's works" represent the greatest challenge for wilderness managers. In four of Vermont's wilderness areas that challenge revolves primarily around the presence and maintenance of the Long Trail and the Appalachian Trail. (The trails are concurrent for almost 100 miles in southern Vermont. Thirty miles south of Breadloaf, the Appalachian Trail veers east toward New Hampshire and Maine.) The Long Trail, in fact, provides the most significant evidence of human activity in the Breadloaf Wilderness today, bisecting the area for more than 17 miles. Five side trails and four overnight shelters have existed within the area's boundaries since early in the twentieth century. Conceived in 1909 by Vermont schoolmaster James P. Taylor as a "footpath in the wilderness" following the main crest of the Green Mountains, the Long Trail is generally considered to be the nation's first long-distance hiking path. In 1986, it was designated a National Recreation Trail.

A genuinely amateur, grass-roots enterprise, the Long Trail has been crucial in shaping a twentieth-century public conception of wilderness in Vermont. Indeed, the trail's presence and tradition predate the creation of the Green Mountain National Forest. The Green Mountain Club (GMC), founded in 1910 to "make the Vermont mountains play a larger role in the life of the people," has been a long-time steward of the Long Trail and the Vermont terrain, both public and private, it traverses. The club's Bread Loaf Section was one of the first local groups to assume responsibility for a defined stretch of the trail; by 1913 it was surveying and building the trail that now spans the Breadloaf Wilderness. Seventy years later, though, some members of the Bread Loaf Section shared the GMC leadership's reluctance to support the designation of Breadloaf and the other new Vermont wilderness areas through which the revered hiking trails pass. Club officials worried that a strict interpretation of wilderness legislation and standards might result in the establishment of a permit system restricting access to the trail, the removal of certain shelters, or even the closing of some stretches of trail altogether.

"My initial reaction to wilderness designation?" recalls Al Stiles, a hiker and trail worker long active in the Bread Loaf Section and other GMC affairs. "I said, 'That's a bunch of baloney.' This area has been cut over, it's been hiked over. You're going to preserve it, lock it up? No. That's the wrong way to do things."

VWA member Wally Elton, who was teaching at Middlebury College during the years of the wilderness-designation battle, also served a stint as president of the GMC's Bread Loaf Section. At his prodding, the local group was the first to break with the club leadership and endorse wilderness designation. "It was kind of a classic case of the membership being far out ahead of the leaders," remembers Dick Andrews, also a GMC member then. Elton and Andrews helped persuade Vermont's congressional delegation to include language affirming that in designated wilderness areas the Long and Appalachian trails "may be maintained." With this assurance, the GMC and the Appalachian Trail Conference (ATC) finally bestowed their cautious blessing on the wilderness legislation. Nonetheless, the key phrase—"may be maintained"—has remained a focus of exacting interpretation and intense debate among Forest Service personnel, trail club members, and other environmental activists.

Russ Eastwood continues over Battell Mountain into Skyline Lodge. The snug log cabin, which overlooks Skylight Pond and the verdant ranges of Vermont and New Hampshire to the east, is a popular, easily accessible destination for hikers of all ages, ambitions, and expectations. Soon after passage of the 1984 Vermont Wilderness Act, the fate of Skyline Lodge provided a test for the legislation's provision concerning the Long Trail. An older lodge, built in the early 1950s, was condemned as unsafe by a Forest Service engineer. After the then-district ranger burned it to the ground one winter, a new set of questions arose: Should the lodge be replaced? If so, should it be rebuilt on the same site, or farther from the pond? Should a more modest structure be built, perhaps an open shelter or tent platforms? When a substantial private contribution spurred the Forest Service to replace the lodge, the construction task fell to Eastwood—who immediately ran into a series of obstacles. Several loads of lumber that had been arduously packed in were used as firewood by dim-witted campers. Eastwood then arranged to have new materials dropped in by helicopter—a motorized use that required the forest supervisor's approval. But when a team from the USFS regional office discovered the lodge under construction, they ordered that the new building be dismantled. At this point, the state's congressional delegation vigorously intervened, reiterating the legislation's explicit intention of permitting maintenance of the trail and shelter system. With the assistance of GMC volunteers, the attractive little lodge was completed in 1987.

Eastwood is proud of his handiwork. But he worries that the popularity of the shelter may be causing serious stress to the surrounding environment. The outhouse has to be moved every year, a backbreaking task on the steep, soggy site. Campers have browsed the surrounding vegetation, cutting live trees, not just deadfalls, to feed the lodge's woodstove. The slope between the lodge and the pond is eroding, revealing the buried debris of the former cabin.

"I really am concerned about what I view as an increasing number of people coming up here for recreation," Eastwood says. "Part of me really wants, at the very least, not to make it more attractive for non-wilderness use." Some hikers enjoying Skyline Lodge might flinch at Eastwood's perception of what constitutes "non-wilderness use." But he takes seriously the objectives of solitude, inspiration, and challenge set forth in wilderness law—even as he complains that the Forest Plan does not provide adequate guidance about how management of the Long Trail should differ, if at all, inside and outside of wilderness areas. By the same token, Eastwood sees benefits in concentrating hikers' use and impacts along the trail corridor and at shelter sites, thereby protecting the remaining wilderness for more primitive, off-trail recreation. "That's why I'm so concerned about monitoring," he concludes.

Monitoring is the foundation of the Forest Service's standard wilderness-management policy—"Limits of Acceptable Change" (LAC). The step-by-step LAC approach acknowledges that human activities, especially recreational use, will inevitably affect the wilderness environment. The process establishes desired conditions and management procedures for specific areas and resources within wilderness. Fundamental to the successful implementation of LAC programs is a comprehensive baseline inventory of resources and facilities. This inventory provides a yardstick for measuring changes in such conditions as trail erosion, the number of persons encountered at shelters and on trails, or the severity of firewood cutting. If monitoring reveals that an activity or resource is approaching or exceeding "limits of acceptable change," wilderness managers may revise their policies.

In the summer of 1992, the Forest Service contracted with the Student Conservation Association to place a "wilderness ranger" on the ground in Breadloaf. Russell Geer, a 35 year-old environmental-studies student at the University of Massachusetts, provides the agency with "eyes and ears," according to district ranger Lundberg. Geer usually camps at or near one of the trail shelters, talking with hikers, inquiring about their use and awareness of wilderness, providing information and advice. He also photographed, mapped, and wrote reports documenting the conditions surrounding the shelters and tent sites—data Eastwood hopes will be incorporated into a consistently applied LAC program for Breadloaf.

"Everyone I talk to has a different impression or understanding of the wilderness idea," comments the serious, soft-spoken Geer. Through-hikers intent on traversing the full length of the Long Trail "come closest to meeting the low-impact ideal," he says, but others seemed "driven," Geer noticed, more intent on "a challenge, an adventure" than on the search for solitude and contemplation. "The trail completely overwhelms the other, more recent wilderness designation."

From Skyline Lodge, Eastwood leads the way over Bread Loaf Mountain. A spur from the main trail, north of the sign marking the Long Trail's midpoint, leads to an open ledge on the mountain's western slope. From here, the view embraces the nearby cluster of yellow buildings comprising Middlebury College's pastoral Bread Loaf campus, the rich agricultural terrain of the Champlain Valley, and New York's Adirondacks. The clearing and maintenance of such trailside viewpoints in Vermont's wilderness areas has been a particularly vexatious issue, pitting the Forest Service and some environmental groups against the Green Mountain Club and the Appalachian Trail Conference. Only a handful of Green Mountain peaks rise above tree line. Hence the rare glimpse of an expansive sweep of landscape is not a minor consideration for many dedicated Vermont hikers who liken the tree-shrouded Long Trail to a monotonous and claustrophobic "green tunnel."

"The stance we're taking is that vistas are a recreational enhancement," says the Forest Service's Diane Strohm, Eastwood's counterpart in the Manchester Ranger District, who has faced the issue while leading a "core group" that drafted the Lye Brook Wilderness Implementation Schedule. Recreation, Strohm maintains, is "a use for wilderness, but it's not the reason we have wilderness." The Lye Brook WIS declares that the maintenance of trailside vistas is "not in keeping with the spirit of wilderness"; therefore, the plan provides, existing vistas "will be allowed to reforest naturally." The trail clubs take a different view of what constitutes "the spirit of wilderness." "I think the Club recognizes that there is a need for a different set of standards in wilderness areas," says Dennis Shaffer, the GMC's Executive Director. Shaffer says that the club may be willing to accept fewer blazes and signs, more blowdowns, the relocation of certain shelters, and other policies designed to reduce trail impacts and enhance wilderness qualities. But he worries that the Forest Service's new policy may mean that the agency "is going to interpret the law in the very strictest sense."

"There's almost a radical ideological wing in the Forest Service, perhaps getting back at those who forced wilderness down their throats," suggests Kevin Peterson, the ATC's New England regional representative. The vista issue has also revealed rifts between the recreation-oriented trail groups and other Vermont environmental activists with different priorities and agendas. "Cutting down trees to get better views inside a wilderness area is completely inconsistent with wilderness designation," says Buck Young, program director of Preserve Appalachian Wilderness (PAW), a group that promotes what it calls the "native biodiversity" of the east. Usually a thorn in the Forest Service's side, PAW has successfully appealed all new timber sales on the forest since the beginning of 1991. On the vista issue, though, the group finds itself in rare alliance with the agency.

The cliffside overlook on Bread Loaf Mountain may be little affected by the new policy. But the Forest Service predicts that other viewpoints within Breadloaf Wilderness, such as Mt. Grant to the north, are more likely to become gradually overgrown. VWA "conspirator" Dick Andrews, once the harshest of Forest Service critics but now a participant in the Lye Brook "core group," relishes the irony of the agency's newfound wilderness purism. "It amuses me to see the Forest Service agonizing over these things," says Andrews. "They planned to strip-mine that thing right down to the ground anywhere there was merchantable number, and now they're worried about somebody cutting a few deadfalls."

"Good fences make good neighbors." I couldn't keep Frost's ironic and too-familiar line from mind when Eastwood led the way down the Emily Proctor Trail. He grimaced when he saw the foot-high, spray-painted, fluorescent-orange "W" with which one of his colleagues had recently blazed a tree at the wilderness boundary. The reason for this garish display was evident a little farther down the trail, where an opening of light revealed a recent logging job. A log skidder was parked at the freshly scoured-out log landing. The first quarter mile or so the trail had been transformed into a fifteen-foot-wide skid road. "This may look bad to you," Eastwood says a little edgily, "but it's a lot better than the kind of thing I used to see five years ago."

Nonetheless, this Spruce Lodge Timber Sale, so close to the wilderness boundary, had been the cause of some intra-office skirmishing. Eastwood learned of its effects when a co-worker dropped the trailhead sign-in register on his desk. "We've closed your trail," the timber man announced. Eastwood won approval to re-open the trail, however, arguing that the Forest Service should be willing to hold its logging practices up to public scrutiny. "If we can't do that," he maintains, "we should probably re-evaluate what we're doing."

Later that summer, just such a re-evaluation took place after Bettina Mattesen visited the site. Reviewing the environmental assessment issued in 1989 for the 55-acre timber sale, she noted that it didn't mention anything about possible effects on the Emily Proctor Trail; the nearby Breadloaf Wilderness; or the New Haven River, classified as a "significant stream" in the Forest Plan and a candidate for designation as a National Wild and Scenic River. All three resources were identified in the Forest Plan as "highly sensitive" areas, subject to management standards and guidelines that weren't addressed in the environmental assessment.

Mattesen's inquiries quickly stirred the interest of the GMC, Earth First!, the Sierra Club, and Preserve Appalachian Wilderness. PAW's Buck Young wasted little time instigating a flurry of media activity. "The sale was conducted illegally," Young stated flatly, alleging Forest Service violations of the National Environmental Policy Act, the National Forest Management Act, and the 1987 Forest Plan.

A planner in the Supervisor's Office at first denied Young's charges. But embarrassed district ranger Paul Lundberg soon admitted that the logging job had in fact been a series of "screw-ups" and "mistakes." The 10-acre clear-cut adjacent to the trail, he insisted, was an appropriate harvest method in the management area, which called for an emphasis on the enhancement of upland wildlife habitat. But he conceded that personnel changes and poor communications among his staff and the logging contractor had overlooked the fact that a former skid road nearby, not the Emily Proctor Trail itself, was supposed to have provided access to the logging job.

The Emily Proctor incident provided a sobering lesson for those who had placed their faith and hopes in the highly touted Forest Plan. "One of the things that's always pleased us is that the plan highlights the importance of recreation and hiking," the GMC's Shaffer told a *Rutland*

Herald reporter. "That's not the way the implementation is working out. We've taken too much for granted. We won't in the future." Indeed, the hiking clubs and conservation groups that differ over some wilderness-management issues found common ground in criticizing imbalances in the forest's budgets and priorities. An analysis by Preserve Appalachian Wilderness charged that the forest's 1991 budget provided up to 120 percent of the funds needed to meet its Forest Plan objectives for timber sales, but only between 30 and 50 percent for objectives involving wildlife protection, resource inventories, and recreation.

The pressure to meet timber quotas and the shortage of funding for other purposes filter down to the district level, taking a toll on morale. "I think there's a lot of tension between the rec[reation] staff and the timber people," Shaffer observed after the Emily Proctor flap. "The recreation budget has been grossly underfunded," Russ Eastwood says. He assures volunteer trailworkers that their unpaid labor isn't a disguised subsidy for timber operations they may oppose. Still, Eastwood states emphatically, "we aren't meeting objectives."

Paul Lundberg says that his office will complete a Wilderness Implementation Schedule for Breadloaf by September 1993. He vows that hiking clubs, environmental groups, and other citizens will play a significant role in planning for and overseeing Breadloaf's future.

"There are good people struggling," grants Bettina Mattesen, who speaks with respect for Eastwood and other hard-pressed Forest Service employees. But in cases like the bungled logging job on the Emily Proctor Trail, she concludes, "they don't have to re-invent the wheel. They can simply follow the law."

"We're growing wilderness," some staffers are wont to say. Over the years, they predict, the contrast between the Breadloaf Wilderness and the surrounding lands, public and private, is likely to become bolder and more dramatic, providing a dynamic benchmark for measuring the condition and health of the region's environment. But the scientific, political, and philosophical ground is always shifting as well. The Breadloaf Wilderness will also provide a benchmark for gauging those subtle transformations in human attitudes, knowledge, and expectations—indeed, in the whole evolving relationship between humanity and nature.

The mountain-loving spirit of legendary Green Mountain guardians like Joseph Battell and James P. Taylor still inspires those who use, care for, and keep a watchful eye on the Breadloaf Wilderness. The Wilderness Act ordains that they may only be visitors. But no law can prevent them from considering Breadloaf, in each individual's distinctive sense, a spiritual home.

(1993)

POSTSCRIPT: When I wrote this article, my wife Nan and I had recently purchased a small house in Ripton, Vermont, adjacent to both the Bread Loaf campus of Middlebury College and the trailhead for the Burnt Hill Trail, which leads directly into the Breadloaf Wilderness Area. With some regret, we sold the property almost 20 years later. The politics and management of Vermont's Wilderness Areas have of course evolved over that time. For one thing, passage of the New England Wilderness Act in December, 2006, expanded four of the state's then-existing six Wilderness Areas, including Lye Brook, Big Branch, Peru Peak, and Breadloaf. An additional 3,757 acres were added to Breadloaf, bringing its total size to 25,237 acres—still the largest of what are now eight Vermont Wilderness Areas. The 2006 law also created two new Wilderness Areas. The 22,245-acre Glastenbury Wilderness is in the southern part of the Green Mountain National Forest; it is traversed by the Appalachian and Long Trails. The 12,333-acre Joseph Battell Wilderness lies immediately to the south of Breadloaf, honoring the philanthropist who had originally purchased and preserved the expanse of mountain terrain that included not only this area but Breadloaf; it is spanned by the Long Trail. Indeed, the New England Wilderness Act reconfirmed that the Appalachian Trail, the Long Trail, and the Catamount Trail, a cross-country ski trail that crosses Vermont north and south, could continue to be maintained in the state's federally designated Wilderness Areas. All told, the eight Vermont Wilderness Areas comprise almost 101,000 acres, representing a quarter of the 400,000-acre GMNF.

The New England Wilderness Act also designated another 15,857-acre parcel of the GMNF immediately to the southwest of Breadloaf as the Moosalamoo National Recreation Area, which also includes some of the lands originally purchased by Joseph Battell. Comprising lower-elevation lands traditionally popular for a variety of recreational uses, the Moosalamoo NRA had been promoted by a local group of property owners and businesspeople, who recognized that protection and management of the area for a balanced array of recreation would help sustain the local tourist and outdoor-sports economy. Some of these uses include activities and facilities not permitted in Wilderness Areas, such as a network of maintained snowshoe and cross-country ski trails, mountain biking trails, snowmobile trails, and developed campgrounds.

Based on my own observations of Breadloaf over the course of two decades, GMNF personnel and policy have pursued good-faith efforts to maintain the wild characteristics of the area, while accommodating the recreational uses and facilities represented by the presence of the Long Trail. The mills of Forest Service bureaucracy continue to grind out new and revised wilderness-management policies, however, reflecting budget constraints and changing political priorities. In 2010, the GMNF issued a Wilderness Interpretation and Education Plan for all eight Vermont Wilderness Areas. The plan was produced partly in response to the 10-Year Wilderness Stewardship Challenge initiated by the Forest Service in 2004. A 2002 agency survey had determined that only 8 percent of Forest Service Wildernesses nationwide met a 60-point "minimum stewardship level," based on fulfilling six of ten management elements, such as air quality monitoring, invasive plant control, fire management, and recreation planning. The Challenge set a goal of 100-percent compliance with the minimum stewardship level by 2014, the 50th anniversary of the Wilderness Act's passage. By 2010, the agency was reporting that 41 percent of Wilderness Areas met the 60-point minimum standard. The Vermont Wilderness Areas fared relatively well for the same year: all six areas (as well as the two new areas created in 2006 but not formally included in the Challenge) met or exceeded the minimum stewardship level. The Breadloaf Wilderness was rated at 76 points.

Of course, numerical metrics and bureaucratic procedures cannot comprehensively gauge the essential qualities and experience of wilderness. The unique public landscapes represented by federal Wilderness Areas continue to provide the settings for individuals to take the measure of themselves and their natural surroundings, according to their own personal standards.

Nothing Small in Nature

The grim consequences of the drought of 1988 were evident early that summer. Sizzling crops, desperate farmers, rising food prices, grounded barges, threatened drinking water supplies—if we didn't feel such effects firsthand, the media daily brought more pessimistic forecasts and worrisome images. The most troubling reports came from atmospheric scientists. With a certain I-told-you-so self-assurance, the researchers suggested that the drought was concrete evidence of global warming—a predicted result of the "greenhouse effect." One ominous projection by the National Aeronautics and Space Administration (NASA), broadcast on television, depicted with dazzling state-of-the-art computer graphics an inexorably catastrophic scenario, in which vast swaths of the earth's land mass seem to be burning up by the early decades of the next century.

By the summer of 1988 there was widespread public recognition of the dismaying chain of climatic events that is apparently turning up the earth's thermostat: increased burning of fossil fuels and the destruction of forests combine to increase levels of atmospheric carbon dioxide and methane, thereby trapping the radiant heat of the sun. The scientists explained the phenomenon (and others equally disturbing, such as the destruction of the earth's ozone layer) with such confidence and their technical wizardry was so impressive, one almost forgot that they were describing a slow-motion apocalypse—an apocalypse quietly creeping up day by day, brought on by our own substantial intervention in natural processes.

While the scientists declared the drought a sure harbinger of global warming, environmentalists used the crisis to renew their faltering campaigns for energy conservation and the development of renewable energy resources. Likewise, nuclear-power advocates experienced fresh hope for that economically and environmentally troubled technology. By a facile exercise of logic, they declared nuclear-generated energy to be safe and desirable because the burning of fossil fuels is dangerous. Editorialists and pundits of all ideological persuasions had a field day, pointing fingers and sounding portentous alarms.

George Perkins Marsh, a man of the world, would not have been surprised by all the ruckus and rhetoric. Nor would he have been shocked at humanity's cumulative influence on what he once described as "the proper working of the great terraqueous machine."

"The earth is fast becoming an unfit home for its noblest inhabitant," he wrote in the introductory chapter of *Man and Nature*, his 1864 classic, "and another era of equal human crime and human improvidence, and of like duration with that through which traces of that crime and that improvidence extend, would reduce it to such a condition of impoverished productiveness, of shattered surface, of climatic excess, as to threaten the depravation, barbarism, and perhaps even extinction of the species."

So far, more than a hundred and twenty-five years after Marsh's warning first appeared in print, we have not yet succumbed to extinction—though some may feel that the verdict is not so clear on the questions of depravation and barbarism. In any event, it might not be too late, during these gradually warming days, to turn to some of the timeless and cautionary lessons George Perkins Marsh so magisterially set forth in *Man and Nature; or, Physical Geography as Modified by Human Action*.

If *Man and Nature* is "the fountainhead of the conservation movement," as critic and historian Lewis Mumford once wrote, it is a safe bet that few but the most ardent of conservationists and the most dogged of graduate students make their way through Marsh's dry, dense text today. But there is another reason besides archaic literary style that Marsh's work and message are not better known and more readily heeded. Like many another neglected and unpopular prophet, Marsh urged his readers, individually and collectively, to take responsibility for the consequences of their actions. He asked his fellow citizens (and Marsh was a prominent public figure who took seriously the duties of citizenship) to take a clear-eyed look at how they lived, the better to mend their harmful ways.

Unlike many other prophets, though, Marsh was no fire-and-brimstone evangelist, no tub-thumping mountebank. His rhetoric was usually subdued, his profuse evidence marshalled with logic and precision, his conclusions equivocal when the data were inconclusive. The style and substance of *Man and Nature* reflected Marsh's legal training, diplomatic background, and resolute faith in the powers of empirical observation and scientific investigation to reveal the path out of humanity's environmental dilemma.

Marsh's eyes were opened to the dynamics of nature, he once recalled, during a boyhood excursion across the countryside surrounding his Woodstock, Vermont, home. His father "called my attention to the general configuration of the surface; pointed out the direction of the different ranges of hills; told me how the water gathered on them and ran down their sides. . . . He stopped his horse on the top of a steep hill, made me notice how the water flowed in different directions, and told me that such a point was called a *watershed*." This simple but profound lesson in physical geography was the starting point for Marsh's sweeping attempt to comprehend the relationship between human activity and natural processes.

Born in 1801, Marsh attended Dartmouth College and was a self-taught lawyer. Restless with the legal profession, he pursued an active but rarely successful business career. He "bred sheep, ran a woolen mill, built roads and bridges, sold lumber, edited a newspaper, developed a marble quarry, [and] speculated in real estate," as biographer David Lowenthal summarized. In the 1840s Marsh served four terms as a Congressman from Vermont, during which time he was influential in the creation and administration of the Smithsonian Institution. A five-year stint as U.S. Minister to Turkey provided him the opportunity to travel in Egypt and Palestine. In 1861, Abraham Lincoln appointed Marsh to serve as American Minister in Italy, a post he held until his death in 1882.

Throughout his life, Marsh, who read twenty languages, pursued a prodigious variety of scholarly endeavors. His prolific writings included a treatise title *The Camel*, based on his firsthand experiences with the creatures and his belief that they might be profitably used in the arid regions of the United States; a groundbreaking *Report on the Artificial Propagation of Fish* prepared for the state of Vermont; an Icelandic grammar; a dictionary of English etymology; and a volume on *The Goths in New England*, in which he attempted to prove a then-popular and unabashedly racist theory that the virtues of American institutions and of the nation's Puritan forebears could be traced to Germanic origins.

But *Man and Nature* (retitled, in later editions, *The Earth as Modified by Human Action*) was the masterwork, the synthesis of Marsh's eclectic learning, extensive travels, and varied experiences. Among the objects of the book, he wrote, besides chronicling "the extent of the changes produced by human action in the physical conditions of the globe we inhabit," was "to illustrate the doctrine, that man is, in both kind and degree, a power of a higher order than any of the other forms of animated life, which, like him, are nourished at the table of bounteous nature." Marsh wrote and published *Man and Nature* at a time when the theological certainty of the natural hierarchy was under attack; the debate over the theory of evolution has only just begun (Darwin's *Origin of the Species* was published in 1859). Marsh reconciled such seemingly conflicting ideas about science and religion—at least to his own satisfaction. His book was a plea that humankind understand and accept its place as the supremely influential species in the global web of life.

Buttressed with the pages of evidence and example that comprise the bulk of *Man and Nature*, Marsh forcefully advanced his argument that humanity was not merely the passive object of geographical forces but the powerful, if usually unconscious, instigator of profound environmental transformations. "Man is everywhere a disturbing agent," Marsh

George Perkins Marsh, ca. 1855-1865. (Courtesy of the Library of Congress.)

wrote. "Wherever he plants his foot, the harmonies of nature are turned to discords."

Marsh composed much of the book in Italy, while the nation he represented was still in the throes of the Civil War and Italy itself was for the first time being governed as a unified nation. It was obvious enough, in his eyes, that history, political struggle, and the state of the natural environment were inextricably intertwined. The long introductory chapter of *Man and Nature* begins with an account of the man-induced environmental disturbances that had contributed to the downfall of the Roman Empire. Marsh's parable of how the Romans laid waste their domain's abundant natural endowments set the moral tone for the rest of his book.

From Rome he led his readers on a long excursion through time and history, ranging across landscapes from his Vermont hometown to the steppes of Russia, exploring "The Woods," "The Waters," and "The Sands," as he titled the book's three central chapters. His linguistic talents and his correspondence with many eminent scientists, scholars, and public figures of his era provided him access to an unusually wide array of sources. (Indeed, some of the most interesting and pointed digressions in the book appear in his extensive footnotes.) Marsh was a pioneer environmental historian. His aim was to sort out, describe, and interpret the complex ecological chains of cause and effect by which mankind had transformed the face of the landscape. And he had a talent for simplifying these connections. Marsh abruptly and periodically punctuated his long, arid expository passages with concise, vivid images that graphically dramatized his theme that there is "nothing small in nature." Consider, for instance, how he distills the long arc of one region's history into a single sentence: "Thus the earth loosened by the rude Abyssinian ploughshare, and washed down by the rain from the hills of Ethiopia which man has stripped of their protecting forests, contributes to raise the plains of Egypt, to shoal the maritime channels which lead to the city built by Alexander near the mouth of the Nile, and to fill up the harbors made famous by Phenician [sic] commerce."

With a skeptic's eye, he compared conditions in his youthful native country with those in the long-settled lands of the Old World. His fellow Americans, he observed, were repeating many of the same mistakes whose grim outcomes could be read on the ravaged landscape of Europe and the Near East. "Let us be wise in time, and profit by the errors of our older brethren!" Marsh warned in a burst of urgency. Unlike Europeans, he noted, Americans had not yet had time to raze all their forests or to build extensive and vulnerable communities in river floodplains.

In the destruction of America's forests, though, Marsh saw a disheartening flaw in the nation's character. He concluded his chapter on forests with a short exhortation under the heading "Instability of American Life," in which he posed a challenge still worth heeding:

> All human institutions, associate arrangements, modes of life, have their characteristic imperfections. The natural, perhaps the necessary defect of ours, is their instability, their want of fixedness, not in form only, but even in spirit. The face of physical nature in the United States shares this incessant fluctuation, and the landscape is as variable as the habits of the population. It is time for some abatement in the restless love of change which characterizes us, and makes us almost a nomade [sic] rather than a sedentary people. We have now felled forest enough everywhere, in many districts far too much. Let us restore this one element of material life to its normal proportions, and devise means of maintaining the permanence of its relations to the fields, the meadows, and the pastures, to the rain and the dews of heaven, to the springs and rivulets with which it waters the earth. The establishment of an approximately fixed ratio between the two most broadly characterized distinctions of rural surface— woodland and plough land—would involve a certain persistence of character in all the branches of industry, all the occupations and habits of life, which depend upon or are immediately connected with either, without implying a rigidity that should exclude flexibility of accommodation to the many changes of external circumstance which human wisdom can neither prevent nor foresee, and would thus help us to become, more emphatically, a well-ordered and stable commonwealth, and, not less conspicuously, a people of progress.

Marsh's message, while well received by other scientists, scholars, and reformers of his era, had a limited immediate impact on a nation still hellbent on expansion, settlement, and the unrestrained exploitation of its natural resources. But his ideas gradually took hold. Indeed, his penetrating discussion of the relationship between forest cover, soil erosion, and streamflow laid down the fundamental tenets of the American forestry and conservation movements of the early twentieth century. Third World deforestation today, and related wood shortages, soil erosion, and flooding, duplicate processes Marsh documented from the Old World's long history and observed personally on the steep hillsides of Vermont.

Despite his exhaustive depiction of the careless and profligate ways of humanity, Marsh held out hope. No enemy of the public ownership and control of natural resources, he pointed to the stirrings of intelligent public regulation and restoration of forests in southern France and elsewhere in Europe. The diking, draining, and creation of land in Holland, he concluded, had been generally benign and successful. And he recounted the experience of the Italian province of Tuscany, which had long been engaged in an effort to prevent floods and restore lost agricultural lands through a flexible, imaginative program of rechanneling the region's much-abused rivers.

There was no question that people would intervene in altering the landscape; the only question for Marsh was whether the result would be beneficial or harmful to humans and their environment, whether such transformations would be pursued purely for private gain or for the commonweal. Marsh's call for active, constructive rehabilitation of damaged landscapes anticipated today's nascent "restoration ecology" movement. Moreover, he echoed the sentiments of those who now worry about the world's exorbitant military expenditures. "[T]he cost of one year's warfare, if judiciously expended," he wrote, "would secure, to almost every country that man has exhausted, an amelioration of climate, a renovated fertility of soil, and a general physical improvement, which might almost be characterized as a new creation."

Influenced by the Transcendental spirit of his native New England, Marsh hewed to a faith that human beings might yet come to comprehend and appreciate their unique place in the natural order. And, in the spirit of his age, he believed in the virtues and benefits of scientific endeavor—the ultimate significance of which, he suggested, was its potential to satisfy humanity's most fundamental spiritual yearning. "The collection of phenomena must precede the analysis of them," he concluded, "and every new fact, illustrative of the action and reaction between humanity and the material world around it, is another step toward the determination of the great question, whether man is of nature or above her."

The questions Marsh posed in 1864 are fundamentally, if not always scientifically, identical to the ones that confront us today. The drought of 1988, the dire prospect of global warming, and other recent environmental calamities, from floods in Bangladesh to the enormous oil spill in Alaska's Prince William Sound—such phenomena dramatize the paradox Marsh well understood before there was a genuine conservation movement or a sophisticated scientific understanding of globe-encircling environmental processes: The technological and economic forces that provide valuable material benefits can also produce the very conditions that undermine the planet's ability to sustain life.

The contemporary significance of Marsh's observations will be evident to those who yearn to preserve and protect the earth's remaining wild places. If, as he proclaimed, "a certain persistence of character" is a requisite for any hope of preserving a healthy, stable environmental order, the complexities of large-scale ecological forces can nonetheless confound the noblest of human intentions. On a globe blanketed with increasing amounts of carbon dioxide and soaking up acidified precipitation, wilderness has no real boundaries or protection, no matter if designated by law and depicted on a map.

His chapter on "Transfer, Modification, and Extirpation of Vegetable and of Animal Species" catalogued the ways human cultures affected the range, distribution, and survival of a multitude of life forms. His arguments in favor of preserving organisms and their habitats anticipated virtually every point made by environmentalists today—from the possible medical uses of little-known organisms and the protection of biological diversity to the spiritual and aesthetic value of undisturbed terrain. And in an era when species are swiftly being rendered extinct while genetic engineers simultaneously attempt to invent new organisms, Marsh's warning about the ecological hubris of his own species has lost none of its cogency. "[W]e are never justified in assuming a force to be insignificant because its measure is unknown, or even because no physical effect can now be traced to it as its origin," he wrote, neatly summarizing the challenge faced by today's scientists as they attempt to understand the earth's intricate atmospheric, biological, and geographical processes.

"The equation of animal and vegetable life is too complicated a problem for human intelligence to solve," Marsh wrote, "and we can never know how wide a circle we produce in the harmonies of nature when we throw the smallest pebble into the ocean of organic life." As we continue throwing pebbles, we should also be keeping an eye trained on the horizon for the first signs of an environmental tidal wave.

The worldly Yankee author of *Man and Nature*, working in his study in a medieval castle near Turin, had a less provincial viewpoint then did many of his counterparts in the pantheon of American conservation history and literature. Marsh's sobersided book, it must be confessed, is not nearly as lyrical or inspirational as other American volumes of environmental scripture, such as the Thoreau's *Walden*, Muir's *The Mountains of California*, or Leopold's *A Sand County Almanac*.

Some students of the American conservation movement, in fact, pigeonhole Marsh as a "utilitarian," who mistakenly places mankind at the center of terrestrial environmental affairs. His ideas, the critics say, hinder the development of a biocentric, truly ecological understanding of humanity's role in the natural scheme of things. Maybe so. Meanwhile, the news pours in and the scientific evidence piles up documenting the link between human activity and environmental degradation. Perhaps Marsh's matter-of-fact candor, expansive perspective, profound historical awareness, and outright common sense accurately reflect the stark facts of life on the planet Earth in this epoch.

Indeed, in his clear-headed analysis of the challenge facing humanity in his time, George Perkins Marsh spelled out some of the indisputably human qualities that are equally necessary today as we plunge headlong into the future: humility about the limits of our knowledge, that "certain persistence of character," and a forthright recognition that there is indeed "nothing small in nature."

(1990)

Canyon of Solace

Eight active, if aging, Rhode Island backpackers, we had gone to the Grand Canyon principally for the physical challenge and adventure—or so we told ourselves. Five men and three women, we were all members of the Narragansett Chapter of the Appalachian Mountain Club. Accustomed to the forests and crags of New England's mountain terrain, we brought high expectations, as well as our share of anxieties, to the South Rim of the Grand Canyon.

Most of us were in our forties, a few edging into our fifties—so we also brought along gimpy knees and several chronic backaches. Among our provisions, large bottles of ibuprofen were as essential as ample supplies of water and food. During meetings to plan our mid-April trip, we had discussed the physical obstacles that might confront us: the ruggedness of those unfamiliar trails, the heat, the rattlesnakes and scorpions, the scarcity of reliable water. "The abyss yawns below your footsteps," read the trail description we had been studying for months. That sentence became our hiking chorus, as our shadowy apprehensions were reconciled gradually with the overwhelming realities of the Grant Canyon landscape.

The abyss did yawn below our footsteps as we headed out along the Boucher Trail, constructed around the turn of the century by the eponymous Louis D. Boucher. A prospector, guide, and desert rat,

Boucher had made Hermit Canyon his personal enclave for some twenty years. Our knees wobbled and our heads spun while crossing washed-out sections of Boucher's old mule trail, a route the National Park Service classifies as "unmaintained." We could well believe, as the trail description continued, that this narrow path represented "probably the most exposed and exciting hiking in the Grand Canyon."

In fact, starting late, giddy with the novelty of the canyon vistas, stopping to photograph every cactus plant and fossil, we immediately fell behind the pace necessary for covering the ambitious nine miles of our first day's plan. By midafternoon, as we descended the tortuous, corrugated trail through the Redwall (this practice of gauging progress in terms of geological stratigraphy was also new to our eastern sensibilities), it became evident that we would not reach our planned campsite on Boucher Creek that night. Some of us were exhausted—perhaps a little afraid that we were, literally, beyond our depth. But there was no turning back. We had no choice but to camp in a dry wash at the head of Travertine Canyon. Our supper and breakfast consisted of granola bars and gorp. We needed to conserve our suddenly meager water supplies.

This proved to be our most serious predicament along the trail. Despite the stern warnings provided by the guidebook and the ranger at the Park Service's Backcountry Reservations Office, the canyon had surprised us. Nonetheless, the challenge also provided us with an early bond. We hiked on, a temporary canyon clan. Our five-day circuit of one small corner of the Grand Canyon soon reached, step by careful step, into the quieter, more private places of our middle-aged souls. We were all, in our guarded ways, seeking refuge in these canyons from other personal spirits, demons, and troubles. On the trail and in camp our conversation usually revolved around the mundane matters of outdoor living: food, route finding, water, setting up camp. But over the course of our excursion, we each revealed some of the deeper concerns that were knit into the fabric of our lives: divorces, past and pending; illnesses, physical and mental, that had afflicted us or our family members and loved ones; deaths; miscarriages; vocational insecurities;

Louis D. Boucher. (Courtesy of the National Park Service.)

worries about our children; worries about *not* having children; romantic disappointments; frustrations about our declining physical capabilities.

The Grand Canyon, of course, is the ideal place to contemplate the passage of time. We were old enough now to appreciate the precious brevity of a single human life span, which represented barely a layer of dust in the canyon's mind-numbing geological stratigraphy. All of us bore a fair share of life's emotional baggage, and the backpacks we lugged, mere physical mass, seemed somewhat lighter by comparison. A sense of urgency had brought us here, an awareness that if we didn't plumb these depths soon, while our bodies still allowed it, we could be burdened permanently with the painful poundage of regret.

For some of us, this trip across country had entailed substantial financial expense and sacrifice. But we had convinced ourselves there was no way to set a price on this opportunity. And here we were, exploring a niche of the Grand Canyon under our own power—righteously congratulating ourselves that we weren't aboard the steady, clattering stream of sightseeing helicopters that started traversing the sky overhead shortly after eight o'clock every morning.

It is a commonplace to say that words fail to describe the Grand Canyon. Hiking along, we loudly exclaimed our own banalities and clichés about the spectacular sights that opened up around every bend in the trail. But if we were more reticent about the darker personal matters that coursed through our minds as we trekked along, we may have shared something with Louis Boucher. A Québec native who arrived at the Grand Canyon about 1891, Boucher was the best-known, but not the first, "hermit" to live in this sere, solitary neighborhood. "A quiet man who lived in an out-of-the-way beautiful place," according to historian J. Donald Hughes, he "had a white beard, rode a white mule with a bell around its neck, and carried the tools of the prospector: a geology pick and a pan, and tools for trailmaking." Boucher's cryptic historical legacy survives mostly in the material remains of his twenty years of labor. For all his evident industry and toughness, though, Boucher apparently also had a romantic streak. He made his home camp at Dripping Springs, at the head of Hermit Canyon, where he kept mules, horses, burros, and sheep. Visitors couldn't help noticing that he also raised goldfish and water lilies in his watering troughs.

Boucher's painstakingly constructed trail—he called it the Silver Bell Trail—connected this well-watered spot below the canyon rim to his graphite and copper claims deeper in the gorge. When, following his trail, we reached Boucher Creek campground a day behind schedule, we explored the vestiges of one of his stone-built cabins and poked our noses into his modest mine. Nothing survived, though, of the lush gardens and orchards he once maintained here. Boucher sometimes rented cabins to tourists at this pleasant setting, but unlike most of the prospectors and promoters of his era who built trails into the canyon, he didn't charge the public a toll for using his path. In fact, according to another Grand Canyon chronicler, Boucher "was a kind, gentle soul who always went out of his way to aid anyone in trouble."

Attending quietly to his own business, shuttling between rim and river, Louis Boucher may have been escaping from some part of his own past. Possibly he found a measure of solace and comfort here—as we did almost a century later. Despite his obvious affinity for canyon living, Boucher abandoned his domain in 1912—the year the Santa Fe Railroad constructed the carefully graded Hermit Trail opposite his more precarious Silver Bell route. The new mule trail brought tourists to the company's elaborate Hermit Camp, which was supplied by an aerial tramway from the canyon rim. Today, of course, the tramway is gone, and a ranger cabin is all that remains of Hermit Camp. Not far away, on Hermit Creek, the Park Service maintains a busy designated campsite, which we shared with a raucous group of Boy Scouts.

Historian Hughes speculates that Boucher departed for Utah because "none of his prospects were pay dirt." Perhaps, though, Boucher left because he felt that Hermit Canyon, overwhelmed with all this new commercial and tourist activity, was no longer a place for a self-respecting hermit—or at least for the sort of hermit who liked to tell visitors that he could see the stars at midday from the bottom of his gorge.

"The abyss yawns below. . . ." We had gone to the Grand Canyon to walk the edge—of space, of time, of our own lives' sometimes rough trails. Louis Boucher had left us a tough path to follow. But we kept our footing. Like him, we had skirted this abyss. And now, like the Grand Canyon's vast, improbable spaces, our lives still stretched out before us.

(1994)

Reflections on the Draft

Ed Miller's recent (November 17, 1978) *Harvard Post* column about "The New Generation Gap," in which he described the ongoing identity crisis taking place among the generation now nearing the age of thirty, reminded me of one particular rite of passage today's 18-year-old boy/man no longer has to experience: registering for—and worrying about—military conscription.

Ten years ago, in that tumultuous watershed year of 1968, an 18-year-male resident of Harvard fulfilled one requirement of the Selective Service Act of 1946 by registering for the draft at the local Selective Service office in Clinton. When I made the trip to that dingy, upstairs office on High Street in 1968 I knew that the simple act of draft registration was no longer an innocent one, that it had become for many 18-year-olds the first important political and moral decision of their lives.

Controversy about conscription was, of course, nothing new, either in this country or elsewhere; but in 1968 the widespread unpopularity of the war in Vietnam was growing. And nowhere were the political and moral tensions of the country felt more acutely than in the consciences and confusion of those young American men who were being called upon to fight in Asia. It was a generation of men for whom the standard American catchwords—patriotism, loyalty, authority, freedom of speech—no longer had any clear meanings, or at least not the same meanings they had for our fathers' generation.

In *The Making of the President: 1968* Theodore White accurately describe how the draft affected those whose lives it controlled:

> The draft policies of the United States have been obsolete for so long as to make World War II's Flying Fortress look like advanced design. . . . America's youth now lives . . . under a system of random, incoherent, confusing conscription in which service, possibly death, is a matter of almost pure chance. The system unsettles all with its sporadic call-ups; it hangs over every college talk, every plan for the future; and service and death, since they come by accident, deprive duty and life of meaning. An almost obscene condition of thought is stimulated in which the best and highest-motivated of the young accept fraud, hypocrisy, evasion, influence and dishonesty as part of the game.

I've never served in this country's armed forces. The reason I haven't is partly a matter of chance and partly a matter of choice. When I turned eighteen in 1968 I had a number of alternatives to choose from in dealing with the Selective Service, each of whose consequences was reasonably clear. I could, as many thousands of my peers did, have accepted 1-A status and either enlisted or waited to be drafted, knowing that by joining the military I would almost certainly be headed for combat in Vietnam. I could have refused to register, hoping that the Selective Service wouldn't catch up with me. I could have left the country, as so many did, refusing to cooperate in any way with the American system of conscription and military service. Or I could have immediately applied for conscientious objector status, as many others did. I might also have sought a 4-F status, if I could prove I had a disability that made it physically or mentally impossible to serve (and there were plenty of stories about people maiming themselves or about sympathetic psychiatrists who could claim that just about anybody was entitled to be 4-F).

Instead, I joined probably the largest group of 18-year-old males, those who received 2-S deferments by attending college. The campus became a sanctuary, though many of us thought only a temporary one, for those who simply wanted to avoid making a decision about what we would do if asked to fight in Vietnam. Those who didn't have the inclination, money, or education to go to college had, of course, to make that decision without delay.

As the war "wound down" to its messy conclusion, so too did the Selective Service. The Nixon Administration, in response to increasing protest against and resistance to both the draft and war, began to tinker with the Selective Service System, first by creating a lottery system in 1969. While admittedly random in its selection, the lottery was supposed to be fairer than the system which chose only those who could not find shelter behind a deferment. And eventually the draft was replaced by an all-volunteer Army: 1973 was the last year any American soldier was inducted under the draft, and 1974 was the last year men eighteen and older were required to register with the Selective Service.

I graduated from college in 1973, the last year of Selective Service induction. And since that time, when worrying about being drafted was an almost constant preoccupation among so many males of my age, I haven't given much thought to the question of conscription and how I would respond to its return. Still unresolved in my mind and conscience are many of the questions raised during the years of the Vietnam war—questions about when it is moral and right to follow the orders of one's government to join the military and take part in the war, and when it is right and moral to resist such orders. The government and the citizens of our country did not settle these questions during the Vietnam debacle; rather, those issues just sort of faded away from the public's consciousness as the war faded away from our television screens. What's clear, though, is that a vast reservoir of mistrust and resentment was created as a result of the Vietnam experience. How will that mistrust and resentment affect the government's next, probably inevitable, attempt to conscript soldiers?

While thinking about the draft it occurred to me to see if my Selective Service file still existed (I knew that the Clinton office was long gone), because during my first two college years I had fattened it up by submitting an application claiming that I was a conscientious objector to war. I was interested to see how my statements on such weighty issues as war, peace, religious belief, and conscience, written while I was still a teenager, would sound to me almost ten years later.

At the time I filed my application claiming C.O. status, it made no immediate difference in my standing with the Selective Service. Until I lost or gave up the 2-S (student) status I held at the time, the Clinton draft board would not consider or rule upon my application. I was taking my claim seriously, though. It was an idea that had been taking shape in my mind while I was still a senior in high school, that I mulled over during my freshman year in college, and that I finally acted upon. I reasoned that if I was serious about the whole matter I should have my application on record as soon as possible; the draft board could not then say later that I was a johnny-come-lately, using any expedient to escape the draft.

I dug out my old *Handbook for Conscientious Objectors* last week—the book I used as a guide in filling out my application; and I was reminded of how much time I spent thinking about the four questions on the Selective Service C.O. application—and about how the Clinton draft board might eventually respond to my answers.

The questions, at first glance, seemed straightforward enough. Yet the first one especially is the one that I'm not sure I could ever answer—either to my own satisfaction or anyone else's. "Describe the nature of your belief which is the basis of your claim," that first question read, "and state why you consider it to be based on religious training and belief." The problem for those who felt sincerely that they were conscientiously opposed to the war in Vietnam—and didn't know how they felt about other wars they hadn't been faced with—was that conscientious objector status could be granted only to those whose opposition to combatant training and service was based on "religious training and belief"; that term, the law declared, "does not include essentially political, sociological or philosophical views, or a merely personal moral code."

The government, in other words, had made a legal determination that only the authority of religion—and not just religious "belief" but

My Selective Service cards: 1968 registration certificate (top left); 1970 1-A
classification (top right); 1972 1-H classification (bottom).

religious "training" as well—entitled one to act on one's conscience. "A
merely personal moral code," as the government put it, did not.

I composed what I thought at the time to be a sincere and reasonable answer to the question, though, "based on religious training and
belief." And I went on to answer the other three questions, which did
not seem so troublesome once I was past the first: "2) Explain how,
when and from whom or from what source you received the religious
training and acquired the religious belief which is the basis of your
claim; 3) To what extent does your religious training and belief restrict
you from ministering to the sick and injured, either civilian or military,
or from serving in the Armed Forces as a noncombatant without
weapons?; and 4) Have you ever given expression publicly or privately,
written or oral, to the views herein expressed as the basis for your
claim? Give examples."

All this I provided the Selective Service, with letters of reference from several high school teachers. In my application I stated that I would accept 1-A-O status, which would permit me to serve in the military as a noncombatant, rather than 1-O, in which a conscientious objector worked in some civilian role. My reasoning at the time I'm sure had more to do with proving to myself that at eighteen I was man enough to face war than with my scruples about whether it was more or less moral to be a C.O. in the military or out.

A few years later, though, I withdrew my C.O application, although it remained in my file. The lottery system had just been established, and my birthday corresponded to a high lottery number. By giving up my student deferment in favor of the much-feared 1-A status, I would be vulnerable to the draft for only six weeks or so; and the Selective Service had promised that only those below a certain number would be called. (The only hitch was whether the agency could be trusted.) I opted for 1-A, waited out my six weeks, and left school for a year, free at last from my own concerns about being drafted. The war, of course, continued.

I called Congressman Robert Drinan's office last week to find out about the existence and whereabouts of my draft file. I learned that, except for a classification card and an index card with my name and address that will be kept on file in Washington until I'm 85 (just in case things are really desperate and the country needs to conscript its 85-year-olds), the rest of the letters and applications I provided the Selective Service had been destroyed within the last two years—or so they say.

Although I was a little disappointed to discover that I would not have one last chance to read my carefully thought out responses to the government's questions about my religious training and belief, I have to admit that I was relieved as well. It is not that I have any qualms about what I wrote ten years ago. It's just that I harbor a certain paranoia about the possibility of a new form of McCarthyism arising in this country, a movement that might use any available information to discredit those who could in any way be identified as "unpatriotic" or "subversive." I never appeared before the Clinton draft board to defend my statements claiming that I was a conscientious objector. And perhaps I could not have justified those claims, at least to the satisfaction of the government's definitions.

But it had begun to dawn on me that the very existence of those statements, if they remained in the government's hands, could someday come back to cause me problems. It's been less than two years, for instance, since Theodore Sorensen, a government-certified conscientious objector who had previously served in the highest reaches of government, withdrew from being considered to head the C.I.A. The question raised by a Senate committee was whether such a man could be entrusted with the nation's security. Can a distinguished American with a conscience be trusted? Evidently not, according to the U.S. Senate.

News reports appearing this week indicate that the Carter Administration is considering a recommendation by the Joint Chiefs of Staff to return to the compulsory registration of 18-year-olds. The Joint Chiefs, according to the *Wall Street Journal*, have won the support of the Congressional Budget Office and the House Armed Services Committee for their contention "that the moribund Selective Service System has dangerously reduced the nation's ability to mobilize for war." Some military officials, the report continues, "believe the registration alone could ease recruiting problems by increasing citizen awareness of the armed services."

What these military officials may be overlooking, however, is that a return to compulsory registration will undoubtedly be accompanied by a renewed search for answers to those questions left unanswered when the country last asked its young men to fight for questionable ends.

(1978)

POSTSCRIPT: On July 2, 1980, partly in response to the Soviet Union's invasion of Afghanistan in December, 1979, President Jimmy Carter issued a proclamation re-establishing Selective Service registration. His order required registration by all male citizens (and male aliens) 18 to 26 years old who were born on or after January 1, 1960. Such draft-eligible men may today register by mail, on-line, at many high schools, or by checking a box on the Free Application for Federal Student Aid (FAFSA) form. The possible legal penalty for failure to register is a jail term of up to five years or a fine of up to $250,000, but prosecutions have been extremely rare. The more onerous practical penalty for failure to register is denial of federal loans, grants, and other benefits, such as Pell educational grants.

The current Selective Service System registration process does not provide a means or opportunity for a registrant to claim conscientious objector status. A draft classification system and process remains in place, however, in the event that the draft is re-activated. At that time, a young man would have the opportunity to file a claim with his local draft board for classification as a conscientious objector. On its web site, as of 2012, the Selective Service System advises that a conscientious objector "is one who is opposed to serving in the armed forces and/or bearing arms on the grounds of moral and religious principles." The "beliefs which qualify a registrant for CO status may be religious in nature, but don't have to be," the agency adds. "Beliefs may be moral or ethical; however, a man's reasons for not wanting to participate in a war must not be based on politics, expediency or self-interest. In general, the man's lifestyle prior to making his claim must reflect his current claims."

The Selective Service System reports that the "last man inducted entered the Army on June 30, 1973." In that last year of the draft, 646 men were inducted. The highest annual level of induction during the era of the Vietnam War was 382,010 in 1966. Since the establishment of the Selective Service in 1917, the highest years of induction during other wars were: 1917 (World War I), 2,294,084; 1943 (World War II), 3,323,970; and 1951 (Korea), 551,806.

Almost four decades have now passed since the demise of military conscription in the United States. As a consequence, an ever-increasing number and percentage of the nation's political leaders, including members of Congress and Presidents (as well as candidates for those offices), have neither served in the military nor been subject to conscription. During the recent long era of voluntary military service, this should not come as a surprise or serve as an invidious distinction. In regard to military service, politicians and policy-makers are similar to most Americans. However, the question of their military service has been a persistent issue, though not a consistently conclusive one, for presidents and presidential candidates from what has been called the "Vietnam Generation"—that is, the estimated 27-million American men who came of draft age between the 1964 Tonkin Gulf Resolution and the withdrawal of American troops in 1973. In one way or another—and in ways that often distorted or obfuscated historical facts—figures such as Bill Clinton, John McCain, George W. Bush, Dick Cheney, John Kerry, and others have been subject to scrutiny, adulation, or attack for their differing approaches to military service during the Vietnam years.

The presidential election of 2012 will be the first for several generations in which neither of the two major candidates has served in the uniformed military services of the United States. Mitt Romney received deferments as a Mormon missionary and as a graduate student during the Vietnam years, then (like me) drew a high lottery number in 1969. Barack Obama, born in 1961, came of age after the demise of military conscription, but "birthers" and other political opponents continued to question the validity and accuracy of his Selective Service registration in 1980. As president, of course, Obama has served as Commander-in-Chief of the nation's military forces.

Very few of my Harvard College contemporaries were drafted or enlisted in the armed forces. In fact, our relative immunity from the direct consequences of war-fighting accentuates a social and cultural chasm that persists in the era of a voluntary military. Journalist James Fallows (class of 1970), who was president of the *Harvard Crimson*, wrote a self-lacerating account of his own experience during his final year in college, when he faced the possibility of being drafted. In his October, 1975 *Washington Monthly* article, "What Did You Do in the Class War, Daddy?" Fallows described his trip with a busload of other Harvard and MIT students to a pre-induction physical at the Boston Navy Yard. Like many of his fellow collegians, Fallows had devised a strategy for disqualification from the draft. By the thinnest of margins, he fell below the weight requirement for a man of his height. A wary, skeptical doctor classified him as unqualified for military service. "I was overcome by a wave of relief, which for the first time revealed to me how great my terror had been," Fallows wrote in 1975, "and by the beginning of the sense of shame that remains with me to this day."

Fallows's sense of shame was brought into sharp focus by the buses that followed his into the Navy Yard. The next group of potential conscripts arrived from Chelsea, "thick, dark-haired young men, the White proles of Boston," he observed. "Most of them were younger than we were because they had just left high school, and it had clearly never occurred to them that there might be a way around the draft." Fallows came to believe that many of us in college in those years, who avoided the draft by legal and/or dubious means, had in effect been complicit in prolonging the war, while our contemporaries from communities like Chelsea were compelled to fight (and perhaps die) in it. The domestic politics of the Vietnam era represented a genuine class war, in which "the children of the bright good parents were spared the more immediate sort of suffering that our inferiors were undergoing," Fallows guiltily wrote. "It is clear by now that if the men of Harvard had wanted to do the very most they could to help shorten the war," he concluded, "they should have been drafted or imprisoned en masse."

Decades later, while America has relied on an all-volunteer force to engage in prolonged military engagements in places like Afghanistan and Iraq, these questions of class, duty, dissent, and military service have not really been resolved or even honestly addressed.

In *Chance and Circumstance: The Draft, the War and the Vietnam Generation* (1978), Lawrence M. Baskir and William A. Strauss, top staffers on President Gerald Ford's Clemency Board, offered a fair-minded, thoroughly documented summary of how those 27-million men of the Vietnam Generation responded to or were affected by the draft and the war. "Fifty-one thousand died—17,000 from gunshot wounds, 7,500 from multiple fragmentation wounds, 6,750 from grenades and mines, 10,500 from other enemy action, 8,000 from nonhostile causes, and 350 by suicide," they write. "Another 270,000 were wounded, 21,000 of whom were disabled. Roughly 5,000 lost one or more limbs in the war. A half million were branded as criminals, more than two million served in the war zone, and millions more had their futures shaped by the threat of going to war."

Of course, as Baskir and Strauss observe, there were among that generation roughly as many women of the same age, all of whom were exempt from the draft. But that does not mean they were unaffected by it. "Only six thousand women saw military service in Vietnam, none in combat," they conclude. "But as sisters, girl friends, and wives, millions of draft-age women paid a heavy share of the emotional cost of the war."

Congressman Robert Drinan, the antiwar Jesuit who represented my district and whose office sought my Selective Service records, retired from Congress in 1980. Though he would likely have been easily re-elected (I interviewed him that year at the outset of what proved to be a short-lived campaign), he instead opted to obey Pope John Paul II's order that Catholic clergy eschew direct participation in politics.

I recently (2011) requested from the National Archives, custodian of some Selective Service System records, any record of my Selective Service history and status. A prompt, terse response enclosed a photo-copy of what was described as my "Selective Service card and extracted information from the registration classification book." The two-sided card documents my registration on March 26, 1968, just a few days after my eighteenth birthday; my status as a high-school student; my height and weight; and the name and address of an aunt in the line requesting designation of a "person other than a member of your household who will always know your address." On the line asking for information about "Other obvious physical characteristics that will aid in identifica-tion," I had written: "wears glasses."

My correspondence with the Clinton draft board is cryptically sum-marized on the form identified as "Extract of Registrant Classification Record." I was granted deferred 1-S (HS) status in May, 1968, while enrolled in high school. By January, 1969, during my freshman year in college, I had been re-classified 2-S, another class of student deferment. On December 8, 1970, I was reclassified 1-A ("Available for military service"). And in August, 1972, during the last year of the draft, I was re-classified 1-H. A table of classifications on the back of the extract form informs me that 1-H status applies to registrants "not currently subject to processing for induction or alternate service." The form also notes that "With the cessation of registrant processing in 1976, all registrants (except for a few alleged violators of the Military Selective Service Act) were classified 1-H regardless of any previous classification." Finally, a hand-written entry on the form next to the heading "Entries from Remarks Column" reads: "RSN 265—22, yr 70." This appears to document my "Random Sequence Number" (265), from the December, 1, 1969 draft lottery, which applied to all men born from 1944 through 1950. The draft-eligibility ceiling for that year—that is, the lottery number above which the Selective Service said it would not induct registrants—was 195. I'm not sure how to decipher the rest of the entry ("—22, yr 70"), but it may refer to the number of days (22) of my 1-A draft eligibility during the calendar year 1970 ("yr 70"). Thus is one man's Selective Service System record encoded for posterity's sake. The comparable records of many other members of the Vietnam Generation would, of course, encapsulate stories much more complex and tragic than mine.

When I wrote this piece in 1978, I was mistaken in predicting that a return to compulsory draft registration would generate significant new questions and doubts about the fairness of and rationale for compulsory military service. Depending upon the times and circumstances, such questions, doubts, and debates are more likely to arise if and when political leaders choose to re-activate the draft itself.

A Little Compton Witch Hunt

Little Compton, Rhode Island, my current home, is tucked away in the southeastern-most corner of this little state. Bounded on two sides by the ocean and nestled into a sort of geographical cul-de-sac next to the Massachusetts state line, the town has remained relatively isolated and its landscape substantially undeveloped—at least by Rhode Island standards. A few dairy and livestock farms, some truck farms and vegetable stands, a vineyard, and the activities of numerous part-time and gentleman farmers maintain much of the town in neat working fields and pastures, interwoven with miles and miles of well-preserved stone walls. Handsome summer estates and "cottages," many of them enjoyed by the same families generation after generation, also lend an air of graciousness, charm, and stability to the scenery. A quaint harbor, home port to a small fleet of fishing boats, is protected behind the rocky point marking the eastern entrance to Narragansett Bay. And the center of town—the "Commons," as it is called here—is a classic New England setting. The white spire of the Congregational church is visible from miles away. Close by are a cemetery (burial site of Elizabeth Pabodie, "The First White Woman Born in North America"); the parsonage; a number of other stately old homes; a genuine general store, complete with pot-bellied stove, butcher, and hardware department; and a busy restaurant—a town gathering place that serves such delectable native fare as jonnycakes, clam chowder, and quahog pie. In all, Little Compton is an appealing place to live. As in many such towns, of course, real estate values have steadily increased; and townsfolk, old-timers and newcomers alike, constantly debate measures to control Little Compton's inevitable growth and change.

Because Little Compton is an oceanfront community, its character changes considerably during the summer. The official year-round population of 3,100 is thought, by some estimates, to triple in the summer—and this doesn't count the day-trippers who come to town simply to take in the scenery or to enjoy a day at the beach. Nowhere is the increased summer population more dramatically evident, especially to us year-round residents, than at the Commons. On any Sunday between Memorial Day and Labor Day, the little intersection surround-ed by the church, the general store, and the restaurant is jammed with activity. Cars line the streets around the Commons as people stand in line at the restaurant for a hearty breakfast or at the general store for the newspapers. (The idea of being deprived of the Sunday *New York Times*, I have observed during my own Sabbath-day visits to the general store, is simply beyond the imagination of some of my fellow citizens. One of the most horrifying spectacles I have ever observed was a near riot that broke out one Sunday morning when the *Times* was delivered late. When word reached those milling about the store that the papers had just been brought in the back door, a small, angry army of tanned and otherwise distinguished-looking executives, lawyers, housewives, and retirees, dressed in chinos, LaCoste shirts, and tennis whites, charged through the store. Pushing each other aside, they snatched up sections of the paper before the storekeepers had a chance to sort them out and otherwise threatened the safety of those of us willing to settle for a Boston, Providence, or Fall River paper. These people were on vaca-tion.) All of this activity is tolerated as a fact of life in summertime Little Compton, where almost everyone seems pretty well satisfied with things just as they are.

This usually quiet town was thrown into a tizzy two weeks ago, though, with the news that Hollywood had arrived. "Some Fear Film Will 'Slime' Town," ran the headline in the *Providence Journal* when word got out that a "location scout" for Warner Brothers Pictures had settled on Little Compton (and especially the Commons) as the ideal site for filming John Updike's novel *The Witches of Eastwick*. The man from Warner Brothers, it turned out, had been negotiating with the town council, the deacons of the Congregational church, and managers of the restaurant and general store to virtually take over the Commons for two weeks in late July and early August. This unspoiled setting, according to Warner Brothers, perfectly filled the bill for certain sequences of the film, which will star Jack Nicholson. (The identity of those cast as witches has not yet been disclosed.)

At a packed town council meeting last week, numerous people vociferously objected to the idea of turning downtown Little Compton into a movie set. One of the main concerns, of course, was that the activities of the movie company would disrupt the center of town during the busiest part of the season. The council president, the chairman of the state's film commission, and the governor had all expressed their support for the film, touting the potential economic benefits. "This will be one of the biggest pictures of the year," the film commission chairman was quoted as saying. "It could add six or eight million dollars to the state's income over eight weeks." The town council president, a redoubtable and outspoken woman who is no stranger to controversy, claimed that opponents of the film-making plans were "the same group of people who are against everything." She didn't name names.

Besides the confusion, traffic, and congestion that the moviemaking might cause, however, there was another concern expressed by some townsfolk—what might be called a moral objection, revolving around the nature, real or imagined, of Updike's novel. The "sexy witchcraft novel," as the *Providence Journal* described it, "is about three contemporary witches who practice their craft and participate in sexual orgies" in a town resembling Little Compton. Most disturbing to some people was that certain scenes might actually be filmed inside the handsome 150-year-old Congregational church. Warner Brothers, according to news reports, had "won cautious provisional approval" from the church deacons. A former president of Vassar College, identified in the *Journal* "as one of the few residents present at the town council meeting who had read the novel," said that "many people regard it as a dirty, dismal, depraved book. It deals with witchcraft . . . devil worshipers who promise to defile in every imaginable way the symbols of Christianity." These attributes apparently did not prevent him from reading the book through to the end. "I ask why any church should offer any cooperation at all," continued this gentleman, pointing out that in the book a church choirmaster plays the devil, who preaches from the church pulpit.

I have not read the book. But my wife has, and I apparently should be more concerned than I have been about the state of her soul. "It's funny," was her sole comment on the novel. She lent our copy to someone but we never got it back. In any event, townspeople who want to judge for themselves the true nature of Updike's fictional intentions can pick up a copy of *The Witches of Eastwick* from the big stack that has appeared next to the cash register at the general store. The Warner Brothers location scout rejected the demand of some townspeople that a copy of the movie's script be left at the town hall for examination by concerned citizens.

In one television news report about the controversy a picture of the church was juxtaposed with a split-second scene from the horror film *The Shining*, based on a novel by Stephen King, in which Nicholson appears as an ax-wielding madman. The news producer, exercising the restraint and sober judgment characteristic of his profession, had selected the most violent scene from one of Nicholson's most lurid movies to give TV viewers some flavor of what might be taking place in Little Compton the summer. This may mark the first time that Stephen King and John Updike have been connected, however tenuously, as artistic equals.

The decision about whether the movie will be made here is in abeyance. The church deacons have reportedly made up their minds about whether they will permit use of the church for the film, but are withholding a public announcement until they have informed the congregation's members by mail. The town council has tabled the matter until its next meeting; the council president claims that four of the board's five members favor giving the film-makers approval to proceed. And opponents of the whole idea have already gathered more than 100 signatures on a petition against the film. As for me, I intend to be the first person in line when the call goes out for extras.

(1986)

POSTSCRIPT: Faced with resistance in Little Compton, Warner Brothers quickly located several seaside Massachusetts communities, including Cohasset, Scituate, and Marblehead, eager to lend their New England scenery and charms to the film's production. The actresses Cher, Michelle Pfeiffer, and Susan Sarandon played the witches of Eastwick. The movie, released in 1987, proved to be a commercial success and a showcase for the comic talents of its stars. John Updike's last novel, published in 2008 shortly before his death, was *The Widows of Eastwick*. Critics were not kind to the sequel, in which the three possessed women return to the community in their later years. The general store in Little Compton still operates, under different ownership. The pot-belly stove was removed long ago and a gift shop has replaced such merchandise as work clothes, animal feed, and serious hardware. The last dairy farm has closed. The population of the town, according to the 2010 census, was 3,492, representing a decline of 101 residents over the previous decade. Little Compton has changed in other ways since 1986.

The Mitten Woman: A Short Story

I barely recognized my own ancient handwriting when Claudia Reed, the town clerk, brought me the old leather-bound journal. Its spine read, "Overseers of the Poor. Town of Atwater," and she had come across the book while moving the town's records to a vault in the new "municipal building" (there had been quite a fuss about whether to call the place the "town hall"). Claudia thought I might be interested in seeing the document before she locked it away for posterity's sake, along with some of the town's other old records.

Those stiff yellowing pages contain the history, however cryptic and sketchy, of the last fifty years or so of the Atwater Poor Farm. The journal consisted almost entirely of lists—page after page of names, dates, inventories, and accounts. And it also included the minutes of the meetings of the overseers of the poor. During the last few years of the farm's existence as a town institution, I had been the person who filled those pages.

I came to the farm fresh out of Atwater Academy in 1921, when I married Hollis Brewster, only a month after my graduation. Hollis, strange as it seems to say, was my brother-in-law before that. But my sister Elvira had died while giving birth to a stillborn child. Hollis and she had been the farm's caretakers for several years, and after Elvira's death, Hollis, who would always been dear to our family, needed help. I came every day after school to cook dinner for the residents and to keep the kitchen clean.

When Hollis, who was twelve years older than I, asked me to marry him, I was shocked, and so were my parents. But he was so modest, steady, and handsome man, it took me only a few days to understand that what I felt for Hollis was what any woman would feel for the man she loved. So, young and inexperienced as I was, I became Hollis Brewster's wife, and together we presided over the last years of the Atwater Poor Farm.

At that time there were only two other people living in the stark but handsome building—a massive symmetrical structure with a large ell extending from each side of the central house. It was erected in 1870 to replace an older and dilapidated farmhouse, at a time when as many as twenty of the town's unfortunates were living there. In some years, according to the journal, more than 300 transients stopped for lodging and food. It had once been a lively, active place, if not always a happy one. By the time I joined Hollis there, however, it was eerily silent, the house's emptiness echoing the melancholy, forgotten stories of its former residents.

In those years the "town farms," or "poor farms," or "almshouses" were closing all over the state, or had long since closed down. They had become financial burdens to towns as the state took on more and more of the functions these institutions had served for so long. Townsfolk, of course, had never broken down the doors to get into the poor farm. Some, in fact, struggled to get out. A big crack in a closet door, the story had it, was made by one of the inmates, who, in a fit of confused anger, rampaged through the building, swinging an ax wildly. There was always a stigma attached to being reduced to such desperate straits as having to take up residence at the farm. A few widows and widowers, cripples, destitute mothers with broods of children, drunkards, the "insane" and the "idiotic," vagrants, men looking for work—such were the folk who sought refuge there at one time or another. Their names and ages and conditions were all listed in this ledger on the table in front of me. My handwriting from that era looked so youthful and innocent to me now, so many decades later. But as I read through what I had recorded during the years I lived at the farm, I saw a name which brought memories of that time back to me in full flood—Lizzy Connors, the sad, sweet, helpless woman who had once, at least for a while, kept the town's conscience alive.

"Lizzy Connor's eyes are troubling her," read the notes of the overseers for April 29, 1911. Six months later the board voted "to change the stove in Lizzy's room and put a wire netting around, so to keep Lizzy from falling on it as she is nearly blind." When I moved to the farm to join Hollis, Lizzy was totally blind, but her perennial good spirits hadn't diminished at all. In spite of the grim and narrow possibilities of Lizzy's life—or perhaps somehow because of them—the town looked after her with what seems, from today's perspective, a remarkable tenderness.

"Frank Callahan died this morning at seven o'clock," reads the entry I made on December 25, 1921—Christmas Day. "His church took charge of his remains and buried them. No expense." Frank Callahan and Lizzy had for many years been virtually the only two residents of the farm, and Frank hadn't even spent all of his time there. A native of Ireland, and a bachelor, he first came to the farm in 1905 at the age of 64. Quiet and "temperate" (in the old sense, that is: not a drinker), he was also a proud man. He paid board to the town, and came and went periodically, doing such odd jobs as carpentry and farm work, as long as his none-too-durable constitution could stand it, which usually wasn't very long. When he died that Christmas Day in 1921, Lizzy Connors became the only remaining full-time resident of the Atwater Poor Farm, other than Hollis and I in our roles as caretakers. I remember well—it hadn't come to mind for years—the next monthly meeting of the overseers.

"What shall we do about Lizzy?" Arthur Harwood, the chairman of the Atwater board of selectmen and thereby of the overseers of the poor, sat at the head of the long table in the Poor Farm's big kitchen. As he asked the question, he looked first at Reuben Quigley, who sat to his right, then at Chester Bickford, who was on his left. Hollis and I sat at the other end of the table, which had been built for the room in the days when twenty or more of the farm's residents would sit down together at mealtime. And Lizzy, the subject of Harwood's question, sat impassively in chair near the stove, rocking steadily, humming her nonsense tunes and knitting, as she did for hour on end, day after day.

Knitting was the one skill Lizzy had, and lucky it had been, too, that a former caretaker's wife took the time and trouble to teach Lizzy years ago. It was something she could keep after even when her eyes were no longer of any use to her. Lizzy had learned to knit mittens—she worked on nothing else. And year after year, at the rate of almost exactly one mitten a week, two pairs a month, she turned them out. When there were more people at the farm, she gave her handiwork to the other residents and transients. In later years, her mittens had gone to Reverend Spaulding, who each Christmas handed them out to those who might be in need. Indeed, as her durable products became known and appreciated, she earned a title around town—the Mitten Woman. In her small but useful way, Lizzy over the years touched the lives of probably hundreds of her fellow townsfolk, returning some of the charity they had extended to her, not always gladly and willingly.

Lizzy, you see, had lived at the farm for almost half a century, outlasting a few generations of selectmen and caretakers. I looked back in the journal and learned that she arrived with her mother and four other sisters in 1872, after the family was abandoned to the town's mercy by one Thomas Connors. Earlier, with another sister, Rebecca, twelve years her senior, Lizzy had spent some time at the town's expense in the Boston Idiotic School, an institution for children like herself. Lizzy and Rebecca were sturdy and healthy girls, but simple and witless ones, just able to care for themselves and, in their younger days, do a few chores around the farm. Their mother, the records show, left the farm a few years later; two of Lizzy's sisters, listed as "sane," were also described as having "run away." Thus were Lizzy and Rebecca left to make their lifelong home at the Atwater Town Farm. Rebecca died in 1910, according to the journal, after a long period of ill health.

"The farm cost us twenty-five-hundred dollars last year," Quigley said. Keeper of the general store, he could always be counted upon to look first at the dollars and cents involved in any matter before the town. "We've been putting this off long enough. I think it's time to put the farm up for sale. Almost every other town in the county has closed down its poor farm. We can find a place for Lizzy over at the state asylum."

"Sarah says she hasn't been well. Doctor Spofford's been here and says she's just getting over a pretty bad case of pneumonia," Bickford pointed out. "If we sent her off now, especially to a place like that, it could be her doom."

Lizzy continued her rocking and humming and knitting. If she had heard and understood the conversation, she made no sign of acknowledgment.

"Well, I've had plenty of complaints. People were unhappy enough when it was just Frank and Lizzy. Now they're asking me whether it makes sense to run the farm for nobody but Lizzy Connors."

Arthur Harwood took off his twisted wire-rimmed glasses and placed them on the table, rubbing the bridge of his nose with his free hand. The other two recognized the gestures as Harwood's way of indicating that he had something he wanted to say.

"Of course, there have always been complaints about the farm," Harwood began, passing his hand slowly over his bald head, as if as if there was still hair there to sweep back. "The town's kept a place for more than 100 years now, as I understand it. I guess we all know that when Lizzy goes, that's the end of it. And that will suit a lot of people, I suppose. 'Let the state take care of it,' they'll say, and we'll end up sending all our sick and retarded and whoever else has problems to live in some cold brick castle up on a hill somewhere, where nobody has to see them or think about them.

"Lizzy was born the same year I was," he continued. "She's lived in Atwater almost all her life. I don't think I'd be very happy if I were shipped out. We've taken care of our own in this town as long as anyone can remember, gentlemen. Times are changing, I know. But sending Lizzy off would be like sending my own kin off. I don't think I have the heart to close the place now."

"We've got to be practical about this, Arthur," Quigley replied. "We can't let our sentiments get the best of us—at least when there are tax dollars at stake. And the money this farm might bring would go a long way towards covering the cost of the new school that's coming up before the town meeting."

Hollis, a laconic man who rarely spoke up at these monthly meetings unless asked a direct question, had something to say. "You don't have to keep the farm going on our account, gentlemen. But, of course, you know that anyway. Sarah and I will be able to find work. We've been thinking about trying to buy some orchard land. But as for Lizzy, I don't think she'd be well looked after elsewhere. This is her home, just as Mr. Harwood says. She's no trouble really. Why, if we had a place of our own and a few extra dollars, we'd take her in ourselves."

Lizzy was old enough to be my grandmother then. But Hollis and I had begun to think of her almost as our child—for, indeed, she was a child. I knew, though, that what he was suggesting was impossible, given our own financial situation. We were lucky to have the town supply us with a roof over our heads, and we were able to provide ourselves with much of our food from the farm's production, but the four-hundred-dollar annual salary for the two of us did not allow for much saving—and we did have a child of our own on the way. I knew how far we were from Hollis's dream of owning his own apple orchard.

"That's all very well and good, Hollis," said Quigley. "Not very realistic, though, and you know it. I'd like to make a motion that we place Lizzy Connors in the state hospital and that we put an article on the town-meeting warrant requesting the town's permission to sell the Atwater Poor Farm."

I was writing quickly to capture the wording of Quigley's motion. Lizzy, I noticed, had folded up her knitting, placed it in the box she kept next to her chair, and begun making her way across the kitchen to the stairway. With the help of a few familiar landmarks and some ropes that Hollis had strung throughout the house to help Lizzy get her bearings, she was wending her way to the bedroom at the other end of the rambling house.

"Good night, Lizzy," I said.

"'Night, Mrs. Brewster," she replied in her slow sing-song voice. "'Night, Mr. Brewster."

"Good night, Lizzy," Hollis said.

Lizzy had nothing to say to the other men, and they only watched her, somewhat uncomfortably, as she shuffled across the room.

"Doesn't she need any help?" Chester Bickford asked me. "How does she know where she's going?"

"She's slept every night in this building for years, Mr. Bickford," I said, feeling more than a little angered at what I consider to be the callousness of Reuben Quigley's motion. "She doesn't need her eyesight to know where she is."

Arthur Harwood was watching Lizzy ascend the stairs, shaking his head side to side slightly. There was a long spell of silence; then he said, "Well, I guess we should put Reuben's motion up to a vote. All in favor?"

"Aye!" Quigley snapped, looking first at Harwood, then at Bickford, who was concentrating on his hands placed flat on the table.

"I vote nay," said Harwood. "Chet?"

"And I vote nay, as well," Bickford said, raising his eyes to look at both men squarely. "I'm not sure the place would bring all that much right now, anyway."

It wasn't a big event in the annals of the town, keeping the farm going for Lizzy's sake. As it turned out, she was to spend just one more year there before the influenza took her. But looking back now, I know that Atwater lost something when Lizzy died and the Poor Farm was sold. Atwater, it seems to me, began to take on some of this century's harshness; we became less of a community, more inured to the difficulties of our fellow townsfolk. I know better than to sentimentalize the Poor Farm. It was not a happy place for most of those who had to live part of their lives there. But for some it was a decent, human place. For a few, like Lizzy Connors, it was the only place they could ever really call home.

The poor farm, so vast and well-built, has, in an ironical twist, been purchased by the town to be turned into housing for the elderly. The building has character, to be sure; but the question of what to call the place is a touchy one—no self-respecting retiree, after all, wishes to use the phrase "poor farm" for an address. So it is called simply Atwater Orchards, memorializing Hollis's efforts. In the end we had purchased the property. Because of the house's size, it had proved difficult to sell, so the selectmen gave us a mortgage on the place on very generous terms. Hollis transformed the accompanying acreage into one of the most prosperous orchards in the area, and during the summer and fall we ran a sort of inn for city folks. When Hollis died, our daughter and her husband continued running the orchard, and I sold the house to fellow who converted it into a few apartments.

I gather that I am eligible to take up residence there, now that the new housing authority owns the property. But I think I will pass up the opportunity and hold onto my little apartment in the center of town—at least as long as I can still make it up two flights of stairs. The memories of the past would be too sharp, too vivid. I would picture Hollis out the window, working among his trees, and Lizzy in her chair knitting, as if none of us had ever left, as if time itself had stopped.

(1988)

POSTSCRIPT: Though this story is a work of fiction, it is inspired by a real person and set of circumstances. In 1975, when I was working for the *Harvard Post*, I wrote a story about the history of the poor farm in Harvard, Massachusetts. The building survives still as a substantial, austerely handsome private home. In the course of researching that article, I reviewed the town's records of the Overseers of the Poor. There, in cryptic form, was the biography of a woman, also named Elizabeth, whose life roughly followed the trajectory and chronology described in this story. That real-life "Lizzy" spent 66 years as a resident of the Harvard Poor Farm. Indeed, some of the quotations from the record of the fictional "Atwater" Overseers of the Poor are used almost verbatim from the Harvard records. My sentimental account of the demise of the Atwater Poor Farm, including such characters as the selectmen/overseers, Sarah and Hollis Brewster, and Lizzy Connors herself, is otherwise wholly a product of my imagination.

The Wilderness Within

"It was a cyst!" My friend called the morning after her surgery, giddy with relief. A decade ago, she had weathered a bout with breast cancer, so she had every reason to expect the worst this time. To the surprise of her doctors, though, the new growth was benign. She had won another reprieve from fear and fate.

The news had been a welcome gift on her husband's 50th birthday. A commercial fisherman, he was accustomed to the hazards and uncertainties of creating a livelihood along our rugged stretch of southern New England shoreline. The long minutes he spent in a clinic waiting room, wondering how the biopsy results might alter their lives, may have been more fearful than his most precarious experiences at sea.

He sets out on his marine rounds from a tiny harbor marking the southeastern point of the Rhode Island coastline. Our small town, Little Compton, is nestled into a geographical cul-de-sac, a quiet corner of this densely populated American state in the heart of the northeastern megalopolis. Bounded on two sides by the ocean, unconnected by bridges, railroad lines, or other major highways to the rest of the region, our community has kept its head down throughout history. It has escaped, so far, the most destructive waves of development that have swept up and down the coast.

The result has been fortunate for the landscape and for those of us who live here. A variety of farms still survive, some adapting to new markets, others providing leisurely retreats for the better off. Conservation groups and government agencies have been at work, buying up beaches, marshes, farms, and other open lands—preserving them undisturbed for future generations. A long-established colony of summer folk flock here to guard zealously their stately old vacation homes and motley little cottages, hoping and expecting that from year to year things will not change.

It is, in certain ways, a community of privilege. But if we dodge some of the social strains and troubles so many other places must endure, we are not immune from other fundamental powers and influences. Poised at the margin of sea and land, ours is an environment where the dynamics of the natural world can never be ignored. Hurricanes and northeasters pummel us with unnerving regularity. Beaches erode, breakwaters are breached, ancient trees are uprooted—but people clean up and carry on.

The town has tried to keep the world at bay. To an extent others envy, we've succeeded. But neither are we exempt from forces—economic, social, political, demographic—which affect the rest of the world and transform the natural terrain.

We learned that, my friend and I, in the mid-1980s when the US Air Force announced its plans to build in our town an antenna installation for the Ground Wave Emergency Network (GWEN). In the nuclear age, every city and village in the world is a potential battlefield. But this fact took on a more ominous and concrete reality when we learned that our community appeared on Air Force maps as a "node" in the military's vision of a nationwide war-communications network. GWEN was designed to function after the "electromagnetic pulse" (EMP) generated by an enemy nuclear attack had knocked out other forms of electronic communication.

The Air Force's proposed site, for which it had already secured a lease, was set between a quiet residential area and the largest undeveloped tract of land in our rural town. This location was an enticement to the Air Force, not an obstacle. To many of us who lived here, the proposal was an outrage—not least because the Air Force's own environmental impact study seemed to rule out just such a setting.

Mustering all the righteousness expected of self-respecting NIMBY crusaders, we mobilized a No-GWEN Alliance, loosely affiliated with groups throughout the country where the Air Force proposed to build similar installations. To the chagrin and surprise of many, we won our battle locally. Stopped cold by a court injunction, the Air Force backed off. And as the Cold War came to an abrupt end, the threat on which the military had based its ghastly nuclear war-fighting scenario virtually evaporated. GWEN was not eliminated, but the program's size was significantly reduced from the Air Force's original grandiose conception. Starting at home, we helped accomplish something important; its effects reverberated across the country.

Our victory and our experiences as activists had created new friendships and bonds, bringing together people who might not otherwise have come to know each other. Idealists all, we learned the practical skills and techniques of political mobilization. We wrote press releases, organized public meetings, appeared at hearings, filed testimony and appeals under environmental law, lobbied politicians, raised money—and met relentlessly.

Perhaps we were inspired by the presence of the town's old Quaker meeting house. Meticulously maintained by the local historical society, the austere but attractive building usually sits empty and unused every day of the year save one. On Thanksgiving, it is the setting for an unpretentious and moving interdenominational service. During our own less peaceable meetings, we borrowed from the local Quaker tradition by talking out our differences, searching for consensus about strategy, tactics, and politics.

At one of our early meetings, as I looked around the room, I realized that of the twenty or so present, many of us, including myself, had at one time or another experienced cancer or some other serious medical crisis firsthand. There may have been others present whose experiences and illnesses I was not aware of. The woman who had bravely stepped forward first to protest publicly the Air Force's plans had only recently lost her husband to cancer. She herself was in remission from breast cancer. Eventually she lost her private battle with the disease—but only after the public battle she initiated had been one.

Many of us were in our thirties and forties. Baby boomers, children of the 1960s, we shared a generational bond. Those of us who had known life-threatening disease shared another unspoken connection as well. "The language of Friendship is not words, but meanings," wrote Thoreau in *A Week on the Concord and Merrimack Rivers*, his first grand reverie on the seamless continuity between one's home and the rest of the cosmos. "It is an intelligence above language."

We relied on such wordless meanings to soothe the sting of barbs flung our way by some fellow townsfolk, who called us unpatriotic, naive, and worse. But epithets and name-calling could not really hurt us. We had weathered more gut-wrenching threats and fears.

We survivors were now impelled to make the most of our time, to seek out and act on essentials and first principles, even if we didn't always succeed. The horizon of our lives had shifted in a manner impossible to communicate to others who hadn't gone through the same experience. We hoped to live out our full span of years. But we knew, for certain, that a year hence, depending upon the cellular roulette wheel embedded in our bodies, we could be gone. This was simply a matter of fact, not something to feel righteous about.

This new awareness of time's essence can be calming, empowering. "Time measures nothing but itself," Thoreau observes in *A Week*, putting time in its place. My own anxieties about career, money, family, and future do not disappear. But I find a degree of liberation and comfort in knowing that time—my lifetime, I should say—is a matter largely beyond my control.

We have since shared in other local battles over our landscape and community. The very source of our vulnerability is also, in fundamental ways, the source of our determination and strength. We know of friends and acquaintances who haven't had our luck. Our memory of them also pushes us on.

We do not feel quite healthy unless we know we are doing what we can to keep our local landscape and community alive. "It may be that the most radical act we can commit is to stay at home," writes Utah naturalist Terry Tempest Williams in her essay "The Wild Card." Some of us stay home with a vengeance. We can measure our sense of well-being by our will to cause trouble.

We are relative newcomers to a town where some families can trace their local ancestry back to colonial times, when settlers had gone to war with the Wampanoag Indians. For a time I served as a trustee of the local library with a man who was only the third person to chair the board in its 115-year history. His two predecessors had been his father and grandfather.

This kind of indigenous rootedness not infrequently stirred resentment and hostility. Us pushy outlanders were regarded as troublemakers and loudmouths. "That's not how things are done in this town," we would hear. If we ignored—and proved wrong—such tenets of local dogma, it was only because we cared for our home place as much as they did.

Recently, the state and The Nature Conservancy collaborated to acquire as a recreational and wildlife preserve the 400 acres that encompassed the proposed GWEN site. Nearby, in what would have been the skeletal shadow of the tower, a number of houses have gone up, providing homes for members of long-time town families. Traveling through this part of town, those of us who took on the Air Force find satisfaction—and a measure of vindication—in our knowledge of what is *not* there: the three-hundred-foot antenna, capped with a round-the-clock strobe light, surrounded by a chain-link fence. A place that would have been a grim benchmark of the nuclear landscape remains woven into the fabric of a living community—comprising people, land, water, wildlife.

Across town, an old lighthouse stands among the reefs and islands that claw into the sea from the harbor. A benevolent counterpart of the phantom GWEN tower, its beacon was extinguished by the Coast Guard years ago. After its abandonment, a private owner maintained the storm-battered structure, then sold it for a pittance to local enthusiasts who hope someday to see its dormant beacon flash again. Some see the effort as frivolous, an expensive exercise in nostalgia. I'm grateful for my fellow citizens' concern and commitment, however. The lighthouse they cherish is a symbol of the place that is our home.

We survivors here have been at the mercy of fate, doctors, medicines, and machines to battle cells run wild. Along the shore, we know that our lives, in every dimension, are always lived on the edge. The dynamic landscape and seascape that enfold us echo the fragile ecology of our individual bodies. Our immediate surroundings combine the wild and domestic, inseparably. There we look for strength and inspiration, to gird against the next cellular storm that may try to overwhelm us.

(1997)

POSTSCRIPT: The collapse of the Soviet Union and the end of the Cold War in the late 1980s quickly undermined the official justification for GWEN. Rapid technological change also rendered the system obsolete. By 1994, Congress had stopped funding the construction of new GWEN towers. The Air Force shortly thereafter stopped building towers for which funds had already been appropriated, and then began to dismantle the system. By the late 1990s, GWEN had been substantially replaced by a satellite communication system called Milstar. The Sakonnet Lighthouse was in fact reactivated in 1997. By 2010 the Friends of the Sakonnet Lighthouse had raised more than $1.5-million, including a substantial federal grant, to initiate a substantial renovation of the structure. Some of the members of the No-GWEN Alliance (not including myself) have been faithful participants in a weekly peace vigil, initiated in 2003 before the American invasion of Iraq, which has met every Sunday morning without fail on the Little Compton Commons.

Goosewing Beach

On a recent frigid Sunday, I laced up my ancient hockey skates and traversed Quicksand Pond, from its northern end for more than a mile due south to the ocean. I glided through the pond's icebound breach-way, which slices across the dunes of Goosewing Beach.

It was a disorienting sensation to skate along the beach, just a few feet from the breaking surf. Only a few days later, when the temperature briefly rose above freezing, the breachway opened, dropping the pond's level several feet. By the end of the week, gulls, Canada geese, swans, and ducks were filling an ice-free expanse of the pond just behind the beach. The breachway was a rushing torrent, spilling into the sea.

Such dramatic natural changes are common along this stretch of the Rhode Island shore, where the sea, sky, and land meet. Indeed, in only a few months the same span of beach on which I skated will be taken over by piping plovers (*Charadrius melodus*). The small, sand-colored shorebird that breeds and nests here has been listed by the U.S. Fish and Wildlife Service as a threatened species, under the provisions of the Endangered Species Act.

Many Rhode Islanders know that this magnificent, easternmost crescent of the state's shoreline has been the subject of much heated rhetoric and controversy in recent years. In 1987 several Little Compton town boards, The Nature Conservancy, and other local conservation groups formed the Goosewing Preservation Coalition, to raise funds to buy various rights to and interests in the beach and the adjoining farm.

The state Department of Environmental Management offered to finance part of the purchase with the proceeds of open space and recreation bonds. The private owners—the Truesdale Trust—had for decades operated Goosewing as a recreational beach open to the public for a fee. The coalition's stated goal was to keep the beach "open for wildlife protection and public enjoyment."

The Nature Conservancy, committed to protecting the habitat of the piping plover and other threatened species, took the lead in raising almost $3 million from foundations and individuals. But the coalition's solidarity began to crack when some Little Compton citizens and town officials raised questions about access to the beach, parking and traffic problems, the status of "historic rights" that town residents may already hold in the property, and the prospect that the state might assume control of the beach.

In 1989, despite such disputed matters, the Conservancy purchased from the Truesdale Trust the 63-acre beach and 12 acres of upland, as well as conservation easements on another 66 acres of farmland and pond shoreline.

Ever since, the status of Goosewing Beach has remained a subject of passionate debate in Little Compton. In 1992, a Democratic-controlled Town Council, over the protests of the independently elected Beach Commission, negotiated a deal with the Conservancy. The Conservancy agreed to transfer to the town its title to the beach without financial compensation.

The Conservancy retained a conservation-and-recreation easement on the property and secured the town's agreement to a detailed beach-management plan. Among other provisions, the plan bound the town to erect a seasonal bridge, purchased by the Conservancy, across a creek separating the parking lot of the town-owned South Shore Beach from the former parking lot at adjacent Goosewing. By these means, nonresidents of the town would have continued access to parking and to the beach. The plan also provided that if the town didn't fulfill its obligations within three years, the Conservancy could exercise a "reverter" clause and reclaim its title to the beach.

Political events and the forces of nature, including storms that battered local beaches, forestalled erection of the bridge. A new Republican-controlled Town Council and a feisty Beach Commission insisted that the management plan gave the Conservancy too much control over what was now supposed to be town property. The Truesdale Trust proclaimed its intention to protect aggressively some of its remaining rights in the property.

Meanwhile, last spring, heedless of the contentious Rhode Island humans, piping plovers winged their way northward toward Goosewing, as they have for untold centuries. And the Beach Commission and the Conservancy, almost in spite of themselves, muddled toward an approach to managing Goosewing that accommodates the recreational needs of beachgoers while protecting the piping plover.

The hard-working volunteer commission and its young staff proved their ability to manage a clean, safe recreational beach. Last summer, the commission stationed two lifeguards on Goosewing, close to the rope fences that Conservancy wardens have erected to protect piping plover nests. While lifeguards patrolled the shore, Conservancy staffers and volunteers kept a close eye on the birds and their human neighbors, educating beachgoers in a soft-spoken manner about the plovers' behavior and life history.

For their part, the plovers flourished. Eight adult pairs fledged 21 plover chicks last summer—more than twice 1992's number and the season's highest fledging rate along the Atlantic Coast, according to Griff Venator, a Conservancy staffer long involved in the Goosewing effort.

In July, in response to some of the town's concerns, the Conservancy proposed to renegotiate certain terms of the 1992 management plan. In a letter to the Town Council, Keith Lang, the group's Rhode Island director, offered to abandon the requirement that the town erect a bridge to the former Goosewing parking area. In exchange, however, the Conservancy sought a commitment that 65 percent of the South Shore parking lot be reserved for nonresidents. Some town officials bridled at this proposal. "Unacceptable," replied the town solicitor. "It's not even negotiable," said the Beach Commission chairwoman. The Conservancy also sought to retain "sole authority" to manage the piping plover habitat.

Last September, an "Ad Hoc Committee on Goosewing Beach," comprising two members of the Town Council, drafted (and the council accepted) a two-page report describing some of the town's concerns. The report barely addressed the specific proposals offered by Lang however, such as the parking alternatives for nonresidents. Except for the possibility of installing new public bath facilities on the Goosewing property and the uncertainty of successfully defending the town's disputed rights to the beach, the council concluded that "there is no value added to the town in granting any concessions to the Nature Conservancy."

The council forwarded its report to the Conservancy, but it has initiated no other direct contacts with the Conservancy or its lawyers. Lang wrote the council again in November, but still has not heard from any town board or official to discuss amending the management plan.

We who live in Little Compton have the good fortune to enjoy daily landscapes and seascapes that others envy. Such blessings are accompanied by responsibilities, though. Perhaps we can view Goosewing as an opportunity rather than a problem, a privilege not a burden.

In any event, Little Compton town officials, including the Town Council and the Beach Commission, should stop dawdling. Rather than complaining and pointing fingers, they should sit down and negotiate with The Nature Conservancy and other interested parties a resolution to the issues surrounding this modest but controversial sliver of Rhode Island terrain.

Many local residents, in fact, believe that Goosewing Beach is now available for public use and enjoyment because of the efforts of the Conservancy and the presence of the piping plover—not, as certain town officials have suggested, in spite of them. But some citizens now fear that the town's reluctance to fulfill or renegotiate the terms of the management plan will force the Conservancy to reclaim the deed to the property next year, as the plan provides. In that event, recreational use of the beach could be much more severely restricted, for residents and nonresidents alike.

Soon, the piping plovers will be returning once again to Goosewing Beach. We in Little Compton can, if we choose, accept the important responsibility of cooperating with the Conservancy and the US Fish and Wildlife Service to preserve the piping plover and its beautiful, subtly complex habitat. At the same time we can help preserve the opportunity for people (no matter their hometown) to use and enjoy the beach.

Our own survival and quality of life may very well hinge on our ability to protect the survival and quality of life of other species, however humble.

(1994)

POSTSCRIPT: In the months subsequent to the publication of this February, 1994 piece in the *Providence Journal*, little progress was made in discussions between The Nature Conservancy and the Town of Little Compton. In December 1995, TNC exercised the "reverter clause" in its 1992 agreement with the town. At that time, it reclaimed its title to the 75-acre beach parcel and conveyed the conservation-and-recreation easement on the parcel back to the Little Compton Agricultural Conservancy Trust, the semi-autonomous town agency that held the easement for several years after the original 1989 acquisition of the property. One of the consequences of this outcome was that projected funding for the project from the Rhode Island Department of Environmental Management was withheld; TNC therefore did not receive expected reimbursement of $875,000, a condition of which had been guaranteed parking for non-residents of Little Compton. Despite some heated rhetoric after TNC reclaimed its title to the beach, the town did not legally challenge TNC's action, nor has it done so since.

As a practical matter, little has changed in the operation and management of the beach in the more than fifteen years since these events. TNC did not seek to prevent public recreational use of the beach, and the Beach Commission continued to provide lifeguard services on at least the western portion of Goosewing Beach. Public access to the beach is available on foot from the town's parking lot at adjacent South

Shore Beach. Town residents have free access to this public lot; non-residents pay a fee. On busy summer days, the parking lot quickly fills up, and some beachgoers are turned away.

For legal and liability purposes, though, the TNC and the town still needed a formal legal agreement to maintain the operational status quo. After reclaiming its title to the beach property in 1995, Doug Parker, Keith Lang's successor at TNC, proposed to the Beach Commission that the two parties adopt a year-to-year agreement, based on some of the provisions in draft documents developed during the previous fruitless negotiations. The provisions of this brief agreement dealt with, among other things, lifeguard services, wildlife management, and the use of an existing shed for storage of equipment by the town. As for questions of legal title and "historic rights," the agreement basically declared a truce. Prior to the 1996 beach season, the agreement was adopted; with occasional minor revisions, it has since been renewed annually by TNC and the Beach Commission.

The Nature Conservancy has continued to devote considerable resources to the management of Goosewing Beach and to the conservation of other lands comprising the watershed of Quicksand and Tunipus ponds. In 1995, TNC helped facilitate acquisition of the Simmons Mill Pond Management Area by the state of Rhode Island. The area comprises more than 450 acres, including the headwaters of the major streams that feed Quicksand Pond. In 2010, TNC dedicated a new Benjamin Family Environmental Center on the site of an old caretaker's cottage directly behind the beach. In addition to its continuing management of the breeding habitat of the piping plover, TNC has also been involved in controlling invasive species such as *Phragmites australis* (common reed) and breaching the outlet of Quicksand Pond in an attempt to bolster the species of alewives and herring that spawn in the pond's watershed streams.

A looming question concerning the future of barrier beaches like Goosewing is the documented process of rising sea level, perhaps related to global warming and climate change. Veteran University of Rhode Island geologist Jon C. Boothroyd in 2008 told the U.S. Senate Committee on Environmental and Public Works that the demonstrably accelerating rate of sea level rise could, by 2100, result in a mean sea level some 3.5 feet higher than today's. Aerial photographs and other direct measurements since the late 1930s demonstrate that the Goosewing shoreline has retreated as much as 100 feet over that period, at a rate of more than one foot a year.

"There will always be a beach," Boothroyd has been wont so say. "It will just be in another place."

Sakonnet Point

The forces of nature and the desires of people collide at Little Compton's Sakonnet Point, the promontory overlooking the entrance of the Sakonnet River. A proposal for the point's development is wending its way through the regulatory and permitting process. If approved by local, state, and federal agencies, the planned Sakonnet Point Club could dramatically alter both the physical aspect of the point and the public's access to the shoreline at this scenic oceanfront locale.

As proposed, the Sakonnet Point Club would be a private marina. Plans call for storage of 94 boats in dry racks on the vacant lot (referred to locally as Lot 433) on the south side of Bluff Head Avenue, which bisects the club's property. The project includes a 63-foot boat-launching pier, a lifting crane, a boat ramp adjacent to the existing breakwater, a floating dock, and parking for 106 cars. A clubhouse and pool would occupy the site of the old Fo'c'sle Restaurant, on a separate lot north of Bluff Head Avenue. (The once-popular seasonal restaurant overlooking Sakonnet Harbor served its last clam fritter more than a decade ago; it is now a dilapidated hulk.) The proposed clubhouse would accommodate a membership that now stands at more than 200 families, according to recent reports. Anyone willing to pay the $6,000 entrance fee, say the club's officials, is free to join.

Proponents assert that the club would improve the appearance of Sakonnet Point, which has never recovered from the restaurant's closing or from failed development plans in the 1990s and the effects of 1991's Hurricane Bob. For some Little Compton residents, both year-round and summer, the club would also address two social and recreational shortages: The few private beach and golf clubs have long waiting lists and escalating fees, and there is also a waiting list for the town's Sakonnet Harbor moorings.

Critics of the club have raised concerns about harbor congestion, the effects on water quality and marine life of a planned desalinization plant, increased motor-vehicle traffic, and the process by which town officials have provided approval for the project.

What seems to unite many of the critics—and may prove a special challenge for the Rhode Island Coastal Resources Management Council in considering the club's application—is the question of public access: to the shoreline (surrounding the seaward boundary of Lot 433) and to the adjacent breakwater.

For decades, the public has been able to drive to Sakonnet Point, park in the lot, and enjoy a spectacular panorama of ocean and shore. The parking on Lot 433 and at the end of Bluff Head Avenue has also provided access to the federally owned breakwater—often crowded with families and fishermen from all over.

This shoreline access may be severely restricted by the club's plans. The club has provided for 77 parking spaces on Lot 433—but for club use only. And the vista from Bluff Head Avenue would be obstructed by four 30-foot-tall boat-storage structures.

The club insists that public access for viewing will be "greatly enhanced" by its plans. Its proposal calls for a walkway around the shoreline perimeter of Lot 433, with two pedestrian-access points on Bluff Head Avenue. "No longer will the public have to trespass in a rubble-strewn asphalt area," the club wrote in a letter mailed to some citizens in July. The club has also provided for six public parking spaces next to its planned clubhouse—but these are not contiguous with the shoreline, the proposed walkway, or the breakwater. Nor do the plans for public parking provide access for the disabled comparable to the access they now have. ("Handicapped access to the public viewing area," the club's architect wrote the Coastal Resources Management Council, "will be accommodated by reservation through the Sakonnet Point Club.")

The CRMC wrote, in a report on its preliminary determination: "Many people believe this area provides one of the premier coastal views in Rhode Island." Calling the club's six planned public parking spaces "inadequate," the CRMC identified public access at the site as a "major concern." It said that a "substantial amount of public parking should be provided on Lot 433 with open views out to the sea."

In response, the club said that public access for cars on Lot 433 "is impossible" and, with the boat-storage operation and members' parking, would represent "an administrative nightmare." "The entire area of Sakonnet Point, both private and commercial, is eminently walkable," added the club, "so that public parking along Bluff Head Avenue to access Sakonnet Point Club's public walkway should not present the public an inconvenience."

As voiced by citizens in letters to the CRMC, the club's assurances of public access are dramatically at odds with their own experience. "This lot has been open to the public for many years," wrote an 87-year-old resident, who lived on Sakonnet Point before the hurricanes of 1938 and '44 swept away her family's home. "During the summer, there is a steady stream of traffic, people enjoying the beautiful view. It should remain open to the public, not just six places to park."

A somewhat younger resident wrote: "I have been able to go [to the point] for 33 years, to fish, to crab, to walk, to feel the cool breeze"—as did her parents and grandparents. "Before my grandfather died," she said, "his only joy was to drive to Sakonnet Point with a beer to watch the sunset and remember all the wonderful times he had had, especially with his wife."

Another resident described the scene on a recent summer Sunday: He counted 71 people on the breakwater—fishing, walking, or simply sitting on lawn chairs. "These are not wealthy people," he wrote; "rather, they are people of many races, colors, and nationalities, from very young to very old. They are just regular people and/or poor people trying to relax by the water and catch some scup, tautog, flounder, or bluefish to eat."

Officers of the club point out that Little Compton voters, at a financial town meeting in 1994, missed the chance to preserve the current level of parking and public access when they rejected funding from the Department of Environmental Management to buy Lot 433. But some residents have recently created a nonprofit corporation, the Sakonnet Harbor Conservancy, in the hope of raising funds to acquire the properties for public use, including parking.

Still, the club proceeds with its plans. If the Sakonnet Point Club is built, opportunities for access to this important Rhode Island seaside setting will shift significantly—in favor of the club's members and at the expense of the public. The club's members and directors are motivated, well financed, and well represented; who speaks for the public interest at Sakonnet Point?

(2002)

POSTSCRIPT: The Sakonnet Point Club received its required permit from the Rhode Island Coastal Resources Management Council in 2004 and opened for business in 2008. At the time, the club claimed a membership of 272 families. The permit provided for the same level of public parking and public access to the shoreline proposed in 2002. The paved walkway around the perimeter of Lot 433 is separated from the club parking and boat storage lot by a wooden rail fence. The club provided the six public parking spaces adjacent to its clubhouse—a building designed to suggest shorefront pavilions more likely to have been seen in, say, Newport a century ago than in Little Compton. The club agreed, at least for the immediate future and perhaps as a reflection of demand, not to construct on Lot 433 the dry racks for boat storage depicted in the original plan. Instead, all boats on the lot are stored on trailers. Though its character changes and evolves, Sakonnet Point remains a busy, crowded area during the summer months.

Time, Memory, Landscape

In July 1621, Edward Winslow and Stephen Hopkins, two leaders of the recently established Plymouth Colony, set out on the Pilgrims' first diplomatic mission inland. Their destination was the village of Sowams, in what is today Warren, Rhode Island, to meet Massasoit, sachem of the Pokanoket Indians. Guided by the English-speaking Indian Squanto, they traveled first to the Indian village of Nemasket, fifteen miles inland from Plymouth, then south along with Taunton River to Mount Hope Bay, home territory of the Pokanokets, a Wampanoag tribe.

Along the way "the Englishman learned that to walk across the land in southern New England was to travel in time," as author Nathaniel Philbrick writes in his deservedly best-selling recent book, *Mayflower: A Story of Courage, Community, and War* (2006). On their trek from Plymouth to Sowams, Winslow and Hopkins noticed the abundance of well-maintained circular holes, a foot deep, all along the well-traveled path. These small man-made pits were not just navigational waymarkers, they learned from their Indian companions, but mnemonic landmarks intended "to inform fellow travelers of what had once happened at that particular place so that 'many things of great antiquity are fresh in memory,'" Philbrick writes. "Winslow and Hopkins began to see that they were traversing a mythic land, where a sense of community extended far into the distant past."

I read Philbrick's passage about the Wampanoag's "memory holes" with particular interest. In July 2005 I spent a stimulating day with the author, traversing Little Compton and Tiverton in search of sites related to some of the events and personalities he describes so vividly in *Mayflower*. Also accompanying us that day was Fred Bridge, a member of the board of directors of the Little Compton Historical Society and a keen student of local history. I felt a certain kinship with Edward Winslow and Stephen Hopkins. Philbrick's fascinating observations challenged me to examine the historical dimensions of a familiar landscape through new eyes.

Philbrick had recently completed a draft of *Mayflower*, so he was traveling the region to test the geographical accuracy of his narrative. His book depicts the years between the Pilgrims' 1620 arrival in Plymouth and the 1676 conclusion of King Philip's War, the brief but bloody conflict when the English colonists effectively wrested the region's lands from the Native Americans of southeastern New England. The events of three-plus centuries ago, especially those of King Philip's War, were fresh in his mind as we toured the local landscape.

Our explorations focused on two local figures who figure prominently in *Mayflower*, Benjamin Church and Awashonks. Church, the original English settler of Sakonnet, is the protagonist of Philbrick's chronicle. An Indian-fighter with a conscience—at least by Philbrick's sympathetic portrayal—he recognized the humanity of his Native American adversaries, even as he captured and killed them. Awashonks, "squaw Sachem" of the Sakonnets, the local Wampanoag tribe, struggled to balance her loyalties between neighboring tribes and Church, with whom the Sakonnets had developed friendly relations. Finally, Awashonks and the Sakonnets cast their lot with Church. That alliance, according to Philbrick, represented the turning point of King Philip's War.

The three of us visited such places as Wilbour Woods, where Awashonks had maintained a settlement; Sakonnet Point; Treaty Rock Farm, site of the parley between Church and Awashonks; the monument on West Main Road marking the site of Church's second Little Compton home; and the stretch of West Main Road further north, near the Friends Meetinghouse, where the aged, corpulent church in 1718 was thrown from his horse, an accident that led to his death.

We prowled Punkatees Neck in Tiverton, trying to imagine the course of the "Pease Field Fight" in July 1675, when Church's small company of soldiers was drawn into a trap by local Indians. After a running skirmish, Church and his 20 men were pinned down by an estimated 300 Indians during a long, hot afternoon, taking cover behind a stone wall near the shore while they awaited evacuation by boat. As bullets flew, two men at a time ferried by canoe to a sloop anchored offshore. Church, the last man to depart, sprinted straight into the Indians' gunfire to recover the hat and cutlass he had left near a well. Then, as he dove into the canoe, "a bullet grazed his hair while another splintered the wooden brace against which he'd nestled his chest, but he reached the sloop unscathed." As Philbrick related this swashbuckling story to Fred and me on the shore of the Sakonnet River, I almost expected to hear the crack of musket fire.

The conclusion of King Philip's War set the stage for development and settlement of the Sakonnet area by English colonists. Church was among the proprietors of the new town of Little Compton who began to divide the land chartered by the Plymouth Colony and purchased from local Indians. The process of land division continued for almost 300 years. Then, in the latter decades of the 20th century, a new set of concerns began to energize the community, altering and in some respects reversing the land-ownership trends set into motion in the 17th century.

By the 1960s and 1970s, "conservation," "environment," "ecology," and "preservation" had become new watchwords of public policy and private activism, nationally and locally. In Little Compton, private organizations like the Sakonnet Preservation Association, The Nature Conservancy, and the Audubon Society of Rhode Island became active in acquiring property for conservation purposes, as did public agencies such as the Little Compton Agricultural Conservancy Trust and the land-preservation departments of Rhode Island state government. Firmly established American traditions and principles of private property began adapting to new, hybrid legal forms of land ownership, such as development rights and conservation easements, in which property owners share rights and responsibilities with these private and public organizations. Locally, the cumulative result of this activity has been dramatic and swift, on the scale of historical events. More than 3,000 acres [almost 3,300 acres, by 2012] of Little Compton's entire land area of more than 13,800 acres are dedicated to some form of legally permanent conservation.

But these significant changes in land ownership and land management raise a new set of challenges for our own generation, which will echo down the years. We can hope that the community will be a more peaceful place than the one depicted in Philbrick's intense and sometimes disturbing book. But will the efforts of today's conservationists result in a future landscape that resembles a theme park, frozen in time, representing the romanticized image of the community as it never really existed? Or will that landscape provide a dynamic, evolving environment where people of all sorts can live, earn a livelihood, and play? And what "memory holes" will we leave for our successor stewards of this terrain to discover and puzzle over, generations and centuries hence?

(2007)

"A Poor Sense of Humor": My Correspondence with the U.S. Attorney

Small-town politics can sometimes turn personal, bitter, intense, and downright menacing. A 1998 incident in Little Compton provided a chilling example of the potentially dangerous confluence of money, political power, and police authority.

During the late 1980s and 1990s, the town received more than $4 million from the Federal Asset Forfeiture Program. The controversial program, which expanded greatly during the long and problematic "War on Drugs," provides participating local police departments a share of proceeds from assets seized in the course of "an investigation or prosecution" for drug trafficking and certain other federal criminal activities. The Little Compton police during the 1980s had gleaned the evidence that first broke open a major international hashish-smuggling operation. For a number of years, the police had maintained surveillance on a local resident of shadowy origins—he was later identified as a deserter from South Africa's army—who had only recently moved to town. A small, relatively isolated town like Little Compton is not necessarily the best or easiest place for a newcomer to avoid scrutiny and suspicion, especially if there is anything even slightly exotic about one's background. In any event, the apparently exasperated wife of the closely watched town resident, who proved to be the local link in a drug-trafficking operation that reached to Pakistan, finally "spilled everything," as a Little Compton police captain told a *Baltimore Sun* reporter in 1998. "She laid out the entire organization for us." (As it happened, the target of the surveillance was an abutter to the property on which my wife and I live. A rumor once circulated that my hashish-dealing neighbor had buried tens of thousands of dollars. In the course of my own outdoor chores and walks through the woods, I remain alert.) As a result of playing a key role in cracking open the case, the Little Compton police department received a substantial share of the proceeds from the take-down and conviction of the kingpins of the far-flung and lucrative drug ring.

The town's enormous windfall represented more than ten times the police department's annual operating budget at the time, a circumstance which federal law and regulations didn't really anticipate. The gusher of federal money also created both opportunities and challenges for town officials. Under the federal guidelines for the asset seizure and forfeiture program, the funds could not be used to cover the normal operating costs of the police department. Instead, the money had to be spent only for supplemental law-enforcement purposes. Our small police department, it soon became apparent, had more money than it knew what to do with. Moreover, a series of town councils offered little resistance to the department's spending priorities. Indeed, those officials were happy to cooperate in stretching Department of Justice forfeiture guidelines to pay for town expenses that possessed only tenuous connections to genuine law enforcement. It was a political bonanza. In addition to purchasing more and flashier police vehicles, boats, and communications paraphernalia, forfeiture funds paid for, among other things, 4th of July fireworks, a woodchipper and a pickup truck for the town maintenance department, and a new sound system for the town hall meeting chamber.

Some Little Compton citizens began to raise questions about the town's spending procedures and priorities under the forfeiture program, however. A 1993 audit requested by the Justice Department as a result of such inquiries identified almost $100,000 in expenditures that represented possible "charges for other than law enforcement activities." In fact, the dramatically disproportionate flow of forfeiture funds to the Little Compton police department made the town something of a national poster child for the program's abuses and distortions. "It's like hitting a mosquito with a hammer," said our own Congressman at the time, Republican Representative Ron Machtley, commenting on the efficacy of spending millions of dollars for law enforcement in a quiet town of less than 3,500 people.

In response to growing criticism and concerns throughout the country, the Legislation and National Security Subcommittee of the Committee on Government Operations of the U.S. House of Representatives in 1993 held hearings on the program. Some of us testified at a public meeting held in town that year to solicit local opinion about the program, and our comments were included in the record of the Congressional hearings. My own concerns focused on how the forfeiture funds threatened to erode and evade the town's traditional means of political accountability. "In a democracy such as ours, civil authorities are not and should never be accountable to the police department," I testified at the time. "The police must always be accountable to civil and civilian authority. *All* of us are accountable to the law, which the police have the responsibility of enforcing. But under no circumstances should other town departments, agencies, or officials be in the position of seeking the police department's approval of funds used for non-police purposes, however worthy those purposes may be." My concerns were not much appreciated or heeded at the time.

One of the uses for which Little Compton officials proposed to use the funds was to build a new combined fire and police station. There was little question that the fire department, which combined paid and volunteer firefighters, desperately needed a new facility; it had operated for years in a cramped building in the center of town that had once been used to garage the town hearse. Use of the federal funds, though, had to serve a law-enforcement purpose. Hence the police chief received permission from the U.S. Department of Justice to spend $1-million of the funds to build a new "police/fire complex," incorporating both departments (even though the police department had only a few years earlier moved into a larger new space in a renovated public building). A variety of sites, designs, and proposals offered by a series of town councils met vehement public resistance and failed to receive political support, however. One citizen, the town's barber, successfully sued the town in state court when a town council attempted to use the federal funds to build the new facility on town-owned land—but without procuring approval of voters at a town meeting, the traditional legal means for authorizing funding for town operations. That legal victory re-affirmed the rights of voters to decide directly the expenditure of all town funds, no matter their source. The law "does not . . . provide the Police Chief and the Town Council with unilateral authority to appropriate substantial amounts of non-tax funds," a Superior Court judge found in the 1992 decision. "Expenditures of such magnitude are inextricably linked to Little Compton's financial affairs and properly the subject of financial town meeting, notwithstanding their character as federal funds."

By 1995, a small group of frustrated citizens, including myself, took advantage of the opportunity provided under the town's home rule charter to place a so-called "citizens' stroke" on the warrant of the annual financial town meeting. By circumventing the floundering town officials, we hoped to break the political gridlock that had stalled resolution of this issue. Despite resistance from some local officials, we also communicated directly with the Justice Department regarding the use and allocation of the drug asset funds for the proposed facility. With a green light from the Justice Department, we won overwhelming voter support to appropriate forfeiture funds to purchase a parcel of land near the center of town as a site for the public-safety project.

Predictably, the budget for the project swelled well beyond the $1-million for which the police chief had originally won approval from the Justice Department. When a proposal was finally presented to voters at the May 1998 financial town meeting, they were asked to approve expenditure of not just the balance of the $1-million already approved by the Justice Department but also a bond of $1.6-million. Some voters balked at the overall cost. Others had reservations about not only its financing (I hoped to use up more of the drug-forfeiture money instead of borrowing funds) but also its design and siting. After an intense debate at that town meeting, the proposal to authorize funding for the project failed by one vote: 137 in favor, 138 against. In the days and weeks after the meeting, as it turned out, frustrations with the razor-thin outcome of the vote were soon expressed in especially objectionable and intimidating ways. My own correspondence with the United States Attorney for the District of Rhode Island documents one such incident.

My letter:

> May 29, 1998
>
> Ms. Margaret Curran
> Acting U.S. Attorney
> District of Rhode Island
> Providence, RI
>
> RE: Police Conduct and the Drug Asset Seizure and Forfeiture Program in Little Compton, RI
>
> Dear Ms. Curran:
>
> On July 8, 1994, I wrote your predecessor, Sheldon Whitehouse [elected to the U.S. Senate in 2006], regarding my concerns about the administration of the Drug Asset Seizure and Forfeiture Program in Little Compton. As I wrote in 1994:
>
>> . . . [S]ome citizens are reluctant to raise their voices and concerns for fear that their comments may be construed as criticisms of the police department. This last is a particularly troubling matter, as some citizens may feel that the police are in a position to retaliate against them for such comments. I personally don't believe that our police department does or would engage in such conduct—but I know that some citizens are concerned about the possibility.
>
> Unfortunately, recent events in Little Compton indicate that town police personnel have engaged in the sort of retaliatory conduct about which I expressed concern four years ago. The Little Compton Police Department as a whole and some

of its individual members are direct beneficiaries of substantial drug forfeiture funds. Moreover, the immediate context of the recent events about which I now write involves the proposed expenditure of forfeiture funds for a planned police/fire building.

I am requesting that the Department of Justice intervene promptly to investigate conduct of at least one member of the Little Compton Police Department which may be intentionally intended to discourage citizens from freely exercising their voting and free speech rights involving a matter of direct interest to the police department and its members.

The following account has been assembled from a variety of sources, which I can provide to you or your representatives upon request:

Sometime on or before the early morning of Memorial Day, May 25, 1998, an effigy was placed on an area of town-owned Little Compton Commons known as "Pike's Peak," where public Memorial Day services were scheduled to take place later that morning. This effigy (photocopy enclosed) was several feet high and, according to the attached computer-printed sign, purported to depict "Bullivant's Parade Uniform." William Bullivant is a Little Compton resident who serves on the Little Compton Volunteer Fire Department, members of which march in the Memorial Day parade around the town Commons. The effigy consisted of a wooden frame, a tee-shirt, a shooting target, the above-mentioned sign, a pair of pants, and a pair of boots set in a block of concrete.

Later on the morning of May 25, before the 10:00 a.m. parade and ceremonies, the effigy was reportedly removed by a police officer to the premises of the adjacent police and fire departments, where it stood outside throughout the day. (The enclosed photograph was taken at around 2:00 p.m. on May 25, immediately outside the police station.) The effigy remained on public property in potential view of hundreds of citizens who attended public activities at adjacent public buildings. The existence and implied message of the effigy were not brought to the attention of Mr. Bullivant that day by any members of the police or fire departments, but rather by the citizens who took the enclosed photograph.

A Little Compton police office has subsequently acknowledged to Mr. Bullivant after a lengthy personal conversation that the officer was himself responsible for creating the effigy and placing it on the town Commons.

Moreover, it appears that the police officer's actions were thoroughly premeditated. On Friday, May 22, while Mr. Bullivant was on the premises of the fire department (which is immediately adjacent to the police department), another volunteer duty person told him that the above-noted police officer, sitting in a cruiser nearby, had just made statements to the effect that Mr. Bullivant should be prepared to wear a "bulletproof vest" and "cement shoes" as his uniform if he expected to march in the Memorial Day parade with other members of the police and fire departments. That is, several days before the appearance of the effigy, town public-safety personnel were apparently making verbal suggestions of bodily harm to Mr. Bullivant, for the apparent purpose of discouraging him from exercising his First Amendment right to participate in the public parade. Mr. Bullivant (who served in the Navy) in fact chose not to march in the parade.

Mr. Bullivant on May 27 had a personal conversation with the Little Compton police chief about the matter, during which the chief acknowledged the responsibility of one of his officers for creating and displaying the effigy on public property. The chief also reported to Mr. Bullivant his intention to place a letter of reprimand in the officer's file and to report the matter to the town council. As of this writing, however, there has been no public acknowledgment by the police department that one of its officers was responsible for this threatening conduct. Nor has any public apology been made to Mr. Bullivant or the rest of the town's citizens for this conduct. I have no personal knowledge, however, whether the police chief has in fact taken any specific disciplinary measures against any police officer for this incident.

As noted above, there is a larger context surrounding this incident. Mr. Bullivant, the target of the effigy, has in recent weeks and months made a number of public statements, during public meetings and in newspaper accounts, expressing his concerns about various aspects of a proposal to build a town police/fire complex on a parcel of land purchased by the town for this purpose using drug forfeiture funds. At the recent May 19 annual financial town meeting, Mr. Bullivant was one of many citizens (including myself) who raised questions and concerns about town council proposals to appropriate additional Justice Department-approved funds and to borrow another $1.6 million to proceed with the construction of a proposed design for the building. After considerable discussion and debate, the bond issue was defeated by a paper-ballot vote of 136 (in favor) to 137 (opposed). After the vote, the town council president moved and the town meeting voted to table the two other warrant items involving the proposed project, one of which called for the appropriation of drug forfeiture funds.

Understandably, many citizens were frustrated with the outcome of the meeting, for a variety of reasons. (This issue has gone unresolved for many years; and it has involved a lawsuit, *Hayes v. Souther*, in which the R.I. Superior Court determined that the expenditure of federal drug forfeiture funds, as least in Little Compton, required appropriation by vote of a financial town meeting.) Public safety personnel are frustrated as well. But any such frustration does not justify conduct by a police officer which effectively represents a threat of bodily harm to a particular citizen. In this respect and context, a threat to one citizen can create a chilling effect on all citizens, thereby discouraging citizens from exercising their right to speak freely and to vote publicly at a financial town meeting on a matter of serious public interest and concern.

I do not know whether any of the police activities described above may in fact represent criminal activity. But these events raise serious doubts that the Little Compton Police Department can conduct a thorough, disinterested investigation of an incident involving the deeply troubling conduct of at least one of its members.

My concern about the chilling effect of the police department's conduct is not theoretical. According to an account in

Effigy placed on Little Compton Commons, Memorial Day, 1998. The printed sign attached to the target reads "Bullivant's Parade Uniform."

the May 28, 1998 *Sakonnet Times*, Police Chief Hawes has stated his intention to present to the Little Compton town council before its June 4, 1998 meeting "a formal request for a special town meeting to revisit the issue of a police/fire complex." Inasmuch as the changed decision of just one citizen could have reversed the outcome of the May 19 vote on the police/fire complex, the threat of violence by a member of the police department against any single citizen, as it becomes known to other town citizens, could well discourage some of those citizens from attending, speaking at, or voting freely at a future town meeting on this controversial topic. Hence the outcome of the democratic process could be directly affected by threatening police activities. And members of the police department will of course be among the principal direct beneficiaries of a new police/fire facility, if and when it is built.

I should add that as a citizen who has been outspoken about and active in a variety of local issues, I am sometimes publicly criticized for my opinions, actions, and alleged motives. On a number of occasions I have run for local office, and I may do so again. Hence, I cherish my right of free speech and respect the free speech rights of others. But the police conduct in this instance seems to far exceed the reasonable limits of constitutionally protected free speech.

Specifically, I again request that the Justice Department investigate police department conduct with regard to the incident described above; the police department's investigation of the matter; and any disciplinary measures taken by the department in response.

Law-abiding Little Compton residents should not under any circumstances be receiving threats of bodily harm from members of its police department. Nor under any circumstances should such conduct be used to discourage citizens from exercising their voting and free speech rights. As I noted at the outset of this letter, this is a matter of particular concern and sensitivity, in light of the substantial financial and law-enforcement resources at the disposal of the Little Compton Police Department through the federal Drug Asset

Seizure and Forfeiture Program, over which your department holds jurisdiction.

Please contact me if you have any questions about any of the facts or representations included in this letter. Thank you for your attention to my concerns.

Sincerely,

Larry Anderson

Copy: Little Compton Police Chief Egbert D. Hawes, Jr.

U.S. Attorney Curran's reply:

June 12, 1998

Dear Mr. Anderson:

We have reviewed your letter of May 29, 1998, as well as additional material sent to us by another concerned citizen of Little Compton and from Police Chief Egbert D. Hawes, Jr.

The facts that raise your concern, as I understand them, are as follows. Over the Memorial Day weekend, an effigy was placed prominently in the town. The effigy consisted of, in part, a stick figure covered by a paper firing range target and what purported to be cement shoes. The effigy may be related in some way to recent debate about the construction of a new police/fire complex in the town. A police officer has admitting constructing and posting the effigy, has apologized to the Police Chief and has been reprimanded by the Chief. The officer maintained that the effigy was the continuation of a joke that had begun the day before and that no actual threat had been implied.

Police Chief Hawes, in a letter to me dated June 2, confirmed that the officer had been reprimanded and that the individual who was the subject of the effigy had accepted the officer's apology. Chief Hawes categorized the officer's action's [sic] as "non professional." I certainly concur with that assessment and believe that police officers should always be mindful of their professional responsibilities, given their unique position as representatives of official authority in a free society. It is apparent that, in this instance, the officer in question forgot those responsibilities.

A review of the facts also leads me to the conclusion that there is no evidence of any violations of federal criminal statutes and therefore no jurisdiction for this office or a federal law enforcement agency to conduct an investigation. The officer's actions were certainly in bad taste and displayed, at best, a poor sense of humor but they do not appear to have violated any federal laws.

If you have any questions, feel free to contact me.

Sincerely,

Margaret E. Curran
United States Attorney

Cc: Chief Egbert D. Hawes, Jr.

As U.S. Attorney Curran's letter suggests, other than the police chief's reprimand of the officer involved, there were no legal repercussions from the Memorial Day incident—except, that is, for the target of the effigy, Bill Bullivant, who in subsequent years was charged by the town police with several alleged violations of law. All these charges were eventually thrown out of court, partly through the intervention of the American Civil Liberties Union. Some of us citizens who protested the conduct and response of the police department at the time of the effigy incident were also publicly (and privately) reproved by some police officers. It was, for some town residents, an eye-opening, nerve-racking, and unforgettable experience.

At a special town meeting in October of 1998, Little Compton voters, by a margin of 297 to 165, approved funding for a somewhat revised version of the proposal to build a new "public safety complex," as the town now calls the facility.

In 2005, the officer who placed the effigy on Little Compton Commons on Memorial Day in 1998 was appointed the town's chief of police, in which position he continues to serve.

(2012)

Town Meeting

Friends and fellow citizens questioned my sanity when I ran for the office of Little Compton town moderator in 2006. In the aftermath of a series of highly contentious financial town meetings during the previous several years, three preceding moderators had resigned, lost bids for re-election, or decided not to seek a second term. Apparently nobody else wanted the job. The worst thing that could happen, I told myself as I pondered the results of my uncontested election (besides offending everyone in town or humiliating myself in public), would be if I lost an attempt for re-election this year [2008].

Town meeting, the time-tested democratic foundation of New England local government, places every voter on equal footing—at least in theory—in determining the town's major business, especially the adoption of an annual budget. For one day each year, every citizen who attends town meeting is a politician and a public official, wielding as much power as any member of a town council or school committee. Town meeting can still provide a direct check on town officials whose decisions and proposals veer too far from the priorities of the community's voters.

Some citizens, however, express reservations about the viability and effectiveness of the "financial town meeting," as Rhode Island describes the institution by law and tradition. Critics of town meetings offer a variety of complaints: Attendance steadily declines. A minority of voters can determine the town's business. Voting blocs or interest groups act in their own self-interest. Many citizens have difficulty attending a potentially lengthy evening or Saturday meeting. Some fear intimidation or retribution for voicing their opinions or casting their votes in public. Others are bewildered by parliamentary procedures, the complexity of issues, or the hidden agendas of public officials. State and federal mandates, collective-bargaining agreements, and the General Assembly's sometimes obtuse, one-size-fits-all approach to municipal issues constrain town meeting's powers.

For all these concerns, though, town meeting has proved to be a surprisingly durable institution in Rhode Island. Of the state's 39 municipalities, according to a 2006 survey by the Department of Administration's Office of Municipal Affairs, 15 adopt their budgets in financial town meeting. Two communities hold public assemblies to debate a town council's proposed budget, which is then placed before voters at a day-long referendum. Two more communities allow for special town meetings by petition of citizens, to vote on or amend the budget already adopted by a town council. Direct voter consideration and approval of town budgets is still at least nominally alive, then, in almost half of Rhode Island's municipalities.

One relatively new challenge to the orderly conduct of financial town meeting is the state-imposed limitation on annual increases in a town's property-tax levy. As amended in 2006, Section 44-5-2 of the Rhode Island General Laws has provided a measure of relief to taxpayers, but the law complicates the traditional approach to the adoption of an annual town budget at a financial town meeting.

The General Assembly probably did not contemplate the potential vexations they were creating for town moderators. By law and long-time practice, the warrant for a financial town meeting consists of separate articles, or budget line items, for different town departments and operations. These separate articles have usually been debated, sometimes amended, and then adopted (or rejected) individually. However, it is a parliamentary challenge to reconcile the tax cap, which sets a fixed budget limit that cannot legally be exceeded, with a traditional article-by-article approach to authorizing a budget; the separately adopted articles may not necessarily add up to the permitted budget cap.

Little Compton's home-rule charter provides that separate articles may be grouped for voting; and town officials in recent years have proposed adopting the entire town budget in one vote. This motion inevitably meets resistance by some voters who believe they are being deprived of a time-honored right to debate and vote on the individual articles. But the majority of town-meeting voters, eager to avoid discord and confusion, have usually been quick to approve the proposed omnibus budget in one vote. Last year, during my first outing as town moderator, the business of the financial town meeting was wrapped up in less than half an hour.

But such expeditious disposition of the town's business may, in a paradoxical way, present another danger to the future of town meeting. If the civic skills essential to the process of democratic self-government are not regularly exercised, they are likely to atrophy. Town meetings have long provided a public forum where citizens both observe and practice the political arts of persuasion, oratory, compromise, organizing, parliamentary procedure, and, ideally if not always in practice, passionate but civil disagreement with their opponents. Public argument and debate, within a commonly accepted framework of decorum and respect, can provide a socially healthy mechanism for the resolution of important community concerns.

Stormy town meetings are nothing new in Little Compton, of course. The conduct of town business by face-to-face voter deliberation has been practiced continuously since the last decades of the 17th century. In May 1803, Little Compton's freeman (the tax-paying male property owners, that is—no women) gathered in the upstairs chamber of the old town hall, which had served the town since the late 1600s on a site at the Commons just north of the Congregational Church. The purpose of the meeting was to elect town officers and the town's two representatives to the General Assembly.

"The Federalists and Republicans, as the rival parties were called, were nearly equal in strength as to numbers," recounted a local historian in 1882. "Benjamin Tompkins held the office of Town Clerk, and

Samuel T. Grinnell was the opposing candidate. The Moderator, Isaac Wilbour, declared Grinnell elected, and ordered Tompkins to vacate the seat, which he refused to do. The Town Sergeant was then ordered to put him out. A scene of confusion ensued that does little credit to the moderation of our ancestors. In the struggle Tompkins lost his coat, but managed to escape with the records. It is said that the freemen came out through the open windows like angry bees from a hive. The party who left the hall organized in the church, and proceeded to elect officers, while the party that remained also chose a set of officers. It is related that Edward Woodman, a man of sharp visage and sharper tongue, opened the door of the church after they had organized, and in a loud voice hurled this significant passage of scripture at his political adversaries: 'My house shall be called a house of prayer, but ye have made it a den of thieves.'

"In this particular," the town historian concluded, "has there not been an improvement in these later times? Less of rancor and bitterness?"

Not all veterans of local town meetings would necessarily agree that we have made progress on the questions of rancor and bitterness. Time will tell whether my own tenure as town moderator will be as brief as that of my immediate predecessors. But I remain hopeful about the future significance and survival of town meeting. One need only read the daily newspaper and watch the daily news to understand that town meeting provides a rare and precious opportunity for local self-government, however frustrating, messy, and circumscribed the venerable institution may sometimes be.

(2008)

POSTSCRIPT: After serving three two-year terms as town moderator, I chose not to run for the office again in 2012.
ADDENDUM (2013): I did not run for re-election in 2012. However, neither did anyone else. I was re-elected with 51 write-in votes.

"Millionaire Aggression" in Acoaxet

Though rich in history, Little Compton has lacked a readable, accurate narrative chronicle of the town's past. That deficiency was finally remedied in 2010 with publication of *First Light: Sakonnet, 1660-1820*, by Janet Taylor Lisle. An award-winning author of young-adult novels, Ms. Lisle, in the first installment of a two-volume "History of Little Compton," combines a brisk, lively style with scrupulous scholarship.

Among the many topics Ms. Lisle clearly explains is the bewildering story of the oft-changing boundary between Rhode Island and Massachusetts, an ongoing legal and political saga that did not finally come to rest until well into the nineteenth century. One important episode of that story was the 1746 decree by King George II that redrew the boundary between the colonies of Rhode Island and Massachusetts. The royal decree was intended to resolve the geographically vague and sometimes contradictory language of the original patents and charters establishing the neighboring colonies.

The 1629 Plymouth patent set as the colony's western boundary "one-half of the River called Naragansetts," which the Plymouth settlers took to be today's Sakonnet River, the eastern passage of Narragansett Bay. The Rhode Islanders, however, had different ideas about the extent of their domain. Their territorial claim, as Lisle writes, was based on that colony's 1663 royal charter, "in which the king had granted the colony land extending 'three English miles to the east and north-east of the most eastern and northeastern parts of Narragansett Bay.'" Such a line, the Rhode Islanders persistently claimed, would be well to the east of the Sakonnet River, thus encompassing much of Little Compton.

Until the 1746 decree, Little Compton had been the southwestern frontier of the Plymouth colony and then the Massachusetts Bay colony, after a 1691 royal charter merged the two. And the boundary between Little Compton and what became Westport, Massachusetts (a town carved from the vast original town of Dartmouth in 1787) was the western shore of the West Branch of the Westport River. Early colonial Little Compton, then, was a peninsula, bounded on the north by Tiverton and on three sides by water: the Sakonnet River to the west, the ocean shoreline to the south, and the Westport River to the east.

George II's decree awarded to Rhode Island most of Little Compton as well as the present towns of Warren, Barrington, Bristol, Tiverton, and Cumberland. But the newly drawn boundary between Rhode Island and Massachusetts immediately generated another political conundrum. When surveyed by a commission from Rhode Island (Massachusetts didn't participate), the new boundary sliced off a triangle of southeastern Little Compton adjacent to the Westport River, leaving it as part of Massachusetts.

"Families along the west bank of the Westport River and around Westport Harbor who had thought they belonged to Little Compton," Lisle writes, "suddenly found they had been left behind in Massachusetts."

The triangle occupied by these overnight exiles was a district traditionally known as Acoaxet and, eventually, Westport Harbor. In order to reach this corner of Westport by land, a traveler must traverse a corner of Little Compton. The northern apex of the triangle can be readily located today in the village of Adamsville: a granite post set into the milldam across the headwater stream of the West Branch of the Westport River. From this point, the boundary between the towns and states extends more than four miles virtually straight southward through

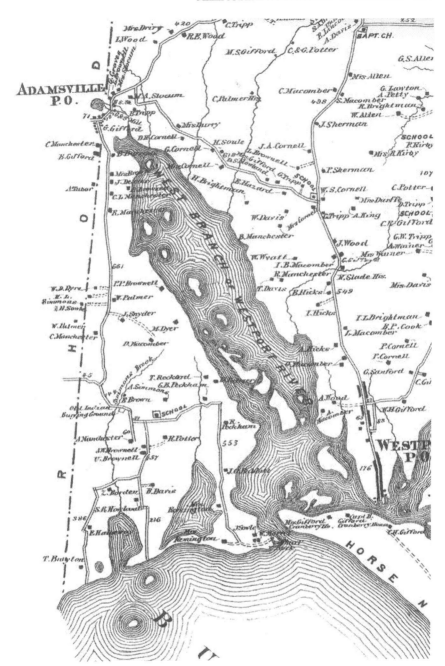

A section of the Westport, Massachusetts, map from *Atlas of Bristol Co., Massachusetts* (F. W. Beers, 1871), depicting the Acoaxet "triangle," bounded west by the Rhode Island–Massachusetts state line, south by Buzzards Bay, east by the West Branch of the Westport River, and north by a point in the milldam at Adamsville Pond.

still-rugged and sparsely settled terrain, reaching the sea at the eastern
end of Goosewing Beach.

The repercussions of George II's decree persisted until the early
twentieth century, when some residents of the Acoaxet triangle attempted to secede from Westport. During the latter years of the nineteenth century and the early decades of the twentieth, a prosperous
summer colony took root at Westport Harbor. The core of the community were members of Fall River's economic and social elite, who built
substantial summer houses, private beach clubs, a party "Casino"
overlooking Cockeast Pond, and, by the early 1920s, a golf course, the
Acoaxet Club.

In those years, though, some of the property owners and residents of
Acoaxet were feeling poorly used. One leader of the Acoaxet community was Earle Charlton, a Fall River businessman and philanthropist who
had parlayed his New England chain of five-and-dime stores into a
substantial ownership interest in the giant F. W. Woolworth Co. After
he built a grand 24-room stone mansion at the harbor, Charlton became
Westport's highest individual taxpayer. Nursing a grievance common
among non-resident property owners in seasonal communities, Charlton
complained that he and his neighbors were paying more than their fair
share of the town's expenses. Their neighborhood, they claimed, paid
one-sixth of Westport's taxes but comprised just one-twelfth of the
town's population.

According to an account of ensuing events by Carmen Maiocco and
Claude Ledoux in *A History of Westport in the Twentieth Century* (1995), 31
of the area's 33 voters eventually signed a petition requesting the
creation of a separate new town, to be called Acoaxet. And the Acoaxet
dissidents succeeded in introducing a bill in the Massachusetts legislature to authorize the secession of their district from the rest of Westport.

But other Westport residents and officials quickly mobilized their
forces and arguments in opposition. The selectmen fought vigorously
against the secessionists, describing the initiative as "millionaire aggression" in a paid newspaper advertisement, according to Maiocco and
Ledoux. A special town meeting was called.

More than three hundred voters crowded into Westport's town hall on January 19, 1926—the largest town meeting in memory, observed town clerk Edward Macomber.   Dr. Henry C. R. Breault offered a motion authorizing the selectmen to oppose "the proposed legislation for the separation of Acoaxet from the town of Westport." Dr. Breault deployed the rhetoric of class warfare in his appeal to townspeople harboring secessionist sentiments. "We don't want to create a taxdodgers' haven," he exhorted, according to a *Fall River Herald News* reporter. "It is un-American and dangerous. Sovietism in Russia grew out of the abuse of the poor by the rich."

Another town elder, Bill Potter, then rose to speak. "You all know Bill," remarked the town moderator. "He's had what he calls another spasm." Potter's spasm took the form of a lengthy poem, in which he targeted the secessionists' patriotism—or lack of it. He noted the plaque in front of the town hall honoring young Westport men who had recently fought in World War I:

> The Boys received a dollar a day,
> And many lost their health.
> The rich man stayed at home engaged
> In doubling his wealth.
>
> And when our lads, at last, came home
> Prepared to settle down,
> They found the rich men ready
> To take part of their town.

The voters promptly voted 281 to 0 in favor of Breault's motion to oppose secession. The original secession petitioners either failed to show up or, sensing the lopsided mood of the town meeting, chose to sit on their hands when the vote was called.

The Massachusetts legislature took no action on the secession bill. Thus the brief revolt of Acoaxet's nabobs was peacefully and efficiently quashed.   The rebels of Westport Harbor retreated that summer to the porches of the Casino and the Acoaxet Club, to commiserate over the continuing assault on their bank and brokerage accounts. Their cool beverages in those Prohibition days may have been fortified with the contraband liquor regularly transported on dark nights across the beaches of Westport and Little Compton.

And the Acoaxet triangle, the eastern vestige of Little Compton's original territory, remained wedded, for better or worse, to the town of Westport and the Commonwealth of Massachusetts.

(2012)

Heritage and Hoopla in Las Vegas

One hundred years ago this past May 15th (2005), a thousand or so people gathered under the scorching desert sun in southern Nevada, beside the freshly laid tracks of the San Pedro, Los Angeles & Salt Lake Railroad, for an auction of building lots at a place called Clark's Las Vegas Townsite. My great-uncle, Sam Gay, was probably among the crowd that day. A 45-year-old bachelor, he had already lived and traveled throughout the American west for a quarter century, since escaping the confines of his native Prince Edward Island, Canada.

In memory of my ancestor—known as "Uncle Sam" in our family—I recently spent a week in Las Vegas to attend some of the centennial events celebrating the founding of the little railroad town that has gone on to become a unique, vibrant, and notorious American metropolis. "What happens in Las Vegas, stays in Las Vegas," according to the city's current promotional slogan. But if "Sin City" represents some of the most disreputable aspects of American culture, it also exemplifies the best traditions of American optimism and economic opportunity. The gigantic, architecturally mind-boggling casino resorts constantly being built and renovated here provide a steady source of new jobs with decent pay. Planned developments now in the works would add 30,000 new hotel rooms to the city's inventory in the next five years. Just before my visit, the newest of these mega-resorts, the sleek, copper-hued, 2,700-room, $2.7-billion Wynn Las Vegas opened on the site of the former Desert Inn (although *Los Angeles Times* architectural critic Christopher Hawthorne was underwhelmed by the building's design, likening it to a "midrise office tower in Houston circa 1983"). The local unemployment rate is under four percent. The state's most recent monthly reports on casino revenues show that gamblers are leaving their money in the city at a record pace. By any measure, Las Vegas's economy is flourishing.

The moving force behind the SP, LA & SL Railroad was the Montana copper magnate and U.S. Senator, William A. Clark. His railroad connecting Salt Lake City and Los Angeles completed one of the last major links in the continental railroad network. He had chosen Las Vegas as a division point for the new rail line because of its abundant supply of water, provided by a series of substantial springs. "The Meadows"—the Spanish meaning of Las Vegas—was a true oasis in this easternmost region of the Mojave Desert. Small bands of Southern Paiute Indians had long lived here. But until the world rushed into Las Vegas in those early years of the 20th century, the place had served primarily as a welcome desert stopover for explorers, mountain men, traders along the Old Spanish Trail, and Mormon colonists. In 1900, the federal census-taker found just 30 inhabitants (including 12 Indians) at what was then called "Las Vegas Ranch."

Like others at the 1905 auction, Sam Gay arrived in Las Vegas in search of a new start. And he found it—not in the form of wealth and power but as a keeper of peace and order. Within months of his arrival in the growing new town, he had been hired as a night watchman for Block 16, the saloon and red-light district Senator Clark's townsite company set aside as the only area in the new townsite where the sale of alcohol was legal. Sam in fact served as a pallbearer for his predecessor, one Joe Mulholland, who had been shot dead in a barroom altercation with a desert rat known as the "Annehauser Kid." Sam proved more effective and durable than Mulholland as a law enforcement officer. In 1910 he was elected sheriff of the newly created Clark County, a

The Arizona Club, Block 16, Las Vegas, Nevada, ca. 1906-1907. Sam Gay is standing fourth from the left.

position to which he was regularly re-elected until 1930, when he decided not to run again.

At a Founders Luncheon for descendants of Las Vegas's earliest settlers, I met Las Vegas native Kathleen Horden Close, granddaughter of John Wesley Horden. In 1905, Horden built the Gem Saloon on Block 16. Later Horden bought a site on Fremont Street, then the town's main business street, where he built the Las Vegas Hotel. The property, Mrs. Close told me, had been owned by her family until the 1990s. John Wesley Horden's business acumen had apparently been fruitful for his descendants. Mrs. Close gave me her card, which included residential addresses in one of Las Vegas's most exclusive suburban neighborhoods as well as in Miami.

The Founders Luncheon was presided over by Las Vegas's colorful, controversial, and popular mayor, Oscar Goodman, who made his reputation as a defense lawyer for notorious organized crime figures. "I am the happiest man in the universe," he convincingly regaled the gathered Las Vegas old-timers. "I love being the mayor of Las Vegas."

The Philadelphia-born Goodman shares with most of his constituents the fact that they are not Las Vegas natives. In the last decade and more, Las Vegas has often ranked as one of the nation's fastest growing communities. An estimated 1.7-million live in the Valley today; ten years earlier, the population was about one million. The sizzling pace of growth of course exacerbates such issues as adequate water supplies, traffic congestion, air pollution, public education, and affordable housing. Development sprawls into the foothills of the mountains that ring the Las Vegas Valley. "Manhattanization"—building upwards not outwards—is the current buzzword employed by Mayor Goodman and other boosters of the city's continuing growth. According to some reports, more than 150 high-end, high-rise condominium projects are in the works in Las Vegas, although some skeptics wonder whether American's frothiest housing market can absorb such a supply.

Later in the week I attended the Helldorado Days Parade, the resurrection of an event that had begun in the 1935 but expired for lack of support in the 1990s. Las Vegas escaped the worse scourges of the Depression when the federal government initiated construction of Hoover Dam in 1931 (the same year Nevada legalized gambling). Local boosters worried, though, that completion of the dam would result in a local economic slowdown. As a tourist attraction, they initiated Helldorado Days, with a rodeo, a parade, and other events exploiting the city's Western heritage.

Some local pundits claimed that this year's parade, while substantial and well-attended, lacked the style and flair of the earlier processions, when the big Strip casinos built elaborate floats comparable to anything in the Rose Bowl parade (with the additional bonus of scantily clad Las Vegas showgirls). As a result of a series of recent mergers, most of Las Vegas's biggest casinos are now or soon will be owned by just a few major companies, whose managers are apparently immune to the sense of community spirit the Helldorado event was attempting to generate. None of the big casinos was represented in the parade. Indeed, one of the few casino floats was a pathetic spectacle from a small, edge-of-town gambling hall. It featured a grotesquely obese "Big Elvis," who waved lazily to the crowd, offering the opportunity to imagine what would have become of the King of Rock and Roll if he had survived to indulge his excessive appetites.

The appetites of contemporary Las Vegans were whetted by another centennial activity—the creation of what was billed as the World's Biggest Birthday Cake (pending substantiation of that claim by the Guinness Book of World Records). The Sara Lee Foods Company had trucked in seven trailers carrying 30,000 pre-baked flat cakes and 34,000 pounds of vanilla icing, which volunteers slathered together into a 130,000-pound, 23-million-calorie slab measuring 102 by 52 feet. Mayor Goodman of course showed up for the completion and cutting of the stupendous confection.

It is only fitting that Las Vegas would choose a speculative real-estate venture to mark the town's founding. On May 15th, centennial organizers staged a re-creation of the townsite auction that had taken place exactly a century earlier. In 1905, the railroad company's local real-estate development subsidiary, the Las Vegas Land and Water Company, had set up a canvas-covered platform at the corner of Fremont and Main Streets, near the single parlor car that then served as the railroad depot. The townsite in 1905 was nothing more than a dusty, flyblown expanse of desert, marked with a grid of wooden stakes defining streets and lot lines.

In the century since that auction, Fremont Street evolved into Las Vegas's early business district and its first casino district—"Glitter Gulch." But as the big resort casinos developed along Las Vegas Boulevard—"The Strip"—in the years after World War II, the fortunes of downtown Las Vegas gradually declined. In an effort to attract tourists and gamblers downtown, the city a few years ago erected a soaring roof over the first four blocks of Fremont Street, creating a sort of pedestrian mall called The Fremont Street Experience. Elaborate light shows are displayed on the canopy every night, a spectacle intended to compete with extravagant attractions along the Strip.

A platform for the auction re-creation was erected under the Fremont Street canopy. The participants in the brief, comic auction skit dressed in period costumes, replicating photographs of the original event. The ubiquitous Mayor Goodman, donning a black Stetson,

Sheriff Sam Gay (second from right) and deputy sheriffs, on the steps of the Clark County Courthouse, Las Vegas, Nevada, ca. 1928-1930.

played the role of railroad owner Senator Clark. A few hundred spectators—a mere fraction of the number attending the original sale—looked on as the mock auction, complete with play-acting bidders, kicked off at ten o'clock on a Sunday morning. At that hour there are still plenty of gamblers patronizing Fremont Street's casinos, most of which cater to a less upscale clientele than do the Strip's megaresorts.

The most earthy and entertaining part of the show was unscripted. As a gesture at creating a sense of authentic Western atmosphere, two horses had been brought into the media enclosure surrounding the auction platform. Just as the skit began, one of the steeds let loose with several forms of equine waste. In 1905, the desert soil would have absorbed such deposits. In 2005, though, the Fremont Street mall is paved with impermeable tile. Sam Gay and his early Las Vegas contemporaries would have chuckled to see the smartly dressed event organizers, in high heels and open-toed shoes, dabbing at the horse droppings with paper towels.

In today's Las Vegas, the Old West is of course long gone, barely even noticed amidst the city's theme-park atmosphere. My great-uncle Sam Gay, as he prepared to lay down his badge and Colt pistol in 1930, knew that the times had caught up with him and were about to pass him by.

"Too many crooks coming to Las Vegas, now they're going to build Boulder Dam," he complained to a Los Angeles newspaperman during the last days of his final term in office. "I've dealt with honest men so long, I wouldn't know how to act around crooks. I'm used to tough hombres who shot each other up once in a while. I'm used to gun fights. But I ain't much good running down racketeers. My notions is too old-fashioned. You can't deal with these new gunmen with a single action .45. Need a machine gun. I'm too old to learn to run one, so I quit."

In 1930, as Sam Gay lamented the changes taking place in the town he had helped to create, 5,165 people called Las Vegas their home. Today, an estimated 7,000 new residents arrive every month. "The greatest city in the history of the world," according to Mayor Goodman, Las Vegas is brashly leaping headfirst into its second century.

(2005)

POSTSCRIPT: The upbeat conclusion of this piece proved to be wildly off the mark. In 2005, only a few lonely and reviled heretics dared question whether the pace of development in Las Vegas could be sustained. As it happened, the wave of growth was then approaching its frothy crest. By 2008 that wave would crash, along with much of the nation's and the world's economy. For Las Vegas and its inhabitants, the consequences were especially grim. The volume of visitors to the city peaked at 39-million in 2007; two years later, that number had dropped by almost ten percent. Population, which had grown at the highest rate in the country for years, leveled off. Ominously, gaming revenues by 2009 had dropped $2-billion from a 2007 peak of $10.87-billion. The unemployment rate, which had been the lowest in the nation, by early 2010 had climbed to more than 15 percent, the highest. The housing boom that had rapidly expanded the ring of residential development into the desert lands surrounding Las Vegas went bust. The region experienced a glut of vacant housing; by early 2011, Las Vegas's home vacancy rate was second only to Detroit's. The foreclosure rate by that time was the highest in the country, a dubious distinction the Las Vegas area had held for more than four years. One in nine Las Vegas housing units received a default notice in 2010, five times the national average. Seventy percent of mortgaged properties were under water.

"Southern Nevada's economy, in our estimation, is at the bottom," declared University of Nevada—Las Vegas economist Stephen Brown at the end of that year. "We're not looking to find the bottom. We are at the bottom. If it's not the bottom, could things actually look worse? I think the answer is 'no.'"

Brown, who heads UNLV's Center for Business and Economic Research, also warned his fellow Las Vegans that their economic destiny was inextricably in the grip of the tourist and gambling industry. "There are thoughts about diversifying our economic base," he observed. "If you could only have one industry for an economic base, tourism is the one you want. It's naturally diversified. People make their money in high-tech, they come and spend it in Las Vegas."

By early 2012, the unemployment rate had receded to 12.2 percent. The tourist and gaming business had gradually begun to stabilize and recover. Though gaming revenue was still below its 2007 peak of almost $11-billion, visitor volume had surpassed previous highs: UNLV researchers projected that more than 41-million tourists would arrive in 2012. But the confidence and faith of Las Vegas in its future have been badly shaken. Rising oil prices, a gambling industry challenged by global competition, declining regional water resources, climate change—these are among the trends and concerns that will determine the fate of "the greatest city in the world." Oscar Goodman, who received 84 percent of the vote when re-elected to his third term in 2007, served as mayor of Las Vegas until mid-2011, his twelve-year tenure ended by term limits. Goodman's wife, Carolyn, easily won election to succeed him in the mayor's office.

During his years as mayor, Oscar Goodman enthusiastically promoted creation of a Las Vegas Museum of Organized Crime and Law Enforcement—"The Mob Museum"—which opened in February 2012, in a former downtown federal post office and courthouse. In Las

Vegas, any portrayal of the city's history and heritage must be viewed with a robust measure of skepticism and caution. I will be returning to Las Vegas to visit the Mob Museum, but by most accounts its depiction of the city's history of crime and law enforcement begins with the arrival of crime syndicates in the 1940s. Sam Gay apparently merits little recognition for his 25 years of colorful service as the town's leading lawman during an era before organized crime held sway in the city.

Acknowledgments

The writing gathered in this collection was produced over more than three decades. I can't adequately thank—or even recall—the many people who in one way or another provided assistance or subject matter for these articles and essays. I can, however, express my sincere appreciation for the support and help I received in assembling and producing this book.

Harley P. Holden, Benton MacKaye's literary executor, provided permission for the use of certain MacKaye manuscript materials quoted and illustrations reproduced here. Holden has been a faithful, genial, and capable custodian of the literary legacy of his late friend and neighbor. The Dartmouth College Library also provided permission to use illustrations and other materials from the Papers of the MacKaye Family. I am especially grateful to Jay Satterfield, Special Collections Librarian of the Rauner Special Collections Library at Dartmouth, and to Phyllis M. Gilbert of the library's staff. I also owe thanks to the Johns Hopkins University Press, and particularly rights manager Kelly L. Rogers, for permission to use material that originally appeared in my book, *Benton MacKaye: Conservationist, Planner, and Creator of the Appalachian Trail.*

Current and former editors of the various publications where many of these articles originally appeared either helped improve them when first published or answered my inquiries about their re-publication in this collection. With apologies to those I am forgetting, such editors include: Jean Martin, Chris Stewart, Robert Whitcomb, Jr., the late T. H. Watkins, Bennett Beach, Kathryn Kulpa, Tom Butler, Bob Sipchen, Robert Rubin, Judy Jenner, Russell Lewis, Margaret Welsh, Holly Camero, and Marc Chalufour.

Other individuals have offered generous support on behalf of their organizations. Brian King, publisher at the Appalachian Trail Conservancy (ATC), has been consistently helpful over many years in providing access to and permission to use a variety of archival material held by ATC. In various ATC publications, Brian has also provided thoughtful, balanced, and well-informed accounts of the history of the organization and the Appalachian Trail. I am grateful to Becky Fullerton, librarian and archivist of the Appalachian Mountain Club, for access to the club's collection of Edward Chamberlain's maps and panoramas. Larry Luxenberg, president of the Appalachian Trail Museum Society and author, has invited me to speak at several events sponsored by the important new historical institution he and his enthusiastic colleagues have created: the Appalachian Trail Museum opened in Pennsylvania's Pine Grove Furnace State Park in 2010. I am also grateful to the Thoreau Society for the opportunity to participate in a panel moderated by Phillip Bosserman at the group's 2004 Gathering. Doug Reeves, Jennifer Wright, and Craig Young of the USDA Forest Service provided current information about Wilderness Areas in the Green Mountain and White Mountain National Forests. Town Clerks Janet Vellante and Marlene M. Samson of, respectively, Harvard and Westport, Massachusetts, helped me find historical records in their towns.

University of Vermont scholar Robert McCullough provided copies of several of the images reproduced here. Bob's deep knowledge and nuanced understanding of Benton MacKaye and related planning and architectural subjects is evident in his book *A Path for Kindred Spirits: The Friendship of Clarence Stein and Benton MacKaye* (2012). I enjoyed an interesting day visiting King Philip's War sites with Nathaniel Philbrick and Fred Bridge. The essay "'Millionaire Aggression' in Acoaxet" originated in a larger project supported by an Independent Research Grant from the Rhode Island Council for the Humanities.

I will always be grateful to Kathleen Cushman and Ed Miller for the intensive crash course they offered me in all aspects of journalism, editing, writing, and publishing.

Finally, friends and family members have patiently encouraged and supported my writing efforts (and other activities). For their numerous acts of kindness and help, I thank in particular Sheila Mackintosh, Abigail Brooks, Mary Lee Griffin, Bill Bullivant, David Mercer, and Bronlyn Jones. My brother Bob's prodigious and exemplary scholarly output sets a standard I can never approach. He has also shared with me his findings and curiosity about our ancestor Sam Gay. For their steady support and for the example of their own engagement in cultural and community pursuits, I am inspired by my son Sam and his wife Kate Freedman. With the deepest, most ardent appreciation, I dedicate this book to my wife, Nan Haffenreffer, for her constant love, support, and encouragement.

Grateful acknowledgment is made to the magazines, newspapers, and other publications in which the following articles were originally published, sometimes under different titles and in somewhat different form:

"Benton MacKaye: Brief Life of a 'Geotect.'" Originally published in *Harvard Magazine*, July/August, 1994.

"Benton MacKaye and the Art of Roving: An 1897 Excursion in the White Mountains." Originally published in *Appalachia*, journal of the Appalachian Mountain Club, December 15, 1987.

"A 'Classic of the Green Mountains': The 1900 Hike of Benton MacKaye and Horace Hildreth." Originally published in the *Harvard Post*, December 19, 1986.

"Where Paths Cross, a Path Begins." Originally published in *Wild Earth*, Spring, 1996.

"Our White Mountain Trip: Its Organization and Methods," by Benton MacKaye. Originally published in *Log of Camp Moosilauke, 1904*, MacKaye Family Papers, Rauner Special Collections Library, Dartmouth College, Hanover, New Hampshire. The complete *Log* is reproduced in facsimile form by permission and courtesy of Dartmouth College Library.

"Bake Oven Knob, 1931: On the Appalachian Trail with Myron Avery and Benton MacKaye." Adapted from "Crossing Paths on Bake Oven Knob: A Pivotal Moment on the Appalachian Trail with Myron Avery and Benton MacKaye," a talk co-sponsored by the Appalachian Trail Museum Society and the Appalachian Trail Conservancy, June 2, 2007, Harpers Ferry, West Virginia.

"'Work and Art and Recreation and Living Will All Be One': Benton MacKaye and Henry David Thoreau." Adapted from a talk at the Thoreau Society Gathering, July 9, 2004, for a panel titled "Influence of Thoreau's *Walden* on Personal Values and Lifestyles," Concord, Massachusetts.

"Lewis Mumford: An Early Trail Champion." Original published in *Appalachian Trailway News*, publication of the Appalachian Trail Conference (now the Appalachian Trail Conservancy), May / June, 1990.

"Hiking with Mark Sanford." Originally published as "How a Leftist Created a Trail That a Rightist Could Love," the *Providence Journal*, August 28, 2009.

"The Spectatorium: Steele MacKaye's Epic Failure." Originally published as "Yesterday's City: Steele MacKaye's Grandiose Folly," *Chicago History*, Fall/Winter, 1987-88.

"Peculiar Work: The Concentric Cartography of Edward G. Chamberlain." Adapted and expanded from "Peculiar Work," *AMC Outdoors*, magazine of the Appalachian Mountain Club, May, 2002.

"Preserving the East's Wild Spirit." Originally published in *Sierra*, magazine of the Sierra Club, September/October, 1988.

"The View from Breadloaf: Fostering a Spirit of Wilderness in the Heart of the Green Mountains." Originally published in *Wilderness*, magazine of The Wilderness Society, Spring, 1993.

"Nothing Small in Nature." Originally published in *Wilderness*, magazine of The Wilderness Society, Summer, 1990.

"Canyon of Solace." Originally published in *Appalachia*, journal of the Appalachian Mountain Club, June 15, 1994.

"Reflections on the Draft." Originally published in the *Harvard Post*, December 8, 1978.

"Little Compton Witch Hunt." Originally published as "Letter from Little Compton: A Witch Hunt," in the *Harvard Post*, May 23, 1986.

"The Mitten Woman: A Short Story." Originally published in the *Providence Journal Sunday Magazine*, January 31, 1988.

"The Wilderness Within." Originally published in *Newport Review*, vol. 5, no. 1, 1997.

"Goosewing Beach." Originally published as "Little Compton: Quit Dawdling on Goosewing Beach," in the *Providence Journal*, February 15, 1994.

"Sakonnet Point." Originally published as "Save Public Access to Sakonnet Point," in the *Providence Journal*, October 7, 2002.

"Time, Memory, Landscape." Originally published as "Sakonnet 'Memory Holes': Traveling in Time across the Little Compton Landscape," in *Little Compton Landscapes*, newsletter of the Sakonnet Preservation Association, January, 2007.

"Town Meeting." Originally published as "Town Meetings both Precious and Messy," in the *Providence Journal*, January 4, 2008.

Made in the USA
Charleston, SC
23 February 2017